INSIDE NORTON NAVIGATOR

INSIDE NORTON NAVIGATOR

Katherine Murray

A Subsidiary of
Henry Holt and Co., Inc.

© 1996 by **MIS:Press**
a subsidiary of Henry Holt and Company, Inc.
115 West 18th Street
New York, NY 10011

All rights reserved. Reproduction or use of editorial or pictorial content in any manner is prohibited without express permission. No patent liability is assumed with respect to the use of the information contained herein. While every precaution has been taken in the preparation of this book, the publisher assumes no responsibility for errors or omissions. Neither is any liability assumed for damages resulting from the use of the information contained herein.

Throughout this book, trademarked names are used. Rather than put a trademark symbol after every occurrence of a trademarked name, we used the names in an editorial fashion only, and to the benefit of the trademark owner, with no intention of infringement of the trademark. Where such designations appear in this book, they have been printed with initial caps.

First Edition—1996

Printed in the United States of America.

ISBN: 1-55828-436-2

10 9 8 7 6 5 4 3 2 1

MIS:Press books are available at special discounts for bulk purchases for sales promotions, premiums, fund-raising, or educational use. Special editions or book excerpts can also be created to specification.

For details contact: Special Sales Director
             MIS:Press
             a subsidiary of Henry Holt and Company, Inc.
             115 West 18th Street
             New York, New York 10011

Editor-in-Chief: Paul Farrell   **Managing Editor:** Cary Sullivan
Copy Edit Manager: Shari Chapell   **Copy Editor:** Betsy Hardinger
Production Editor: Maya Riddick   **Assoc. Production Editor:** Brian Oxman
                  Development Editor: Mike Sprague

DEDICATION

To Jim,
   my favorite martian.
                        K

Acknowledgements

The actual work that goes into writing a book is a pretty straightforward process—you plan out what you need to say, do the necessary research, and say it. But the entire phenomenon of creating a book—from the original spark of "Hey, we need to do a book about..." to the final relieved sigh as the editor says a quick prayer and sends the finished pages off to the printer—is a complicated and sometimes arduous process that requires the work, insight, and cooperation of a number of talented people.

Thanks to the professional staff at MIS:Press for making *Inside Norton Navigator* such a pleasant and problem-free process. Michael Sprague, Aquisitions Editor, is an extremely talented and capable mastermind: he believes in his projects and in his authos, and to say that he's great to work with really sells the experience short. Maya Riddick, Production Editor, did a terrific job of shepherding the project through editing and production, making sure the pieces were in the right places at the right time, which—especially in publishing—is often not a simple thing to do. Also for the clear design and attractive layout—the result is a clean, easy-to-navigate book that invites readers to stop in and stay awhile. And Betsy Hardinger, Copy Editor, came through with a great line-by-line edit, clarifying things I stumbled through and asking questions that will help make concepts and procedures much easier for readers to understand.

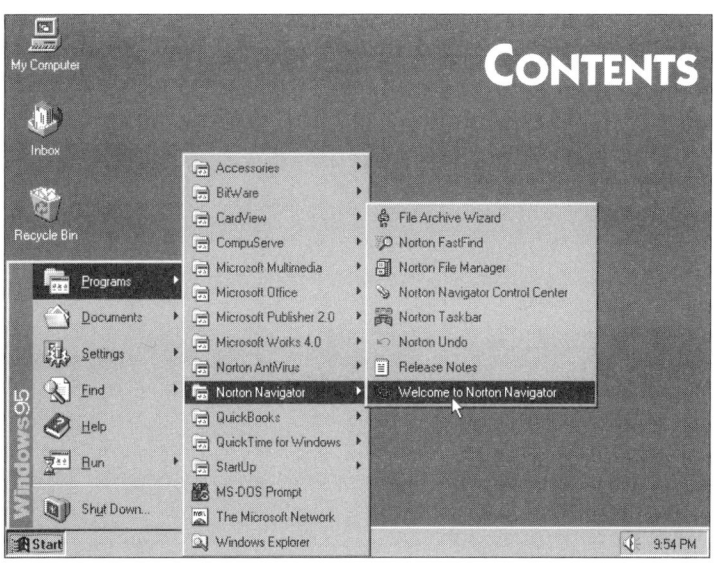

CONTENTS

INTRODUCTION 1

    How Should You Read This Book? 2

    How Is This Book Organized? 2

    Watch for These Signs 3

    A Few Assumptions... 3

PART ONE: NORTON NAVIGATOR BASICS 5

CHAPTER 1: WHAT IS NORTON NAVIGATOR? 7

    Welcome to the Navigator 8

    The History of Navigation 13

    How Will I Use the Navigator? 13

    Where Windows 95 Leaves Off... 15

    What Do You Need to Run Norton Navigator? 16

    Norton Navigator Picks Up the Slack 16

    The Next Stop 19

Chapter 2: A Norton Navigator Overview 21

But First, an Assumption 21
Starting Norton Navigator 22
Do I Have to? (On-line Registration) 24
Taking the Tour 24
    Taking a Side Trip through an Example 26
    What to Do with the Information Once You've Found It 27
Something Worth Exploring 29
    Cutting the Tour Short 30
What's in It for You? 30
Starting with the Taskbar 30
    Finding the Norton Navigator Desktop 32
    Displaying the Norton File Manager 32
    Displaying the Control Center 34
    Escaping the Control Center 42
    Finding the QuickLaunch Area 42
And All the Help You Need 42
    Using the Help System 42
    Symantec Technical Support 46
The Next Stop 47

Chapter 3: When You Need to Do It Now 49

Starting Out 50
Using the Control Center 52
    Displaying the Taskbar at Startup 52
    Adding Norton Quick Menus 52

Adding Norton Explorer Extensions 56
A Do-It-Fast Task Compendium 58
    Displaying the File Manager 59
    Formatting a Disk 60
    Scanning a Disk 62
    Selecting Files 66
    Zipping Files 70
    Viewing Disk Contents 73
    Copying a File 73
    Deleting a File 75
    Exiting the File Manager 77
The Next Stop 77

PART TWO: NAVIGATION AT ITS FINEST: THE CONTROL CENTER 79

CHAPTER 4: A CONTROL CENTER OVERVIEW 81

What Is the Control Center? 82
Displaying the Control Center 83
Exploring Control Center Options 85
    Norton Taskbar 85
    Norton Quick Menus 87
    Norton Folder Navigator 89
    Norton Explorer Extensions 90
    Norton SmartFolders 93
    Norton FileAssist 96

Norton LFN Enabler 98
  Norton Indexing 100
  Norton Undo 100
 Closing the Control Center 101
 The Next Step 102

CHAPTER 5: CUSTOMIZING THE SCREEN DISPLAY 103

 Working with the Taskbar 104
  Displaying the Taskbar 104
  Understanding Taskbar Elements 105
  Changing Taskbar Properties .106
  Getting Taskbar Help 109
 QuickLaunching Applications 110
  Adding Items to the QuickLaunch Area 111
  QuickLaunching 112
 Changing the Start Menu with Quick Menus 114
  Adding Quick Menus 115
  Setting Up the Documents History List 116
  An Applet a Day... 118
  Back to the real world 119
 The Next Stop 119

CHAPTER 6: ALTERNATE REALITY OR ALTERNATE DESKTOP? 121

 Understanding Multiple Desktops .122
 When Will You Use Alternate Desktops? 122
 Creating a New Desktop 123

Changing to a Different Desktop 125
Choosing Desktop Backgrounds 126
Choosing a Screen Saver 129
Help! I'm Locked Out 130
Adding Items to the Desktop 133
Using Desktops from Other Programs 139
The Next Stop 140

CHAPTER 7: WORKING WITH FOLDERS 141

What Are Folders? 142
Using the Folder Navigator 146
Creating and Using SmartFolders .149
What Is a SmartFolder? 149
Creating a SmartFolder 149
Updating a SmartFolder 154
Using a SmartFolder 154
Moving SmartFolders 155
Removing a SmartFolder 156
The Next Stop 157

PART THREE: THE FILE MANAGER EXTRAORDINAIRE 159

CHAPTER 8: FILE MANAGER BASICS 161

Displaying the File Manager 162
Understanding the File Manager Window 163
The Menus 164

    The Toolbar 166
  Working with the Tree and List Display 169
    Changing the Tree Display 169
    Methods of Navigating through the Tree Area 172
    Adding Folders to the Tree Area 173
    Using the List Display 175
    Changing the List Display 176
  Using SmartTabs 178
    What's a SmartTab? 178
    Using the Default SmartTabs .179
    Creating a SmartTab 182

CHAPTER 9: WORKING WITH FILES 185

  Selecting and Tagging Files 186
  Copying Files 188
  Moving Files 189
  Deleting Files 189
  Renaming a File 190
  Displaying File Properties 190
  Comparing Files 191
  Zipping and Unzipping Files 194
  Undeleting Files 196
  The Next Stop 198

CHAPTER 10: WORKING WITH DISKS 199

  Disk Basics 200

Simple Disk Procedures 200
    Selecting Disks 201
    Copying Disks 203
    Labeling Disks 206
    Formatting Disks 207
    Scanning Disks 210
    Working with Network Drives 215
The Next Stop 216

Chapter 11: Special File Procedures: Searching, Sorting, and Indexing 217

Using FastFind to Locate Files 218
    Using Indexes to Speed Up FastFind 221
    Saving Searches 225
    Using an Existing Search 226
    FastFind Search Options 227
Sorting Files for Easy Access 228
    Using Sort Filters 231
The Next Stop 232

Chapter 12: Mapping FTP Internet Sites 233

What Is an FTP Site? 234
    FTP Differences 234
Starting Out with FTP 234
What Do I Need before I Connect? 235
Connecting to the FTP Site 236

Displaying the FTP Log Window 236
Transferring Files to Norton File Manager 237
　　Disconnecting from an FTP Site 238
Adding a New FTP Site 239
　　Setting FTP Properties 241
Removing an FTP Site 242
The Next Stop 243

APPENDIX A: INSTALLING NORTON NAVIGATOR 245
Starting Installation 246

APPENDIX B: COMPARING WINDOWS 95 AND NORTON NAVIGATOR 249

INDEX 259

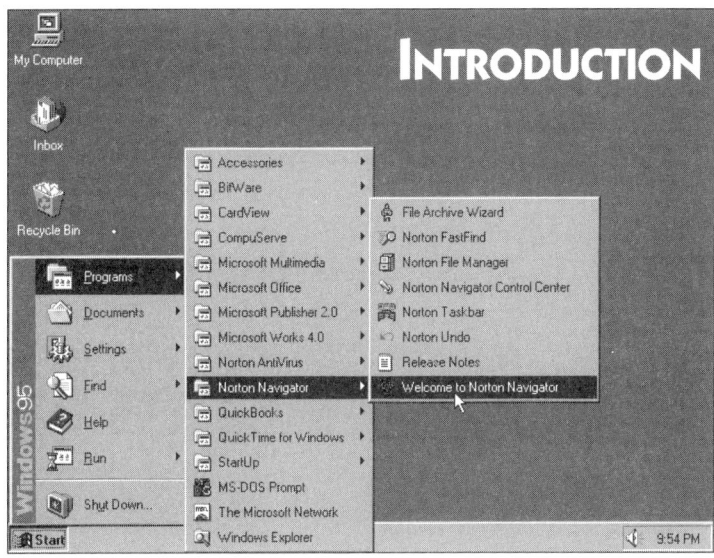

Introduction

With the arrival of Windows 95, the computing world is experiencing a rash of new software releases. Every software manufacturer who can take advantage of the advancing technology is doing so. People who are accustomed to the Windows look-and-feel want a similar look-and-feel in all their Windows applications. And even though Windows 95 is faster to use, streamlined, and more flexible than older versions of Windows, there's still room for improvement.

Enter Norton Navigator.

Norton Navigator for Windows 95 is a collection of utilities that enable you to work faster, cleaner, and smarter in Windows 95. *Inside Norton Navigator* will help you find the best features of the program and get up to speed with them as quickly as possible.

How Should You Read This Book?

Inside Norton Navigator is organized into three parts, each with chapters grouped around a single theme. If you are interested in finding out more about Norton Navigator in general, check out Part One, "Norton Navigator Basics," before you do anything else. Chapter 1 will be particularly relevant if you are considering purchasing the program but have not yet done so. If you want a broad overview of Norton Navigator tasks and plan to start in the Control Center, check out Part Two, "Navigation at Its Finest." If you are looking for the File Manager, see Part Three, "File Manager Extraordinaire." All chapters in Part Three relate to various tasks in the File Manager.

In short, use this book the way you use Norton Navigator—find the piece of information you need and use it. Unless you're interested in everything there is to know about Norton Navigator (or, perhaps, you are really bored), we don't recommend reading the book from cover to cover. Just use the index, the table of contents, or the close-your-eyes-and-point method to find the item you need quickly, and then apply your new-found knowledge and get on with life.

How Is This Book Organized?

Inside Norton Navigator is organized with a building-block approach, although you don't have to follow the chapters in sequence. If you're going to read anything straight through, tune into Part One, "Norton Navigator Basics." In this part, you learn what Norton Navigator is and how it fits into the spectrum of file- and data-management utilities. You get an overview of program features in Chapter 2, and a quick run-through using Norton Navigator in Chapter 3.

Part Two, "Navigation at Its Finest: The Control Center," focuses on the Control Center, the hub of the various file and disk utilities. Chapter 4 begins with an overview of the Control Center, and Chapter 5 explains how to customize the screen display. Chapter 6 shows you how to create alternate desktops and switch between them; and Chapter 7 explains how to work with folders in Norton Navigator.

Part Three, "The File Manager Extraordinaire," is where many of the features of the program really shine. Learn the basics of file management in Chapter 8; work with disks in Chapter 9; search and sort files in Chapter 10; index and archive files in Chapter 11; and map FTP Internet sites in Chapter 12.

The book concludes with three appendixes, a glossary, and an index.

WATCH FOR THESE SIGNS

Means that a shortcut or workaround is available for the highlighted process.

Lets you know where to turn in the book for more information about the topic under discussion.

Provides you with a definition for an often-used term or other handy information of note.

A FEW ASSUMPTIONS...

As we begin this book, let's state a few assumptions. First, we are assuming that you have loaded Windows 95 and are fairly proficient with the new menus, new look, and new features. (If you are not, see Appendix C for information on installing and working with Windows.)

We also assume that you don't have much time to spend reading a book about computers, so the descriptions and step-by-step tasks are simple to understand and use.

Furthermore, we assume that you've successfully installed Norton Navigator. If you have the program but haven't installed it, you can use Appendix A, "Installing Norton Navigator," to get started.

Now let's start navigating.

PART ONE

NORTON NAVIGATOR BASICS

Chapter 1: What Is Norton Navigator?

Chapter 2: A Norton Navigator Overview

Chapter 3: When You Need to Do It Now...

CHAPTER 1

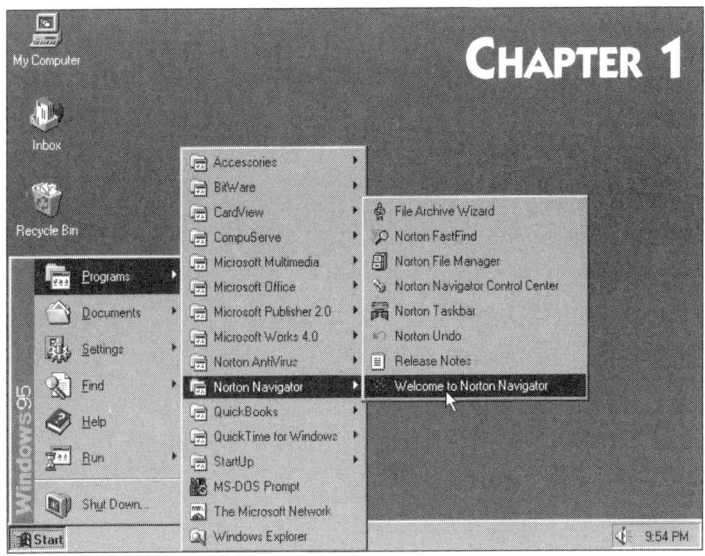

WHAT IS NORTON NAVIGATOR?

Imagine that you've just upgraded to Windows 95. You're happy with the new look, the easy-to-find-and-use features, and the enhanced speed and functionality.

Now imagine that you can do your work faster, spend less time working with Windows and more time using your programs, zip and unzip files (saving you valuable disk space), and even work with the Internet, without adding any new complexity to your Windows tasks.

Too good to be true? Read on.

Welcome to the Navigator

Norton Navigator is one of the programs that, once you settle in to using them, make you wonder how you ever made it through the pitfalls of computerdom alone. No more wondering about renegade viruses; no guesswork about how much room is left on drive D. Zip and unzip your files easily—there are no cryptic multifaceted commands to master. Just click and zip.

You start Norton Navigator from Windows 95. Simple to find and simple to use, Norton Navigator will load its AntiVirus utility—or all its utilities, for that matter—automatically if you let it. The commands for autoloading are found in the Navigator Control Center. Figure 1.1 shows where you find the commands for Norton Navigator startup. As you can see, the Navigator package includes a number of utilities:

- File Archive Wizard
- Norton FastFind
- Norton File Manager
- Norton Navigator Control Center
- Norton Taskbar
- Norton Undo
- Release Notes
- Welcome to Norton Navigator

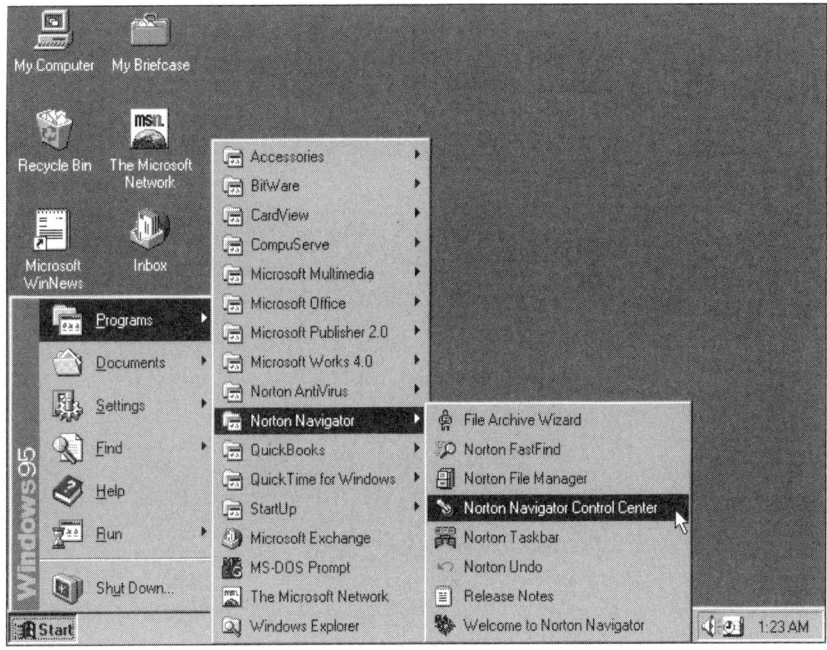

FIGURE 1.1 GETTING NORTON NAVIGATOR STARTED FROM THE WINDOWS 95 TASKBAR.

The File Archive Wizard walks you through the process of archiving—or compressing and putting away—files you no longer need direct access to. Norton FastFind helps you locate a specific file or types of files; you can also search for a particular word or phrase in a file. The Norton File Manager, shown in Figure 1.2, is a feature-rich utility that enables you to do all sorts of file-management tasks, including zipping, encoding, associating, undeleting, and much more. You can also use the File Manager to map FTP sites, which allows you to use Internet login sites as though they were just another drive on your computer.

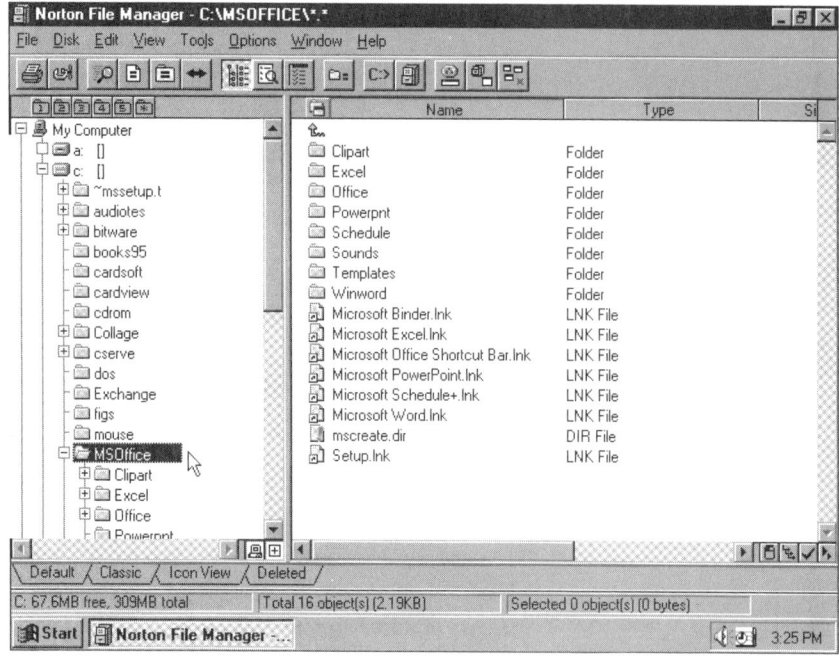

FIGURE 1.2 THE NORTON FILE MANAGER TAKES YOU ABOVE AND BEYOND THE LIMITATIONS OF THE WINDOWS EXPLORER.

The Norton Navigator Control Center is just what it sounds like—a clearinghouse for settings and controls about the way Norton Navigator works with you, your computer, and Windows (see figure 1.3). The Norton Taskbar is Norton's version of the Windows Taskbar, including additional icons you can use to move between desktops or elicit help from other Norton commands. Figure 1.4 shows a picture of the Norton Taskbar. No doubt you'll be using it often.

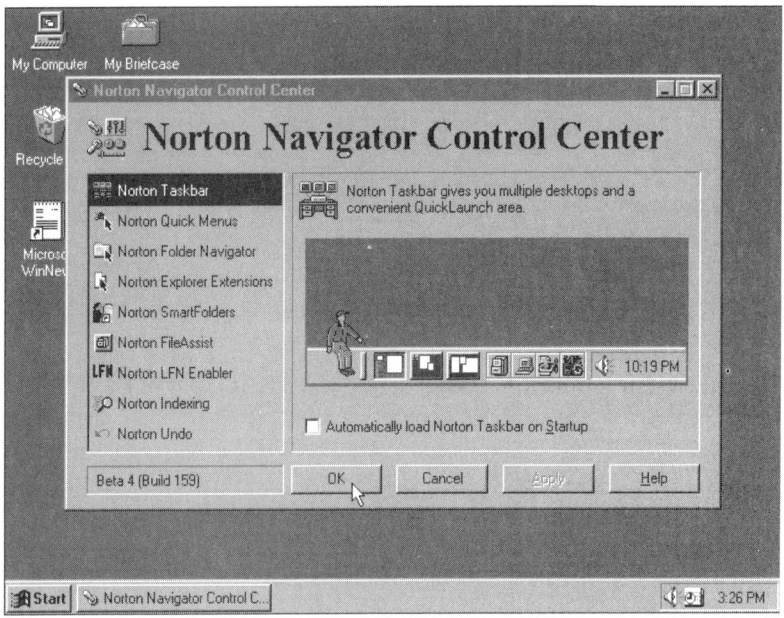

FIGURE 1.3 THE NORTON NAVIGATOR CONTROL CENTER—A COMMANDING PRESENCE.

12 Inside Norton Navigator

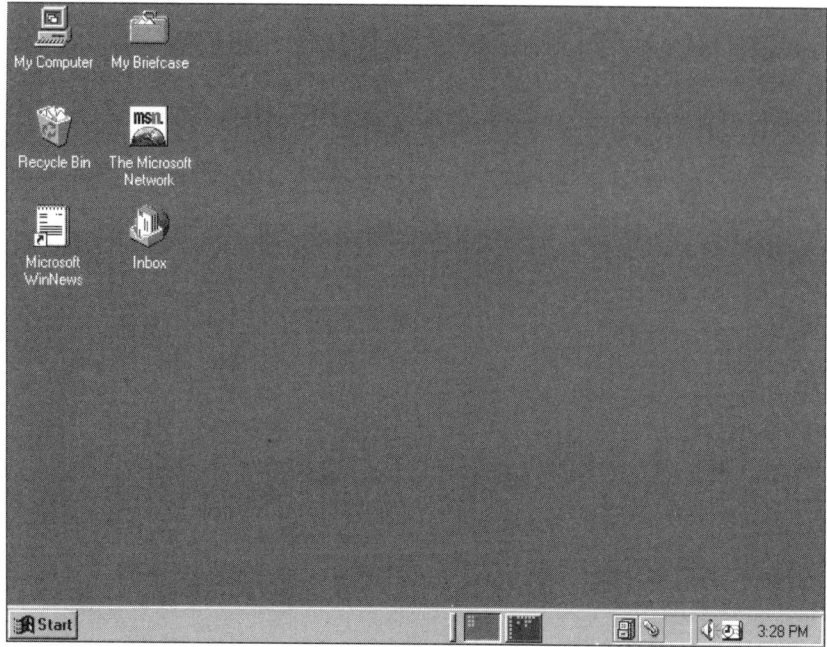

FIGURE 1.4 THE NORTON NAVIGATOR TASKBAR INCLUDES ICONS DIFFERENT FROM THOSE IN THE WINDOWS 95 TASKBAR.

Norton Undo is a reverse-it utility that undoes your last operation. The Release Notes file includes read-me text about the most current version of Norton Navigator. If you haven't already done so, take a moment and read this file before you install Norton Navigator. The version notes often discuss software "bugs" that can cause trouble during installation or program execution. Finally, the Welcome to Norton Navigator option kicks off the Norton tutorial, an overview program that introduces you to the key features of Norton Navigator.

To find out about starting and taking the Navigator tour, see Chapter 2, "A Norton Navigator Overview."

ROAD MAP

The History of Navigation

What happens when you combine the products of two companies that have had successful disk and file management utilities? You get the best of both wrapped into one.

Norton Navigator represents the combined brainpower shown in PC Tools for Windows (by Central Point Software) and Norton Desktop for Windows (by Symantec). Each of these former competitors now fully complements the other in a disk and file management program that balances power with personality, functionality with ease of use.

PC Tools for Windows was one of the earliest packages to add on extra functions and features to Microsoft Windows. Picking up the Windows slack, PC Tools for Windows performed regular backups, checked disks and files for potential viruses (and fixed them when they were found), wiped files away (a complete delete program), and helped you monitor your system's resources.

Norton Desktop, another fine integrated utility, has been around the proverbial computer chip a few times. A powerhouse of file and disk-saving utilities, Norton broke into the forefront with Disk Doctor, UnErase, and the File Manager. Many of the stronger features—in particular, the File Manager—you'll find in new and improved versions within Norton Navigator.

How Will I Use the Navigator?

If you're like many people, you may not think about breaking down and purchasing a disk and file management utility until you absolutely need one. You're getting weird errors and are afraid it's a latent virus, seeping through your system. (It's possible!) Your hard drive locked up last Tuesday and you had forgotten to do a recent backup. You've learned the hard way about the importance of a regular, routine backup of files you may need in the future.

When you begin scouting your options, you realize that Norton Navigator has far and away the greatest number of features for the smallest amount of effort. And even though the number of features is almost staggering, the reassuring fact is that you don't have to use them until you're ready. If you want only the virus protection right now, fine. You might want to try the extended filename feature later, or perhaps the alternate desktops will appeal to you. Whatever your interest or level of experience with computers, you'll find Norton Navigator has just what you need to take premium care of your disks and files.

Specifically, Norton Navigator helps you with the following operations:

- ✦ Working with files
    - ✦ Zipping and unzipping files (file compression)
    - ✦ Viewing files
    - ✦ Encrypting files
    - ✦ Coding and decoding files
    - ✦ Associating files
    - ✦ Undeleting files
    - ✦ Displaying a file history list
    - ✦ File searching
    - ✦ Moving and deleting files

ROAD MAP

See Part Three, "The File Manager Extraordinaire," for information on working with files.

- ✦ Copying, cutting, and pasting files
- ✦ Archiving files
- ✦ FTP site mapping

- Working with folders
    - Comparing folder contents
    - Synchronizing folders
    - Adding cascading menus to folders
    - SmartFolders

ROAD MAP

See Chapter 7, "Working with Folders," for more about basic folder operations.

- Working with desktops
    - Multiple desktops
    - Using the Taskbar

ROAD MAP

Please see Chapters 5 and 6 for more information on working with the Norton Desktop and the Taskbar.

WHERE WINDOWS 95 LEAVES OFF...

If you were an avid Windows 3.1 user before the reinvention of the wheel, you may be pleased—or perhaps perturbed—by the changes in the software you used so often. In the last several years, we've seen DOS programs shirked away like old shirts from Windows-eager users. Windows offers a familiar face, a predictable gait, and a known commodity. If you figure out how one Windows program operates, you can pretty much guess how the others will work. The File menu in Microsoft Works, for example, isn't much different from the File menu in Microsoft

Word. You point and click. Many of the same quick keys work in a similar fashion from program to program.

These benefits are still in place in Windows 95. But Windows 95 grows us up into a faster world of processing (we may as well face it while we can catch it), puts a new streamlined look on our screens, and replaces the old, friendly, windowed desktop with slick popup menus that just seem to make more sense. (I never did figure out what we were doing with the windows-on-the-*desktop* analogy anyway. The windows in my office are built into the *walls*, not positioned on my desk.)

All this is to say that if you haven't tried Windows 95, try it. You'll like it.

WHAT DO YOU NEED TO RUN NORTON NAVIGATOR?

Before you can try Norton Navigator, you must upgrade to Windows 95. You'll need the following things:

- Windows 95 installed on your computer
- A PC-compatible 486/50 or higher computer
- At least 8MB of RAM
- A hard disk with at least 8MB free disk space (but much more than that would be better)

NORTON NAVIGATOR PICKS UP THE SLACK

Microsoft Windows 95 brings to the table new features and functionality in its operating environment. No longer a dueling duo, Windows 95 overtakes DOS (although you can still use DOS if you like) and replaces it as your computer's operating system. Depending on the features of your computer, Windows 95 may run faster or slower than old Windows.

CHAPTER 1 WHAT IS NORTON NAVIGATOR?

(It's meant to work faster, but it may chug along on systems that are just squeaking by in the requirements department.)

Norton Navigator builds on the new Windows 95 desktop look and Taskbar approach by giving you the option of choosing alternate desktops and working with the Norton Taskbar. In fact, if you created and used other desktops in, for example, PC Tools for Windows or Norton Desktop for Windows, you can copy these desktops into Norton Navigator by using a special importing program included with the new Norton Navigator. The program is called Norton Importer, and it is available on your program disks or CD-ROM.

There are so many ways that Norton Navigator surpasses the Windows that we'll just gloss over them quickly here. You'll read more about the features in detail as you begin to peruse later chapters. Here are just a few added benefits:

- You can add quick command buttons to Open and Save dialog boxes in all your Windows programs. These buttons give you a point-and-click method of retrieving or depositing files in their appropriate directory without climbing through the Windows Explorer directory tree to find the right location.

- You can use long, sensible names for your files—which means you will someday be able to tell what a file contains without opening it (a novel idea!). Anyone who has ever spent a frustrated half hour opening and closing files with names such as **02FRE47.DOC** looking for one specific file knows how valuable it is to name a file in a way that makes sense.

- You can now zip and unzip files with a click of the mouse. No longer do you have to wander down into the **PKWARE** subdirectory to find the PKZIP and PKUNZIP programs—they are built right in to Norton Navigator. There's even a **Zip** button on the toolbar, so you simply highlight the files you want to zip and click the button. There's not much in life that's easier.

✦ FTP site mapping. If you are a traveler on the Information Superhighway—or at least on the Internet—you'll be interested in Norton's FTP site mapping feature. FTP stands for *File Transfer Protocol*, a common term in Internet language. This application enables you to transfer files in all their forms—documents, binary data, video, sound, entire programs—from the host computer to your personal PC. When you use Norton Navigator to map an FTP site, you are establishing a route to a specific FTP site you will use. When you access the site, it is treated just like another drive on your computer, making Internet access much easier.

ROAD MAP

For more about working with FTP site mapping, see Chapter 12, "Mapping FTP Internet Sites."

✦ The Norton Navigator also gives you the option of working with multiple desktops. Particularly if you're a person who wears many hats—manager, writer, personnel director, chief cook and bottle washer—being able to compartmentalize your programs and files is helpful when you have a number of programs to organize. Suppose, for example, that you work from an office at home. You have all kinds of things on your computer desktop—Microsoft Office, which you use for work; BOB, which you use for home; and all kinds of Zork-like games your kids love to play. You don't need all these icons cluttering up your desktop when you're trying to work. Similarly, you don't need your kids accidentally clicking the Office icons and putting your reports in the Recycling Bin. Multiple desktops are safety guards for logical—and safe—computing.

THE NEXT STOP

In this chapter, you've learned about some of the eye-opening features you'll be exploring on your trip with Norton Navigator. In Chapter 2, you'll check out Taskbar elements, take a quick peek at a few utilities, and learn how to get help in the midst of file and disk management crises. (Not that we're anticipating any!)

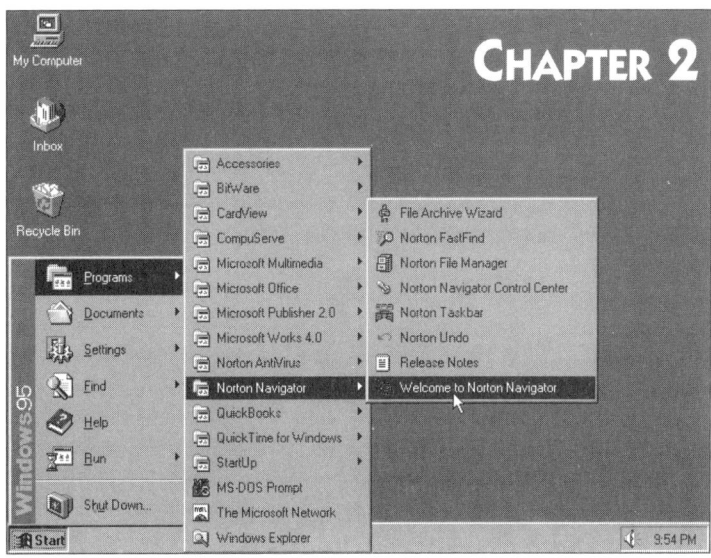

CHAPTER 2

A NORTON NAVIGATOR OVERVIEW

OK, you're psyched. You're ready. It's time to start making sense of all these files and folders and whatnot. This chapter takes you from startup through exploration of the entire Navigator system, giving you usable information and a bird's-eye-view of features you'll want to return to later.

BUT FIRST, AN ASSUMPTION

Notice that you haven't seen the word *installation*. That's because we've taken the liberty of assuming Norton Navigator is already installed on your computer. If it's not, you need to stop here, find the software, and install it.

How? Insert the CD in your CD-ROM drive, open the CD-ROM window, and double-click the **Setup** icon. The Navigator installation program will walk you through the process. For more in-depth information on installation, see Appendix A.

Take your time. We'll wait.

STARTING NORTON NAVIGATOR

The Windows 95 Start menu seems a logical place to begin. Click **Start** to open the menu and move the pointer to Programs. As soon as you highlight **Programs**, another menu appears to the right of the Start menu. This menu lists the various programs you have on your computer. Scan through the list (it's alphabetical, by the way) until you find Norton Navigator; then move the mouse pointer to that point.

The Norton Navigator submenu opens to the right of the Programs menu. You see all the different Norton utilities you can choose—which one should you try first? Since they have the welcome mat out for us, let's begin with Welcome to Norton Navigator (see Figure. 2.1).

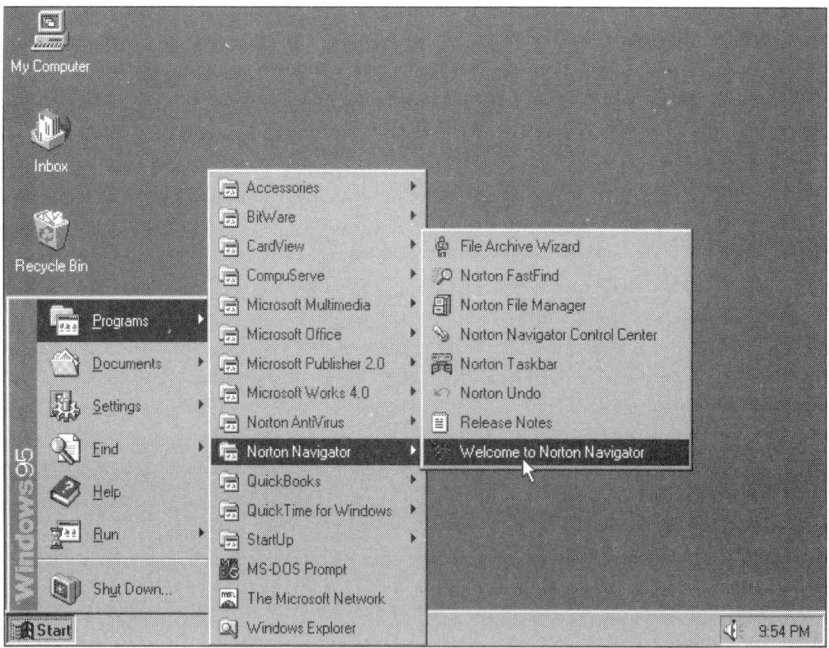

FIGURE 2.1 GETTING STARTED USING NORTON NAVIGATOR.

After you click the command, the Welcome to Norton Navigator window appears (see Figure 2.2). In the center of the window, you see a tip that offers advice or shortcuts for using different utilities. On the right side of the window, you find five command buttons:

- **Introducing** leads you to the Norton Navigator tour (train now boarding!).
- **Configure** displays the Control Center so that you can make various selections about the way you work with the program.
- **Online Registration** enables you to use your computer's modem to call Symantec and register your software. It's quick, easy, and relatively painless.
- **Next Tip** displays, as you might expect, the next tip.
- **Close** shuts down the Welcome to Norton Navigator dialog box.

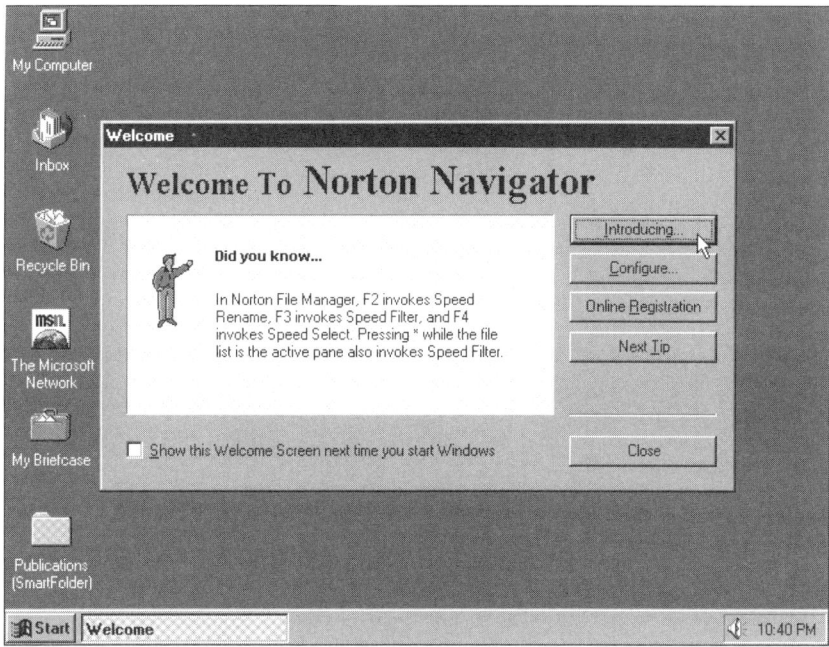

FIGURE 2.2 THE WELCOME TO NORTON NAVIGATOR WINDOW.

One other option in this window is worth mentioning: the **Show this Welcome Screen next time you start Windows** checkbox. If you'd rather see this screen than the standard "Hi—I'm Windows!" welcome screen, click the checkbox to add a check mark. Otherwise, leave it blank. (If you've seen one Welcome box, you've seen 'em all.)

Do I Have to? (On-line Registration)

If communications isn't your thing, the idea of using a modem to call a major software company and offer up your product registration may seem like a Big Deal. It isn't. On-line registration is almost ridiculously easy. You click the button and wait while Norton Navigator dials the parent company, uploads information, and disconnects. Pretty simple. When all is said and done, the process takes less than a minute. And now you're on the list for future updates and product enhancement information.

Taking the Tour

It's nice to know that, true to its style, Norton Navigator leaves you in the driver seat even through its own tutorial. Some programs "take over" when you buckle in for their tutorials—you see animated features, you're told when and where to click the mouse button, and you exhibit Pavlovian-style response to the prompts you see on-screen.

Norton Navigator is different. When you click the **Introducing** button in the Welcome to Norton Navigator window (go ahead, click it), the Introducing Norton Navigator screen appears, as shown in Figure 2.3.

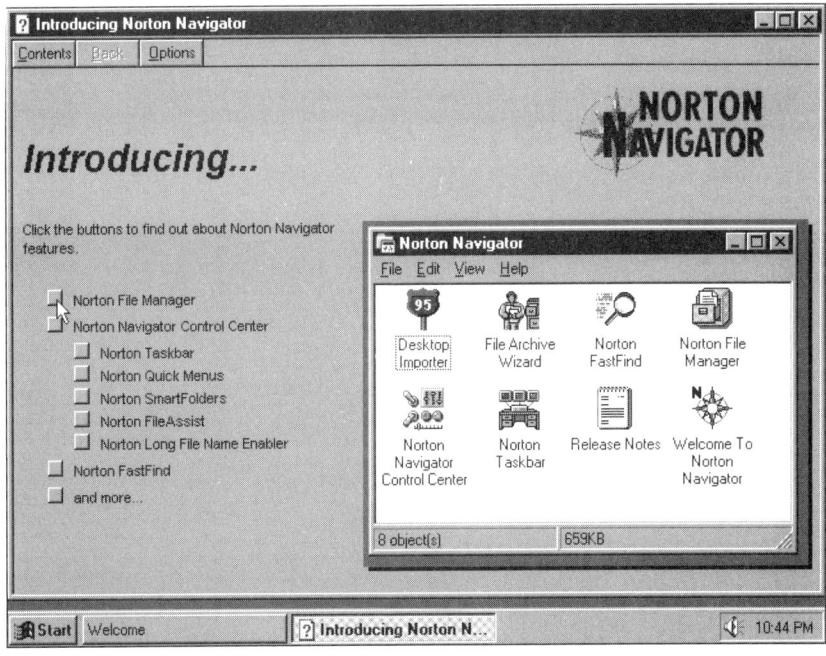

FIGURE 2.3 THE CALM AND COLLECTED INTRODUCING NORTON NAVIGATOR WINDOW.

The Introducing screen gives you the option of selecting any item you want to see more information about. Like Navigator, we'll leave you to explore the items on your own, but be sure to check out the following:

+ Norton File Manager
+ Norton Control Center
+ Norton Taskbar

When you are finished reading about a particular item and you want to return to the Introducing window, click **Back** in the upper-left corner of the window.

Taking a Side Trip through an Example

Let's try an example. Choose **Norton Taskbar**, since that's where we will start when we begin our own tour in a moment. The Introducing Norton Taskbar screen appears, giving you the key points related to the Taskbar, focusing on benefits such as multiple desktops, shortcuts, and hot keys (see Figure 2.4). If you want to see more about the Taskbar, click **More>>** and a second screen of information appears, this one explaining QuickLaunch.

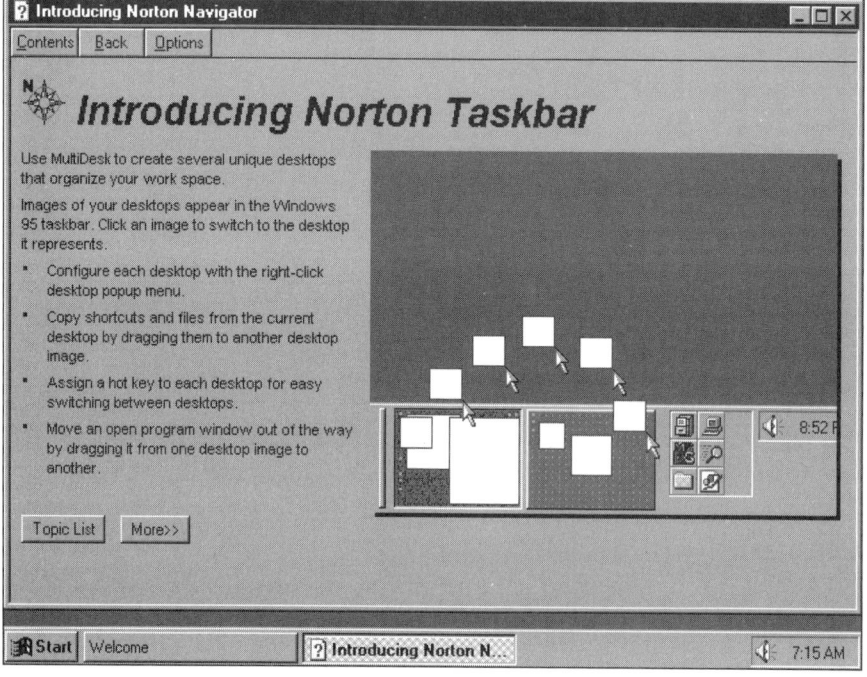

FIGURE 2.4 GETTING OUR INTRODUCTIONS STRAIGHT.

When you're ready to return to the main Introducing Norton Navigator window, click the **Topic List** button.

CHAPTER 2 A NORTON NAVIGATOR OVERVIEW   27

What to Do with the Information Once You've Found It

Because the Introducing Norton Navigator tour is offered in basic Help format, you have a number of options available for what you can do with the information displayed on your screen. For example, you can use any of three command buttons just below the title bar at the top of the window to perform different functions:

- **Contents** returns you to the first screen of Introducing Norton Navigator (but we've already done that).
- **Back** moves you one page back in your tour process.
- **Options** displays a popup list of commands you can select to work with the information displayed in the window (see Figure 2.5). For a detailed look at your choices in the Options menu, see Table 2.1.

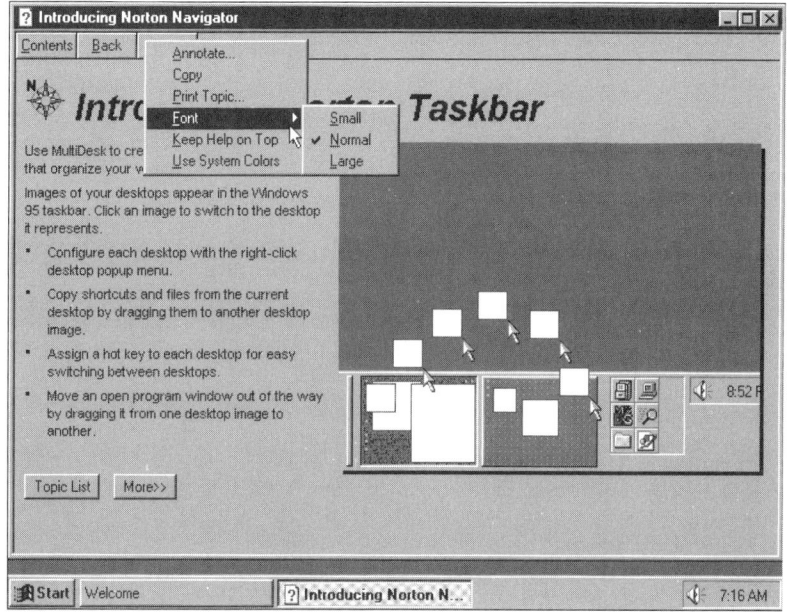

FIGURE 2.5 DISPLAYING OPTIONS FOR WHAT YOU'LL DO WITH THE INTRODUCTORY INFORMATION.

TABLE 2.1 EXPLORING HELP OPTIONS.

Option	What It Does	Why Do That?
Annotate	Displays a popup box in which you can add notes that will be attached to the topic.	To remind yourself that you want to set up three desktops: one for home, one for work, one for kids.
Copy	Makes a copy of the selected topic	To copy the information to the Windows clipboard and paste it into an employee handbook you're creating.
Print Topic	Displays the Print dialog box so that you can print the topic displayed on the screen.	To print information you think you or other users may need often; keep in a folder or with your program documentation
Font	Lets you change the size of the font used for on-screen text. Choose Small, Normal, or Large. Normal is in effect when you first start the program.	Depending on the size of your display, you may want to enlarge (for small screens, such as laptops) or reduce (for large screen monitors) the text.
Keep Help on Top	Lets you choose whether you want the Help windows on top of other windows during your work session.	When you are working through a procedure you find confusing, having Help on top makes referring to it easier.
Use System Colors	Changes the colors used to display Norton Navigator. You are asked whether you want to restart Help with the new colors. Choose **Yes** or **No**.	When the lighting and/or quality of your display makes the default colors hard to read.

Something Worth Exploring

Here's a neat feature you may use often: Annotate, in the Options menu of any Help window. This new Windows 95 lets you add your own notes in Norton Navigator. When you click **Annotate**, the Annotate window appears. Type your notes and click **Save**. You are returned to the Help screen, and a small paper clip icon is displayed beside the title of the window. When you want to display the annotated note, click the paper clip (see Figure 2.6).

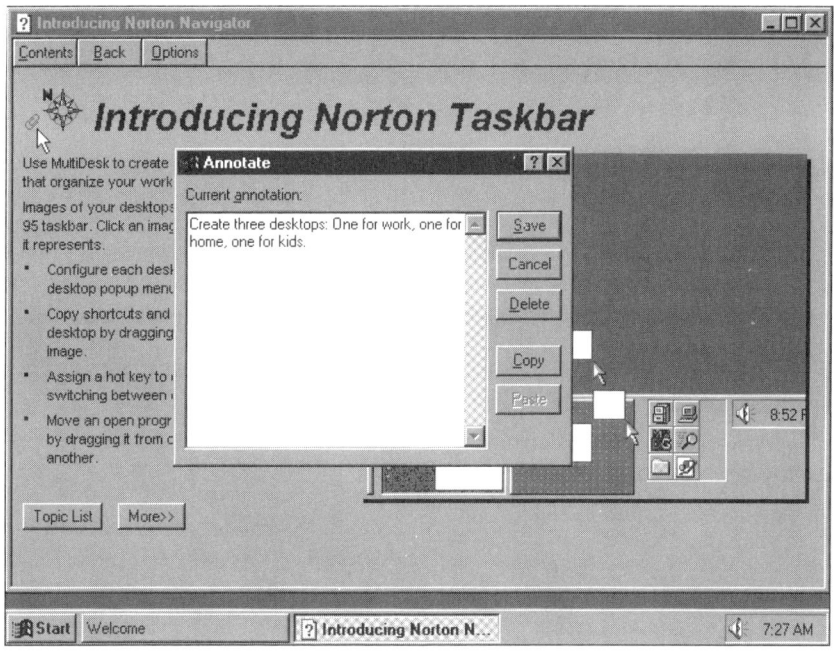

FIGURE 2.6 CLICK THE PAPER CLIP ICON AND THE ANNOTATE WINDOW APPEARS.

Cutting the Tour Short

When you've seen all you care to see by way of Introductions, click the **close** box in the upper-right corner of the Introducing Norton Navigator window. The Help window closes and you are returned to the Welcome to Norton Navigator window.

In the next section, you take a self-guided tour through various program elements. We'll take this at a fairly quick clip, so wear comfortable walking shoes. (And don't forget your sunscreen!)

What's in It for You?

Norton Navigator, as you have no doubt surmised, is packed full of a variety of features. Some make your life easier. Others protect your programs and data. Still others let you organize and get around in your computer with greater fluidity. All Norton Navigator features take working with your computer—with Windows 95 and all your application programs—a step closer to being what you would design if you designed programs.

In this section, you learn about the features that take Norton Navigator beyond the normal software realm. You'll learn where to find and start each of these items and learn a few cursory (no pun intended) facts on how to access them on your own. Look for the roadmap icon for more information about where you can find full-blown descriptions of these features in other parts of the book.

Starting with the Taskbar

The Norton Taskbar is a fully customizable bar that you use to move easily between programs and desktops. Based on the Windows 95 Taskbar approach but taking things several steps farther, the Norton Taskbar gives you access to the Norton Desktop Manager and QuickLaunch features.

To start the Taskbar, display the Windows 95 Start menu. Choose **Programs** and then choose **Norton Navigator**. From the Norton Navigator group, choose **Norton Taskbar**. First the Norton opening window appears; then it disappears; and when you look down (you may not even notice the difference, it's so slight), your Windows Taskbar has been replaced with something slightly different (see Figure 2.7).

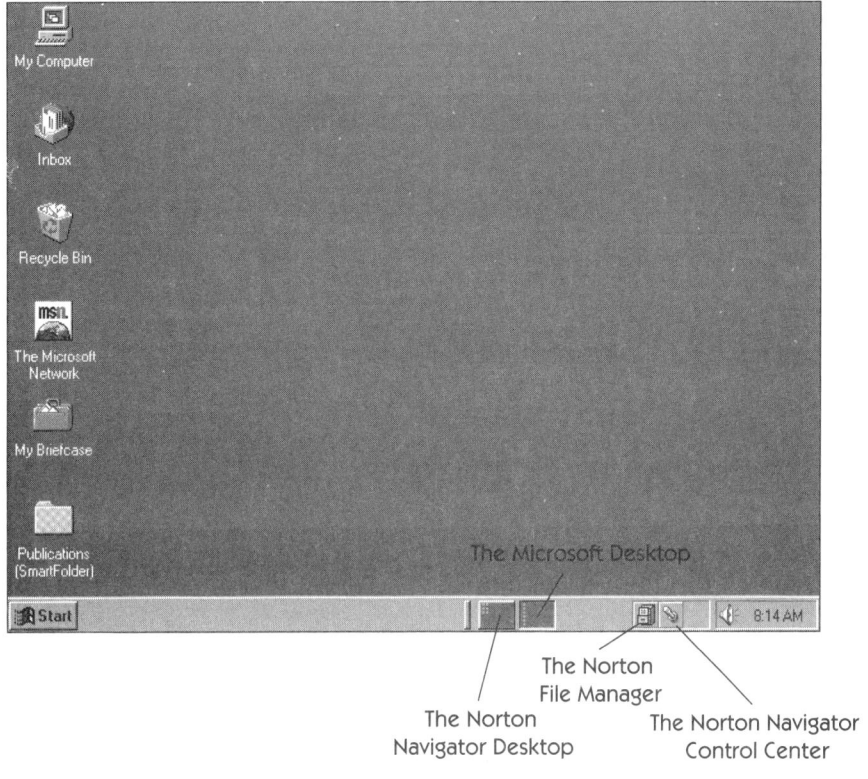

FIGURE 2.7 THE NORTON TASKBAR.

Finding the Norton Navigator Desktop

To move between desktops using the Taskbar, you simply click the desktop icon you want. Until you organize and divide programs, assigning different programs and folders to their respective desktops, the desktops may look similar.

You can add a new desktop easily by positioning the mouse pointer on the Taskbar and clicking the right mouse button. A popup menu appears, and you can select **New Desktop**.

You can create new desktops that help you organize your work, perhaps creating a new desktop for each major project you're working on. You also can customize each desktop so that each one looks different, with individualized backgrounds, different passwords, and so on.

ROAD MAP

For more information on creating, customizing, and using multiple desktops with Norton Navigator, see Chapter 6, "Alternate Reality or Alternate Desktop?"

Displaying the Norton File Manager

To the right of the desktop icons in the Taskbar, you see a small filing cabinet icon. Click this icon to access the Norton File Manager (see Figure 2.8).

CHAPTER 2 A NORTON NAVIGATOR OVERVIEW   33

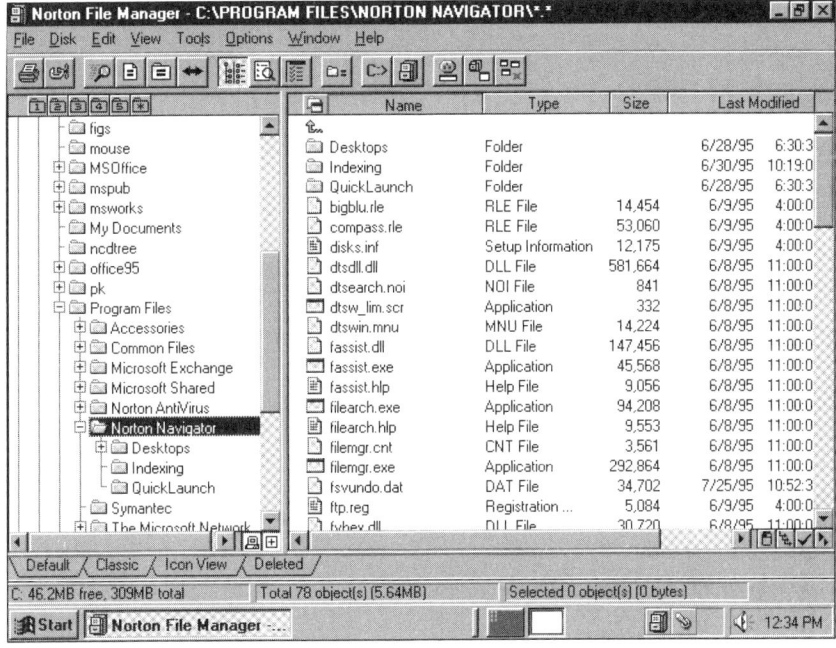

FIGURE 2.8 DISPLAYING THE NORTON FILE MANAGER FROM THE TASKBAR.

You will use the File Manager to work with files, folders, and disks; to zip and unzip files; and to view, archive, delete, search for, and recover files. In the file manager you can also perform routine disk management tasks such as copying, labeling, formatting, or scanning disks and can arrange for network file coordination.

ROAD MAP

For more about working with the File Manager, see Part Three, "The File Manager Extraordinaire."

To skim through the available folders and drives on your system, click the up-arrow in the vertical scroll bar in the center of the File Manager window. Click a different folder and the file list in the window on the right side of the screen will change to show the contents of the new folder.

When you're ready to exit the File Manager, open the File menu and choose **Exit**. The File Manager closes and you are returned to the Norton Navigator Taskbar.

Displaying the Control Center

To the right of the **File Manager** icon, you see the Control Center icon. Click it. The Norton Navigator **Control Center** window appears, as shown in Figure 2.9.

The Norton Navigator Control Center gives you a convenient central location for many of the Norton utilities you'll use often. You can display or modify Taskbar defaults, elect to add Quick Menus, use the Norton Folder Navigator, and add Explorer Extensions to popup menus and dialog boxes; use FileAssist to locate a specific file; use long filenames with LFN; create an index of selected files; or undo something you've just done. We've already discussed the Taskbar, so we won't repeat it here, but the following sections introduce you to each of the remaining features.

Chapter 2 A Norton Navigator Overview   35

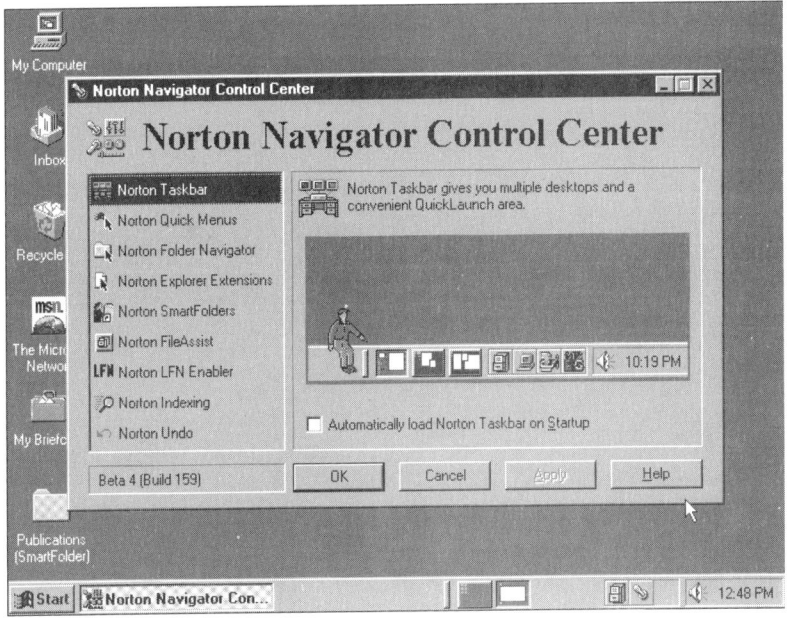

Figure 2.9 The Norton Navigator Control Center.

SHORTCUT

If you want to have Norton Navigator load its Taskbar automatically each time you start Windows 95, click **Automatically load Norton Taskbar on Startup** in the Control Center window.

Norton Quick Menus

Norton Quick Menus give you a further level of organization by adding submenus to the Windows 95 **Run** command and the Documents menu, both of which are available from the Start menu. Click **Norton Quick Menus** and notice the change in the right side of the Control Center window.

Quick Menus can display your most recently used files, organized by application. For example, all Word files are grouped together under the option Microsoft Word Document so that you can see the names of files you've used most recently (see Figure 2.10).

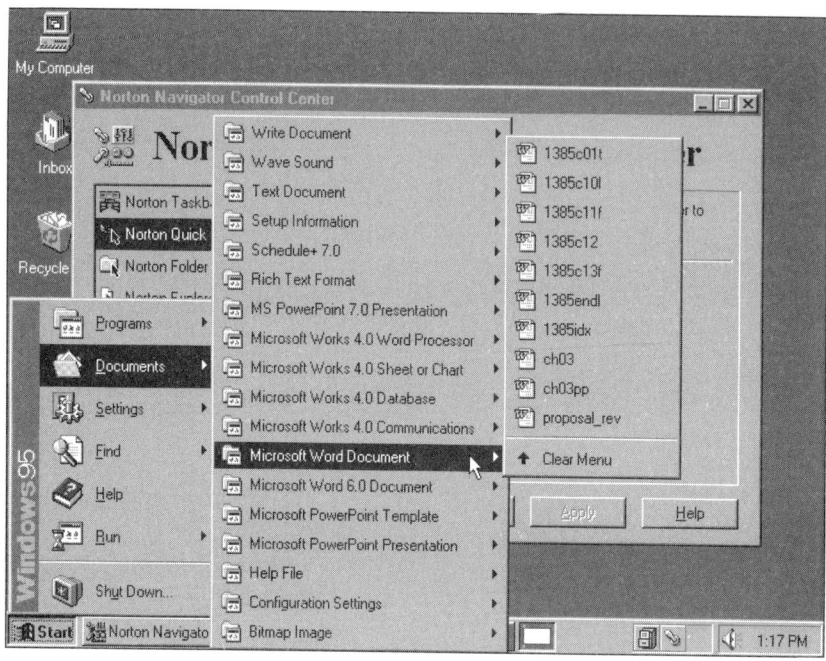

FIGURE 2.10 QUICK MENUS HELP YOU ORGANIZE YOUR FILES SO THAT YOU CAN ACCESS AND USE THEM MORE EASILY.

ROAD MAP

For more about working with Quick Menus, see Chapter 5, "Customizing the Screen Display."

Norton Folder Navigator

The Norton Folder Navigator makes it easy for you to move from folder to folder by using cascading menus. Once you turn on this feature in the Control Center, you can display a cascading menu by clicking the right mouse button on a folder or file. The menu contains commands that let you copy, move, or open files and to create shortcuts to folders and other files.

Norton Explorer Extensions

The Norton Explorer Extensions add extra functionality to the shortcut menus you display by clicking the right mouse button. You can add commands to file menus, folder menus, or even drive menus. Choose the commands you want to include by selecting **Norton Explorer Extensions** in the Control Center and then clicking the **Commands** button for the item you want to change (files, folders, or drives).

If zipping and unzipping files quickly would be helpful for you, for example, you can add these commands to the file's shortcut menu. Figure 2.11 shows a file's shortcut menu.

ROAD MAP

Find out more about Norton Explorer Extensions in Chapter 3, "When You Need to Do It Now."

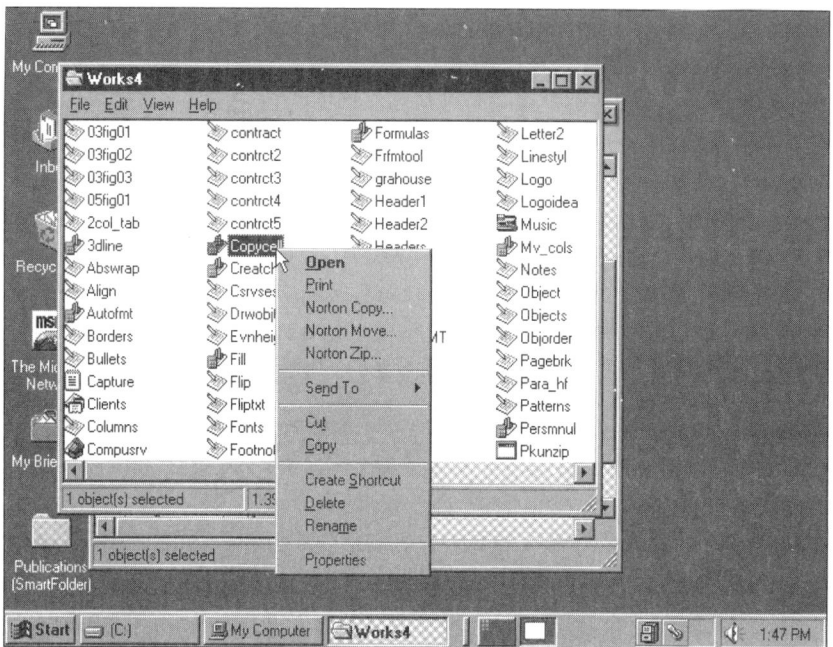

FIGURE 2.11 YOU CAN ADD COMMANDS TO A FILE'S SHORTCUT MENU BY ADDING NORTON EXPLORER EXTENSIONS.

Norton SmartFolders

Norton SmartFolders group file shortcuts together so that you can find certain files easily. For example, suppose that a major part of your work involves editing publications. You can add a SmartFolder to store all the publications on your system, even though they may be spread among many different directories.

Norton Navigator uses a wizard to walk you through the process of creating a SmartFolder. First choose the type of file; then choose the folders in which you want Norton to look. After you're finished with the wizard, the SmartFolder you created is deposited on the desktop, as Figure 2.12 shows; you can access a file in the folder by opening it and double-clicking the file's shortcut.

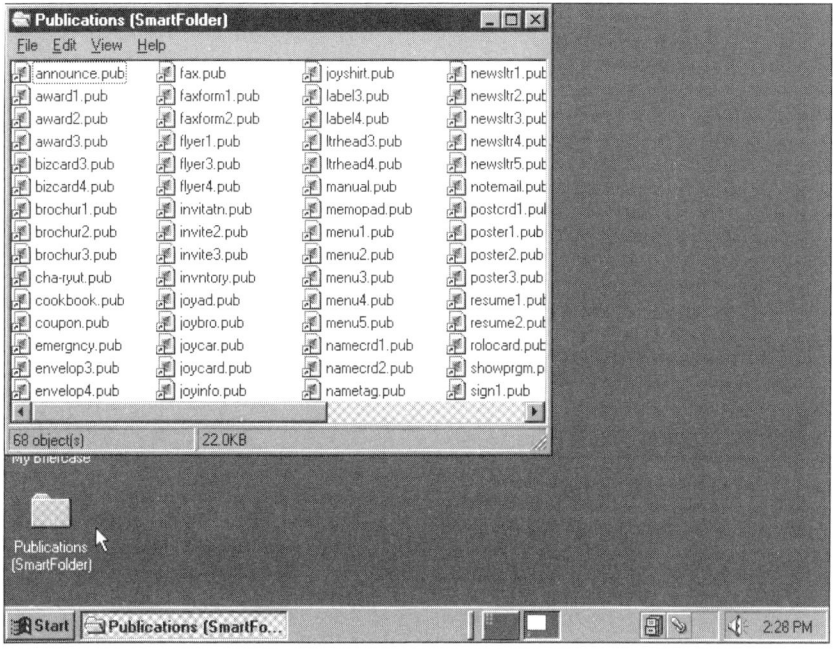

FIGURE 2.12 THE SMARTFOLDER APPEARS ON THE DESKTOP, READY FOR ACCESSING.

NOTE A *wizard* is Microsoft-speak for an automated utility that leads you through a specific operation. The SmartFolder Wizard creates the SmartFolder for you by asking you a series of questions. When you answer the questions, the wizard puts it all together and voila...a SmartFolder. You'll see other wizards in Norton Navigator.

Norton FileAssist

FileAssist is another utility available in the Control Center that adds file-management buttons to the Save As, Open, and Browse dialog boxes in other programs. You can add three different buttons:

 Command Menu button

 Document History button

 Folder History button

When you click the **Show Command Menu** checkbox in the File Assist window, you can also opt to customize the commands displays in the Command menu by clicking the **Commands** button. This lets you choose the commands that are most important to you and add them to the Open, Save As, and Browse dialog boxes in your other Windows programs.

The other two options—**Show Document History Menu** and **Show Folder History Menu**—add buttons that display the most recent files and folders you've used.

 For more about FileAssist, see Chapter 4, "A Control Center Overview."

Norton LFN Enabler

LFN Enabler sounds cryptic, but LFN is just short for "long filename." Windows 95 makes it possible to use descriptive names for your files, so you have a shot at remembering their content later without opening the file.

The Norton LFN Enabler makes long-filename extensions possible for even those programs that are not Windows 95–based. If you have an old version of Word, for example, or an older DOS program, you can still use long, descriptive filenames with the programs using the LFN Enabler.

Norton Indexing

Norton Indexing works hand-in-hand with Norton FastFind, a find-it-fast feature that locates files you're looking for. Create an index by using an index wizard, and you'll locate your files in FastFind with lightning speed. The indexing feature helps Norton Navigator perform file searches as much as 10 times faster than the search capabilities of previous versions of Norton Utilities.

Norton Undo

The Norton Undo feature has saved many of us from that unexpected bolt of panic when you realize you've done something you wish you hadn't, such as deleting the current copy of the annual report and not as you intended, or copying over a database file with all of last year's client information.

Norton Undo keeps an eye on all Norton activities, so if something goes awry in Norton Navigator, you can easily salvage the situation. But Norton Undo also offers you the option of monitoring all Windows 95 activities, so you're doubly protected.

Escaping the Control Center

After you've taken all the time you want and looked around the Control Center sufficiently, close the window by clicking the **close** box. You are returned to the Norton Navigator Taskbar, where we will resume our tour.

Finding the QuickLaunch Area

To the right of the Control Center icon in the Taskbar is yet another area of interest, but don't look—you won't find it. The QuickLaunch area is that blank spot between the **Control Center** icon and the volume control to the left of the clock.

With QuickLaunch, you drag any program's icon to the QuickLaunch area. You can then start the program easily from the Taskbar with a single click. But until you add your own program or file icons there, the space remains blank.

AND ALL THE HELP YOU NEED

The overall breadth of Norton Navigator is not too overwhelming. What is likely to confuse you is the sheer number of features the program includes. How do you remember whether what you need is FileAssist or FileFind? Do the Norton Extensions have anything to do with LFN? With all the different elements that make up the program, it's easy to get confused.

Luckily, Norton Navigator includes a built-in Help system that can answer questions about Navigator basics. Symantec also offers three different kinds of technical support, which we'll cover later in this section.

Using the Help System

You can display Help in the Control Center by clicking the **Help** button in the lower-right corner of the window. The Help Topics window appears, as shown in Figure 2.13.

CHAPTER 2 A NORTON NAVIGATOR OVERVIEW

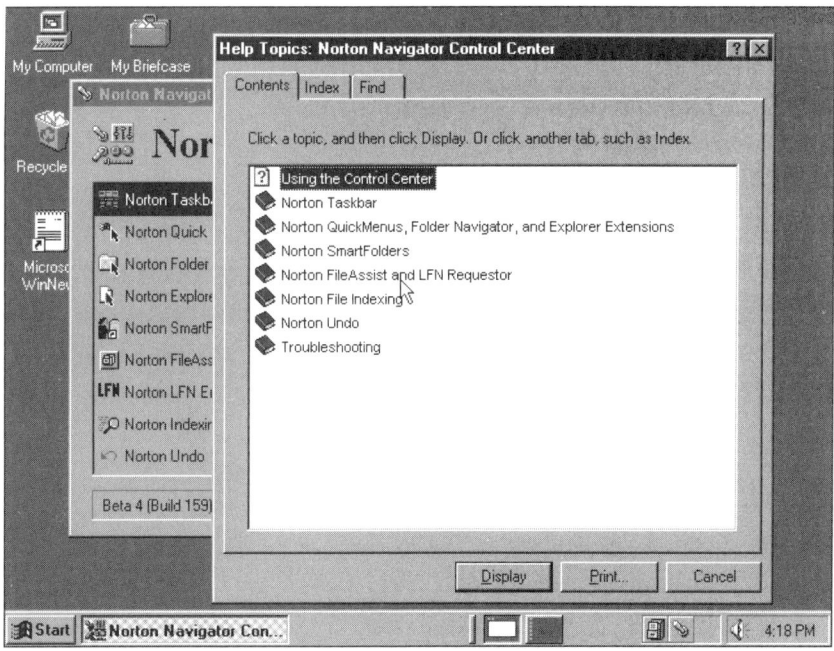

FIGURE 2.13 GETTING HELP FROM NORTON NAVIGATOR.

Because you were in the Control Center when you yelled "Help!" the topic **Using the Control Center** is automatically highlighted, and a number of subtopics related to the Control Center are displayed.

You can get help three ways:

✦ In the Contents window (currently displayed), you choose the topic and then click **Display**. If a list of subtopics appears, select the one you want; then click **Display** again. The topic you selected is displayed in a window along the side of the screen (as shown in Figure 2.14). You can now return to the Contents window, print the information, or choose **Options** to use the information in other things. (See the section "What To Do with the Information Once You've Found It" earlier in this chapter.)

44   Inside Norton Navigator

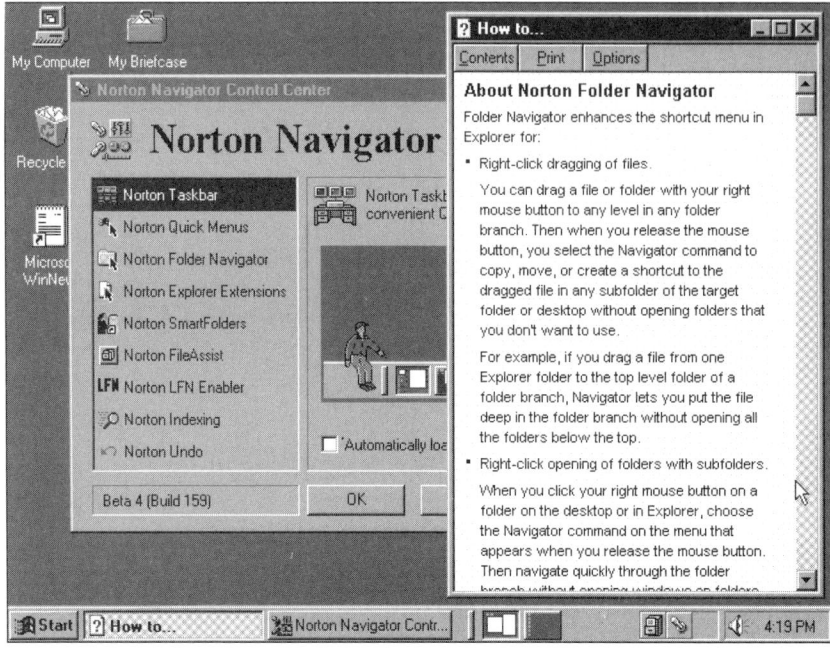

FIGURE 2.14 AFTER YOU SELECT A SUBTOPIC, THE HELP FILE APPEARS.

✦ You can use the **Index** tab to search for a topic by entering the first few letters of the word you're looking for. As soon as you begin typing, Norton starts the search. Figure 2.15 shows an example of the **Index** tab in the Help Topics dialog box. Once Norton locates the topic you want, click it (if there's a subtopic beneath the topic, choose the one you want to see) and then click **Display**. The help appears in a small popup box.

CHAPTER 2 A NORTON NAVIGATOR OVERVIEW   45

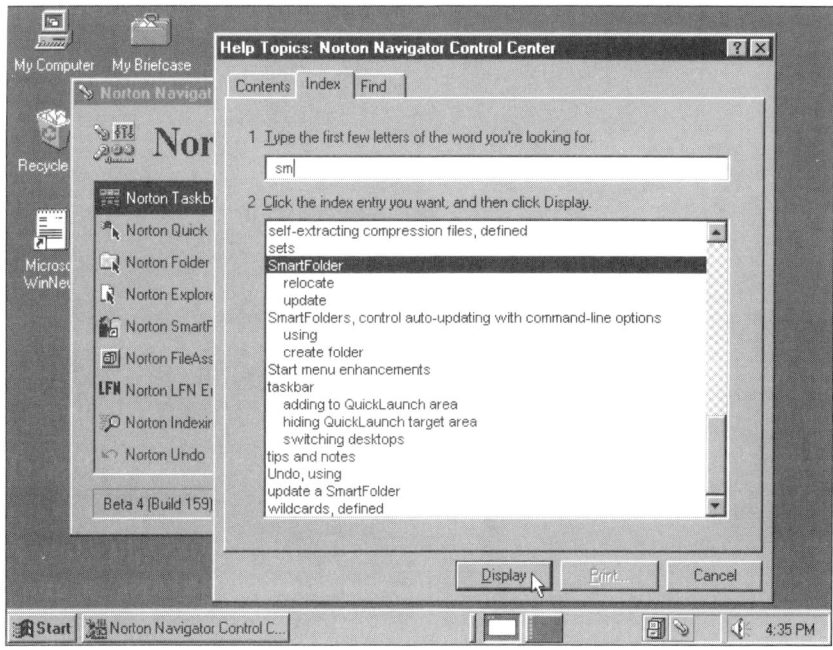

FIGURE 2.15 IN THE INDEX TAB, YOU CAN LOCATE A TOPIC BY TYPING A KEY WORD.

✦ You can also get help by clicking the **Find** tab. A wizard screen appears, telling you that before you can use **Find**, you must allow Windows to create a database that will store all the possible words you may want to find. Choose whether you want a minimum, maximum, or custom-sized database; then click **Next**. When the **Find** tab returns, the database has been generated and Norton Navigator is waiting for the text you want to find (see Figure 2.16).

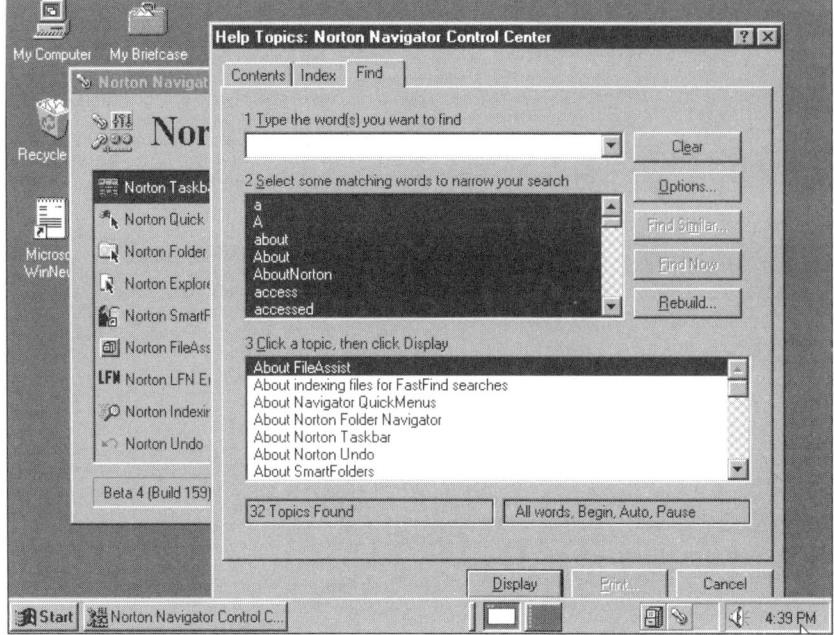

FIGURE 2.16 USING THE FIND UTILITY IN HELP TOPICS.

Symantec Technical Support

Any good software manufacturer wants to do its best to take care of its customers and answer questions as they come up. Symantec offers three different kinds of technical support. Depending on the nature of your business or computer usage and on how much help you need, you might find that one of these plans will fit your needs.

StandardCare Support

StandardCare Support is available to all registered users of Norton Navigator for Windows. At no cost, you have limited phone access to technical support lines, both automated and interpersonal. You can access bulletin boards, leave E-mail messages, or phone in with questions about operations, problems, or services.

PriorityCare Support

PriorityCare Support is a technical support plan that offers fast-access support for people who call infrequently. The charge is a per-minute fee, and you are met with quick, results-oriented answers that sleuth out the problem and get you back on the trail to productivity.

PremiumCare Support

PremiumCare Support is a technical support plan that, for a yearly charge, gives you unlimited phone access and fast access to technical expertise.

For more information about any of the technical support plans offered by Symantec, call 800-441-7234.

THE NEXT STOP

Now that you've had a leisurely stroll through Norton Navigator features, we'll concentrate on doing this quickly in Chapter 3, "When You Need to Do It Now," which focuses on common file-management and organization tasks.

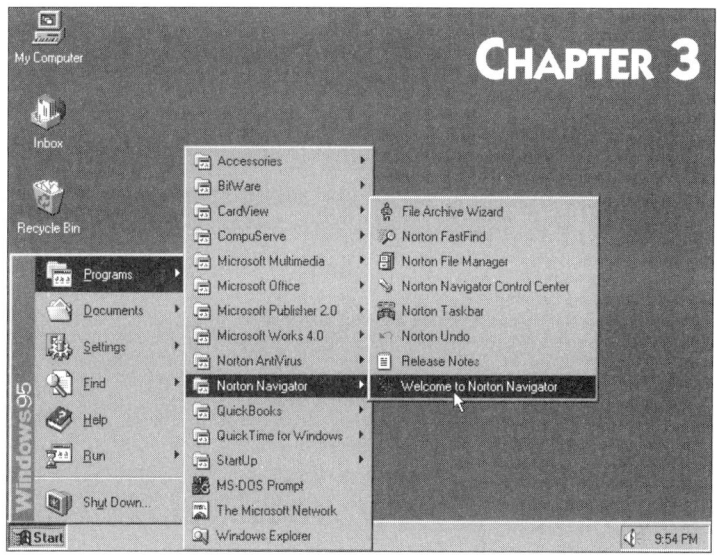

CHAPTER 3

WHEN YOU NEED TO DO IT NOW

Chapter 2 took you through a slow startup of various Norton Navigator features. This chapter concentrates on a faster track: here, you'll learn to perform a number of routine tasks you often need to do quickly, such as

- ✦ Moving among directories
- ✦ Formatting a disk
- ✦ Scanning a disk
- ✦ Selecting files
- ✦ Zipping files
- ✦ Copying files to disk

Additionally, you'll learn how to speed up the way you work with Windows 95 by enabling the Quick Menus feature and by adding Norton Explorer Extensions to file, folder, and drive menus.

STARTING OUT

In Chapter 2, you learned to start Norton Navigator. As you recall, it's a four-step process:

1. Open the Windows 95 Start menu.
2. Select **Programs**.
3. Select **Norton Navigator**.
4. Choose the utility you want to work with from the displayed list (see Figure 3.1). First, choose the **Taskbar**.

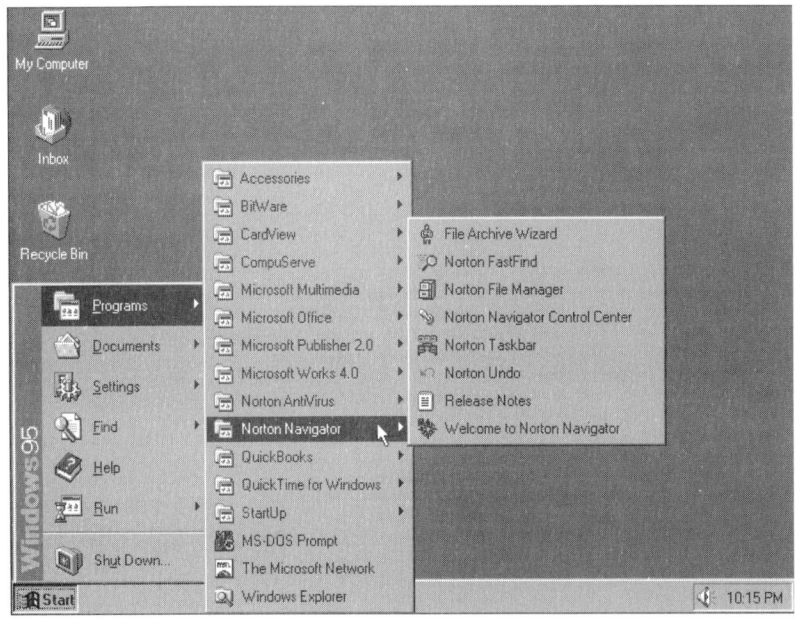

FIGURE 3.1 THE UTILITY YOU START DEPENDS ON WHAT YOU WANT TO DO.

For the purposes of this chapter—introducing you to procedures you may need to do quickly and often—we use only the Control Center and the File Manager. But Table 3.1 lists the various choices in the Norton Navigator group window.

TABLE 3.1 STARTUP CHOICES WITH NORTON NAVIGATOR.

Utility	Use to
File Archive Wizard	Compress and remove unneeded files taking up room on your hard disk.
Norton FastFind	Do lightning-fast searches of files, folders, and disks.
Norton File Manager	Perform a wide range of disk, file, and folder management tasks.
Norton Navigator Control Center	Move among Norton utilities and control screen display, add and subtract features, and so on.
Norton Taskbar	Navigate between alternate desktops and the Norton Desktop; select File Manager and Control Center easily; use QuickLaunch.
Norton Undo	Reverse your most recent operations in both Norton Navigator and Windows 95.
Release Notes	Review changes made in the newest release of the program (Note: This is a text file and not a utility.)
Welcome to Norton Navigator	Take a simple introductory break and explore the different aspects of Norton Navigator.

USING THE CONTROL CENTER

You got a good look at the Norton Navigator Control Center in Chapter 2. Now let's put some of that understanding into action. Start by clicking the **Control Center** icon in the Norton Taskbar. (It's the icon to the right of the **File Manager** icon.)

Displaying the Taskbar at Startup

First, make sure that the Norton Taskbar is highlighted. (It is highlighted automatically by default.) If you want to have the Norton Taskbar loaded automatically when you start your computer, click the **Automatically load Norton Taskbar on Startup** checkbox. A check mark appears in the box. Then click **Apply**. This action applies the new setting to Windows so that the next time you start your computer, the Norton Taskbar will appear.

Adding Norton Quick Menus

Anything named "quick menu" has to help speed things up. Norton's Quick Menus change the way two elements of the Windows 95 Start menu—the **Run** command and the **Documents** command—look and function.

To start Quick Menus, click **Norton Quick Menus** in the Control Center window. The right side of the window changes to show your choices (see Figure 3.2).

CHAPTER 3 WHEN YOU NEED TO DO IT NOW 53

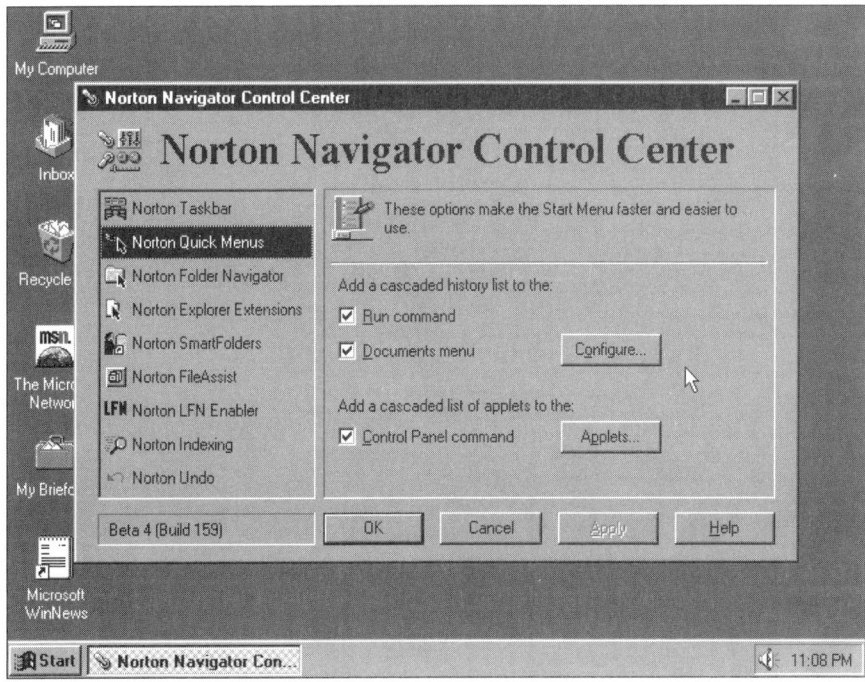

FIGURE 3.2 ADDING NORTON QUICK MENUS TO THE WINDOWS 95 START MENU.

The Quick Menus give you three big enhancements:

✦ You can add a list of the most-recently-run programs to the popup **Run** command window.

54 Inside Norton Navigator

+ You can add a list of the most-recently-opened documents to the Documents menu, arranged according to the program that created them.
+ You can add Norton applications—called *applets*—to the **Control Panel** command in the Windows 95 menus.

To add the most-recently-run files to the **Run** command, click the **Run command** checkbox. To add a document history to the Documents menu, click the **Documents menu** checkbox and then click the **Configure** button. The Document History Configuration popup appears, as shown in Figure 3.3.

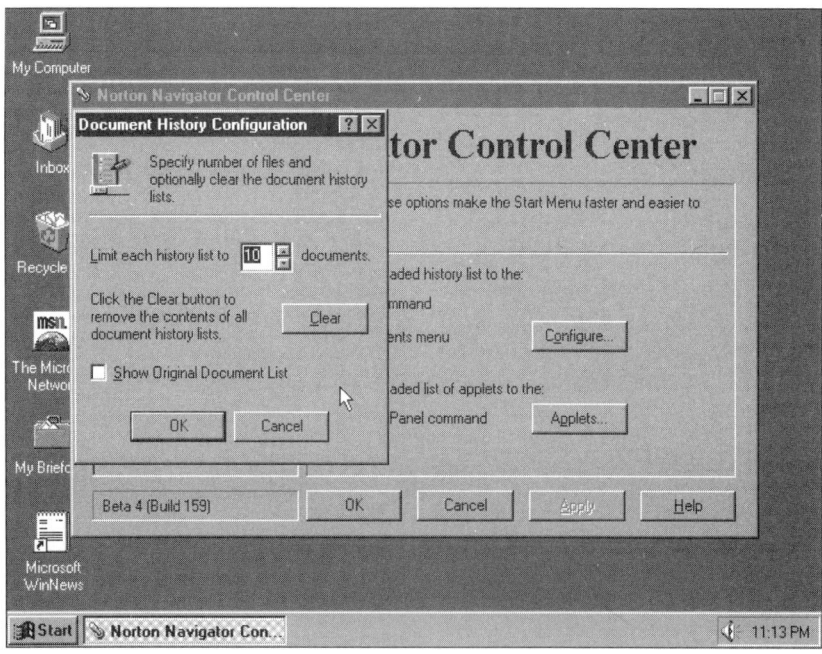

FIGURE 3.3 IN THE DOCUMENT HISTORY CONFIGURATION POPUP, YOU CAN DEFINE HOW MANY FILES YOU WANT DISPLAYED OR CLEAR THE HISTORY BOOKS.

To clear the display of all past Documents, click **Clear**. To specify a different number of documents to display in the history list, click the up- or down-arrow beside the numeric entry in the upper portion of the popup. If you want to return to the original document display, you can click **Show Original Document List**, but this is better left blank. When you're finished entering information, click **OK** to return to the Control Center.

Now, when you go to look for a document in the Documents menu, things look a little different, as Figure 3.4 shows.

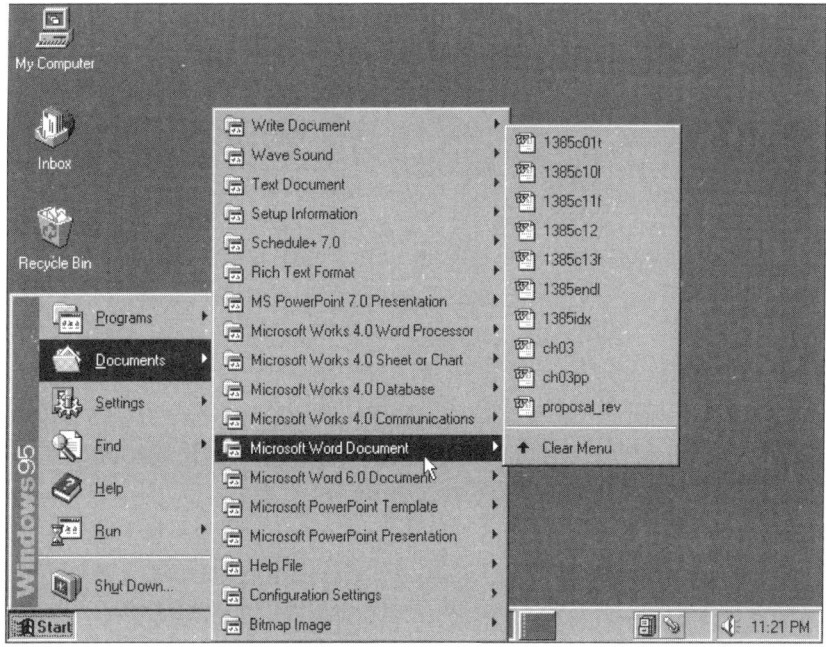

FIGURE 3.4 THE MODIFIED DOCUMENT MENU.

If you want to add applets to the Control Panel, click the **Control Panel command** checkbox and then click the **Applets** button. The Control Panel Applets popup box appears on the screen (see Figure 3.5).

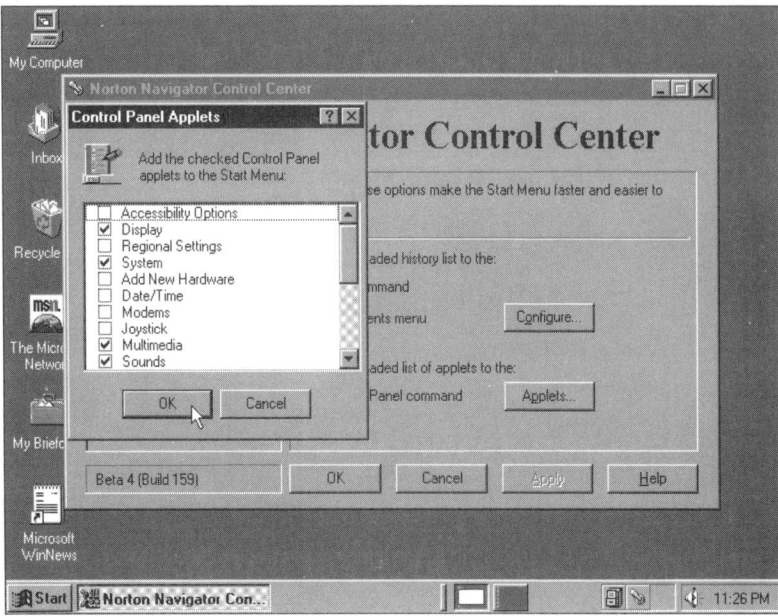

FIGURE 3.5 CHOOSING THE APPLETS YOU WANT TO ADD TO THE CONTROL PANEL.

Adding these applications to the Control Panel will save you time and trouble you might otherwise spend searching the necessary folders for the right information. Scroll through the list, clicking the ones you want. (If you see applets included that you want to remove, click the option with the check mark to turn the feature off.)

When you've chosen the items you want, click **OK**. The Control Panel will now display the applets you specified.

Adding Norton Explorer Extensions

The Norton Explorer Extensions are another "speed-'em-up" feature that you find in the Control Center. The Explorer Extensions add commands to the file, drive, and folder popup menus (which you activate by clicking the right mouse button).

For example, to add file-management commands to the popup menus that appear on files when you position the mouse pointer on a file and click the right mouse button, first click **File Popups** (if it's not already marked with a check mark). Next, click **Commands**. The File Popup Menu Commands dialog box appears, allowing you to choose the commands you want to include automatically in the file popup (see Figure 3.6).

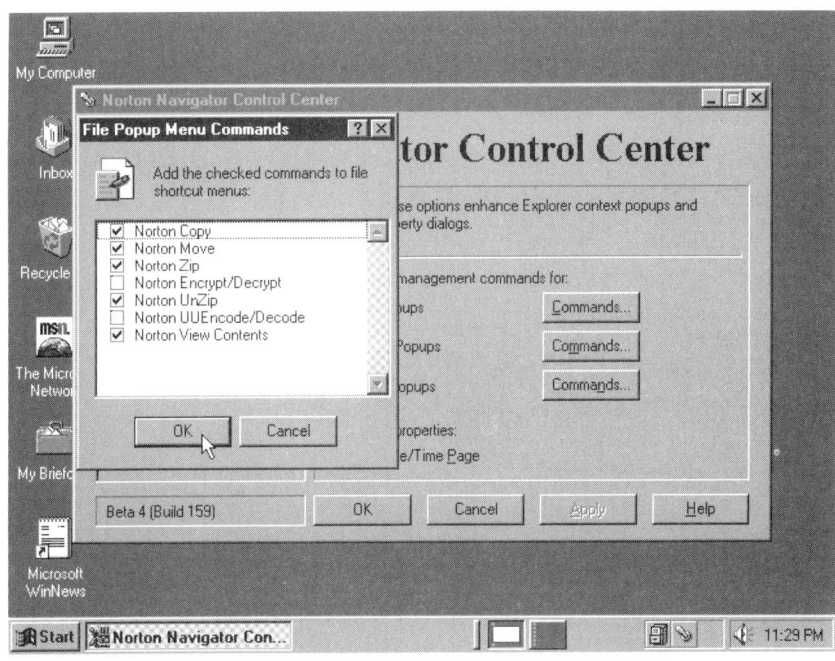

FIGURE 3.6 THESE COMMANDS ARE SELECTED BY DEFAULT. YOU CAN CHOOSE FEWER COMMANDS, IF YOU WISH.

Click the commands you want, placing a check mark beside the commands you want to include and removing any check marks from those commands you do not want to include. When you've checked the commands you're interested in, click **OK**.

The procedure for Folder Popups is the same, although the commands are different. When you choose **Folder Popups**, these commands are available:

- Norton Compress Folder
- Norton Copy
- Norton Move
- Norton File Manager

Again, when you're finished, click **OK**.

The **Drive Popups** command has even fewer available commands. Here you choose from only two:

- Norton Copy Disk
- Norton File Manager

Both commands are selected by default. If you want to disable either one, click the check mark beside the command to remove it.

NOTE: The last remaining option in the Explorer Extensions involves adding a File Date/Time Page to the file properties. This is selected by default and is generally a good thing to include with your files.

A Do-It-Fast Task Compendium

The rest of the procedures in this chapter are geared toward the types of things you routinely do in your computer work—things you may be comfortable with in Windows 3.1 or even in DOS. Now you can use the newest technology of Norton Navigator for these tasks.

You'll be amazed at how much easier file management and organization is when you use Norton Navigator. Just as the Extensions and QuickMenus add functionality and save you time, the Norton File Manager—where you'll perform the rest of the procedures in this chapter—makes using and working with folders and files more intuitive than ever.

Displaying the File Manager

Now that you've displayed the Norton Taskbar, getting to the File Manager is easy. Just position the mouse pointer on the **File Manager** icon (it's the small filing cabinet on the right side of the Taskbar) and click. After a moment, the Norton File Manager appears, as shown in Figure 3.7.

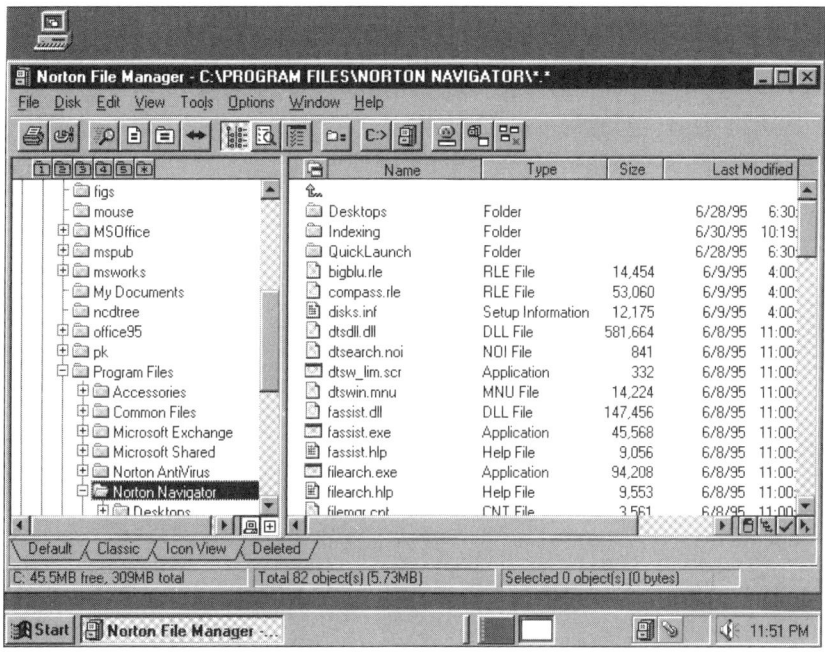

FIGURE 3.7 THE NORTON FILE MANAGER.

SHORTCUT

When the File Manager first appears, the window is not displayed in maximum size. To enlarge the window to its largest size, click the **Maximize** button in the upper-right corner of the File Manager window (to the left of the **close** box).

Changing the Directory Display

One of the first things you may want to do when you display the File Manager is to change the level to which folders are displayed. On the left side of the File Manager window, you see the File Manager Directory Tree. Along the top of the Directory Tree window you see six folder icons. These icons represent the level of detail—or the level of subdirectories—that is displayed in the Directory Tree.

Click level **1**. Everything on the Directory Tree disappears with the exception of My Computer and FTP Sites. These two items represent the highest-level directories on the computer.

Now click level **2**. Sublevels appear beneath My Computer. Now you can see the drives you have available, as well as a CD-ROM if you have one.

Clicking level **3** displays another level of directories. You get the idea. You can continue clicking level by level or choose the level you need to access the files you want to work with.

ROAD MAP

For more about working with the File Manager, changing the File Manager display, and performing a variety of tasks in file and disk management, see Part Three, "The File Manager Extraordinaire."

Formatting a Disk

One of those inescapable procedures (unless you're lucky enough to have purchased a drove of formatted disks that you never have to reuse) is that of formatting disks. Norton Navigator makes it as quick and painless as possible.

When you're ready to format a disk, follow these steps:

1. Insert the disk in drive **A**.
2. Open the Disk menu.
3. Choose **Format Disk**.
4. The Format dialog box appears, as shown in Figure 3.8. Notice that Norton Navigator automatically senses the size of the disk as well as its capacity.

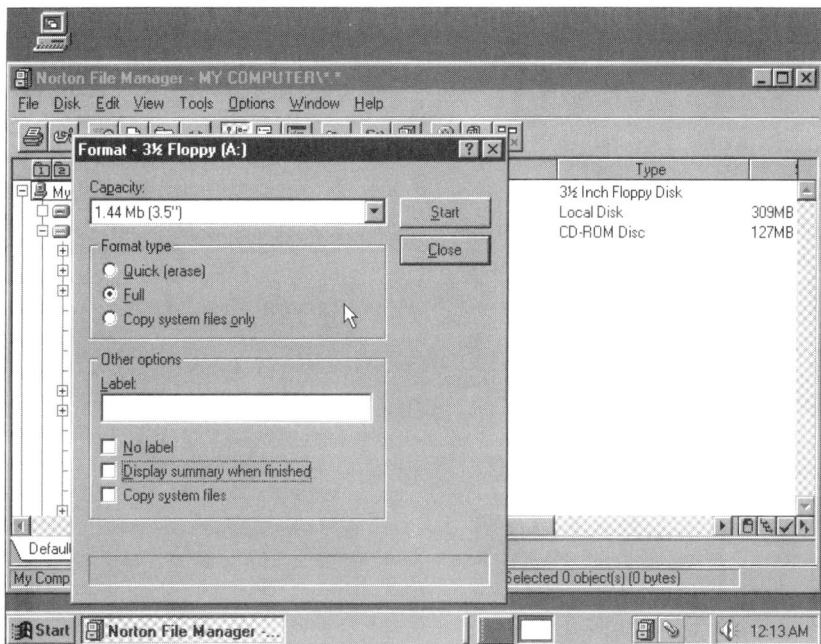

FIGURE 3.8 GETTING READY TO FORMAT A DISK.

5. Choose the **Format type** you want. **Quick (erase)** removes any existing data and prepares the disk quickly. **Full** removes all data

on the disk and formats the disk from scratch. **Copy system files only** does not remove the data on the disk; instead, it copies only the system files to the disk so that you can use the disk as a startup disk in the future.

6. Add a disk label in the **Label** textbox.
7. If you don't want a label, click the **No label** checkbox.
8. Click **Display summary when finished** to see the statistics on the format procedure. (You can use this report to tell whether there were any bad spots on the disk.)
9. **Copy system files** adds startup files to the disk so that you can boot your computer from the formatted disk.
10. When you're ready to start the format, click **Start**. Norton File Manager begins formatting the disk. A **Formatting...** status bar appears at the bottom of the Format dialog box, showing you the progress of the format.

Scanning a Disk

If you're having trouble with a disk or if you simply want to check its health before you use it on your machine (not a bad idea), you can use ScanDisk to check the disk before you use it. Start ScanDisk by opening the File Manager's Disk menu and choosing **Scan Disk**. The ScanDisk dialog box appears, as shown in Figure 3.9.

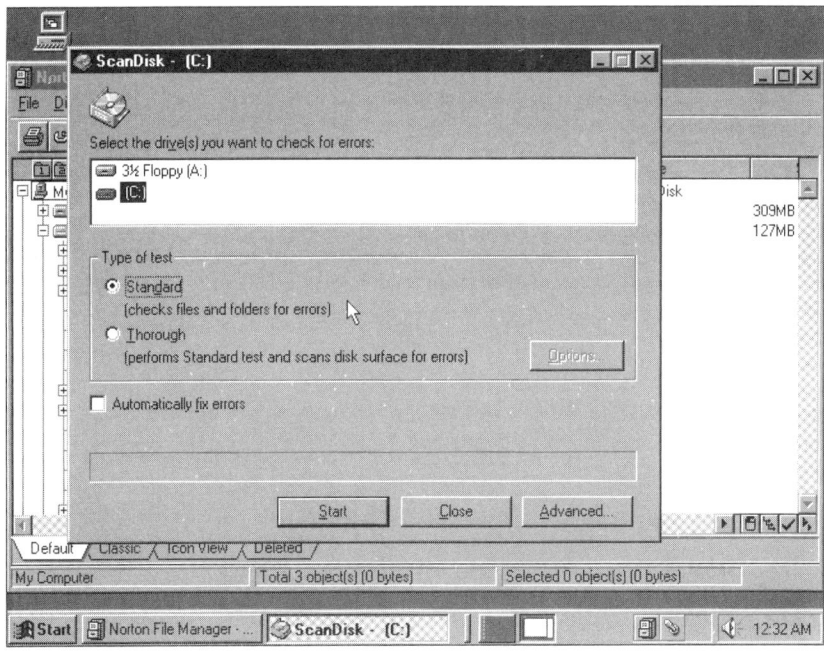

FIGURE 3.9 SCANNING A DISK FOR ERRORS.

ScanDisk will allow you to search for errors in the files and folders stored on a disk as well as the disk surface itself. Here are the steps:

1. Start by inserting the disk in drive **A**.
2. Choose the drive you want to check.

3. Select the **Type of test** you want to perform. A **Standard** test looks through the files and folders stored on the disk; the **Thorough** test checks all the files and folders and examines the physical surface of the disk for problems. **Standard** is selected by default. If you choose **Thorough**, the **Options** button becomes available. When you click **Options**, the Surface Scan Options dialog box appears, giving you a number of options for how you want Norton Navigator to do the surface scan of the disk. You can choose from among these options:

   + Scan the disk system and data storage areas.
   + Scan only the system area of the disk.
   + Scan only the data area of the disk.

NOTE If you have been having trouble with a disk or if the information on it has been garbled or unreliable, your best bet is to check both system and data areas. The time required isn't much longer than doing a more isolated scan, and you can be sure you've checked everything there is to check on the disk.

Still in the Surface Scan Options dialog box, if you want to skip write-testing (meaning that ScanDisk won't test the drive's ability to write to the disk), click the **Do not perform write-testing** checkbox. If you want ScanDisk to refrain from repairing any bad sectors in hidden and system files, click that checkbox. Then click **OK**.

NOTE What's a bad sector? A disk records information on its surface in tracks and sectors. Sectors are divisions of individual tracks. When you have a bad sector on a disk, it means that part of the disk cannot record information. ScanDisk has the capability of fixing most bad sector problems so that data can be stored in that area.

5. If you want ScanDisk to fix the errors it encounters automatically, without any intervention from you, click the **Automatically fix errors** checkbox.

6. Click the **Advanced** button to determine whether you want to change any of the Advanced options (see Figure. 3.10). You can specify when a summary is displayed; choose whether the log file kept as a record of the scan is replaced or added to; make copies of any cross-linked files; convert lost clusters to files; and look for invalid filenames, dates, and times. Finally, a checkbox that tells Norton Navigator to check the host drive first is displayed in the lower-right side of the dialog box. It is selected by default. Click **OK** when you're ready to return to the ScanDisk dialog box.

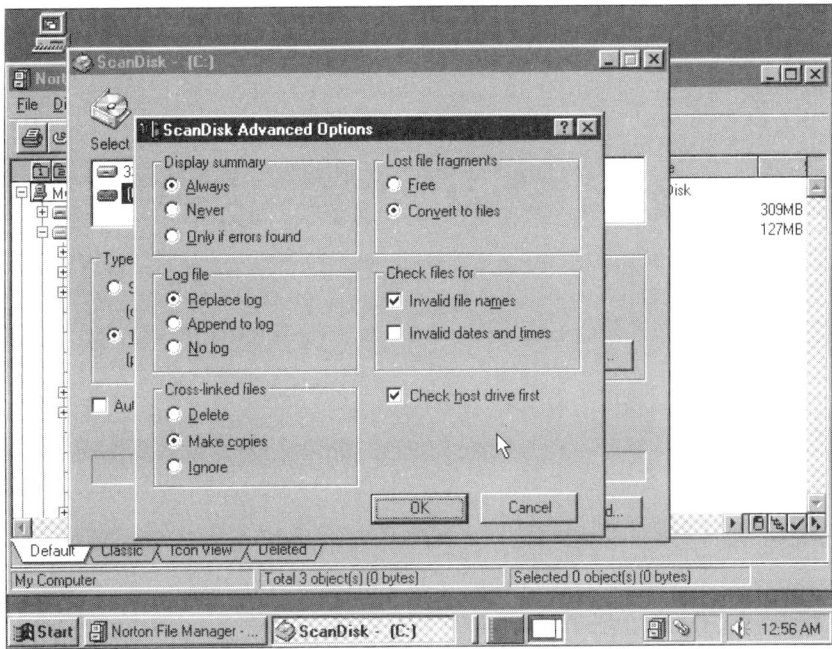

FIGURE 3.10 SETTING SCANDISK ADVANCED OPTIONS.

7. Click **Start** and ScanDisk begins the scan.

You see a message that ScanDisk is checking folders, then file allocation tables, then folders again, then disk surface...you get the idea.

NOTE If you are scanning your hard disk—especially if you have a large-capacity hard disk—be prepared to wait for 10–30 minutes for ScanDisk to complete a Thorough test.

Selecting Files

Before you can perform routine file-maintenance tasks, such as copying, moving, deleting, or zipping files, you must know how to select the files you want to work with.

Norton Navigator's File Manager gives you several ways to do this. You can use commands in the Edit menu to select and deselect the files you want to work with. Open Edit and choose **Select**. A small popup menu appears beside the menu (see Figure 3.11) giving you the choice of selecting **All** (this means folders and files), **All Files**, or **Some** files. If you choose **Some**, the Select Files dialog box appears so that you can specify the files you'd like to select. Type the files you want in the **Files:** area; then click **Select**.

CHAPTER 3 WHEN YOU NEED TO DO IT NOW   67

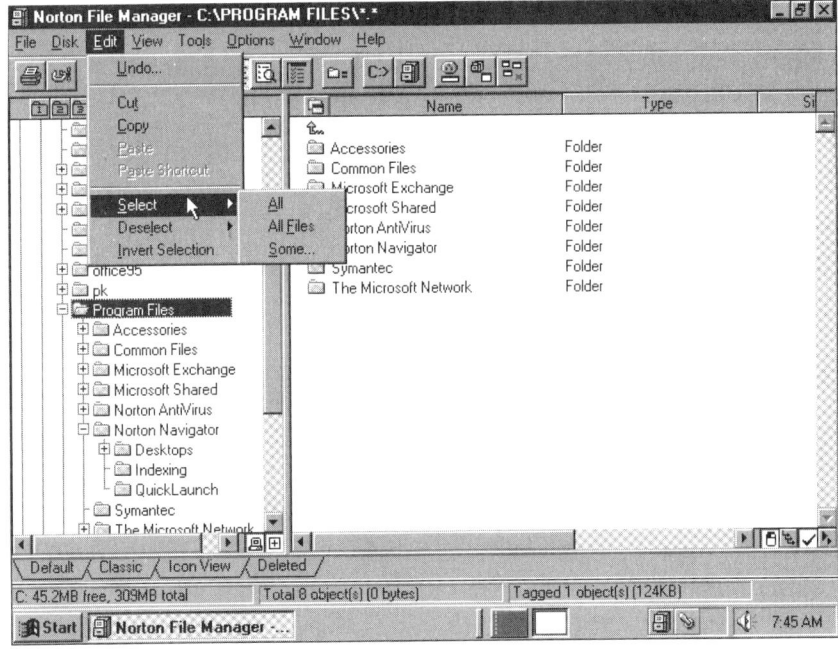

FIGURE 3.11 THE POPUP SELECT MENU.

SHORTCUT

You can deselect files easily by opening the Edit menu and choosing **Deselect**. You then choose whether you want all selected items deselected or only some items. Norton Navigator removes the highlight or tags from the items you specified.

In the **List** area of the File Manager window, you see a set of four buttons along the bottom right side of the window. These buttons further affect how you select and deselect files (see Table 3.2).

TABLE 3.2 FILE SELECTION BUTTONS IN FILE MANAGER.

Multiple Select	If you want to choose several files that are not contiguous—that is, they do not appear all together in one block—you can click the **Multiple Select** button and then choose the files you want to work with by pointing to and clicking each file.
Show Entire Branch	You can change the display of the files in the right portion of the File Manager window by clicking the **Show Entire Branch** button. All files in that particular directory branch are displayed.
Tag Mode	When you want to tag selected files in order—perhaps to perform multiple operations with them—click **Tag Mode**. Each file you click is highlighted, and a check mark is placed to the left of the filename. You might use tagged files, for example, when you are selecting files for searching or indexing operations.
Outline Mode	When you click **Outline Mode**, Norton File Manager displays the files according to their file types. Files are summarized so that you see, for example, how many **.exe** files you have and how much memory they use, how many **.txt** files you have, and so on.

Selecting All Files

When you want to select all the files in the displayed list, open the Edit menu, choose **Select**, and choose **All Files**. All files in the **List** window are highlighted.

Selecting a Block of Files

You can select a contiguous block of files by clicking the first file in the block, pressing and holding the **Shift** key, and clicking the end file in the block. All files between the two points are highlighted.

Selecting Multiple Noncontiguous Files

If you need to select a few assorted files from the list but they aren't together in a group, first click the **Multiple Select** button. Then move the pointer to the list area and click the files you want to select. Norton File Manager highlights only those you click.

Tagging Files

In some operations, such as when you're searching for particular file elements or want to index files, you may want to create a subset of files that you use for certain purposes. You can tag the files to mark them as part of this subset; then you can perform a variety of operations on the files you've tagged.

To tag files, first click the **Tag Mode** button in the bottom of the list area. Then move the mouse pointer to the files you want to tag and click. Norton File Manager highlights the selected files and tags them with a check mark preceding the filename. The status bar tells you how many files you've tagged and how much storage the files occupy (see Figure 3.12).

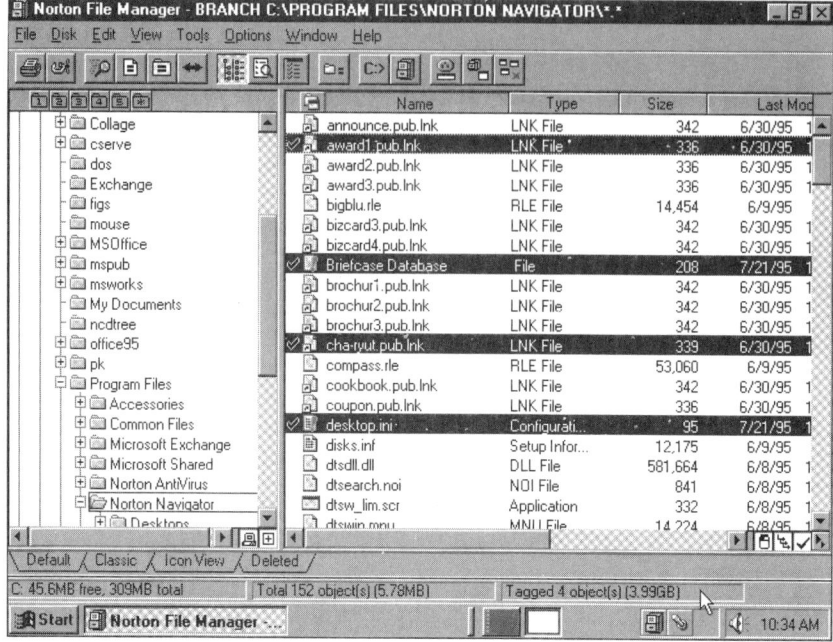

FIGURE 3.12 TAGGING FILES.

SHORTCUT

To untag files quickly, simply click the **Tag Mode** button again.

Zipping Files

Just a few years ago, file zipping was a relatively uncommon practice. Today, almost everybody needs to zip a file once in a while.

The process of zipping a file compresses the file into a fraction of the space normally required by the file in its expanded state. File compression lets you copy large files to disk, compress many files into one for easier handling, and free a considerable amount of storage space on your hard disk.

The advent of multimedia has brought with it enormous creativity, enormous opportunity, and enormous files. You just can't fit graphics, sound, and text into a small space unless you have a utility that compresses file data into the smallest possible package.

Norton's File Manager includes Norton Zip, a utility that compresses the data. Norton UnZip is the partner utility that expands the data when you're ready to use it. The commands for using Zip and UnZip are housed in the File menu, but you can also use Zip from the Norton File Manager's toolbar.

Here's how to zip files:

1. Select the files you want to zip.

You can zip one file or many; any file you need to compress to preserve space can be zipped.

NOTE

2. Click the **Zip** tool (second from the left on the toolbar) or open the File menu and choose **Norton Zip**. The Norton Zip dialog box appears, as shown in Figure 3.13.

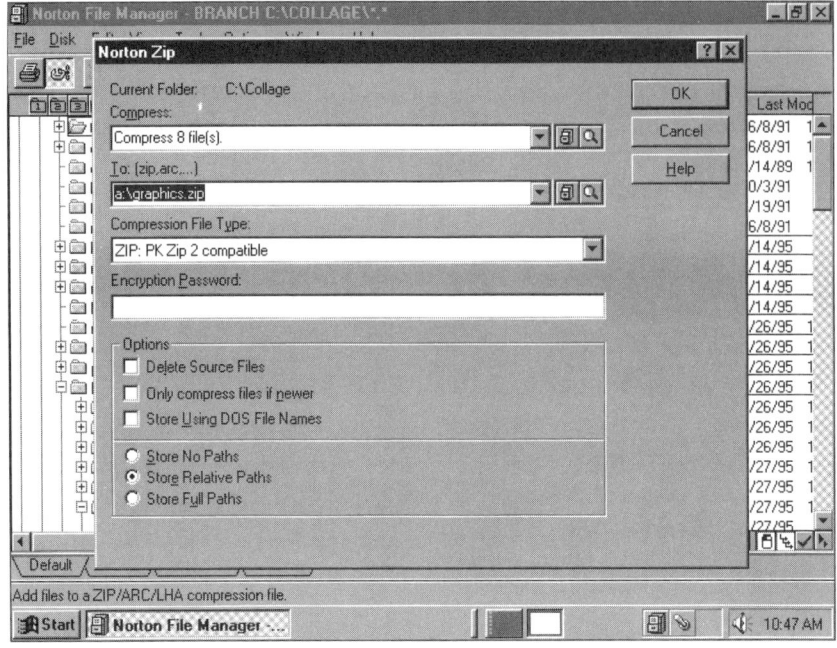

FIGURE 3.13 ZIPPING FILES.

3. In the **To:** textbox, enter the location and name you want to assign to the Zip file created when the files are compressed. In this example, we name the file **GRAPHICS.ZIP** and want it saved to drive **A**.

4. Click **OK**. Norton Zip begins zipping the files. A small animated icon shows you the progress of the compression. When the task is finished, the Norton Zip dialog box closes and you are returned to the File Manager.

Zipped files take on an unusual appearance in the File Manager. You'll notice that they are a kind of "electric" green color. When you click the file, you will see the file's contents—so you can easily double-check the files you zipped to make sure that you included everything necessary.

CHAPTER 3 WHEN YOU NEED TO DO IT NOW   73

This brings us to our next task. Let's display the contents of drive **A**.

Viewing Disk Contents

Until now, you've learned to navigate through the directory tree, but that's been on your hard disk. How do you display the contents of a disk in the disk drive?

Position the mouse pointer in the vertical scroll bar that divides the directory tree window and the file list window. Click the up-arrow, scrolling up to the top of the directory tree. Beneath My Computer, click **a:**. After a second's delay, you see the zipped graphics file (assuming you zipped some files and had them placed on drive **A** in the last section) beneath the drive name. Additionally, in the file list window, you see the zipped file.

When you want to change back to drive **C** (or move to another drive), simply click the drive you want.

NOTE If you seem to be missing a drive—perhaps Norton File Manager isn't displaying your CD-ROM—make sure the **Show All Drives** button, in the bottom of the directory tree window, has been selected.

Copying a File

Now that you know how to display the different disks and directories (or folders), copying a file is simple. First, click the drive or directory that stores the file you want to copy. For example, suppose you want to copy the **GRAPHICS.ZIP** file from drive **A** to the **MSPUB** directory of drive **C**. (You won't have that directory unless you have Microsoft Publisher installed on your computer.)

First, click drive **A** and display the **GRAPHICS.ZIP** file (see Figure 3.14).

74 Inside Norton Navigator

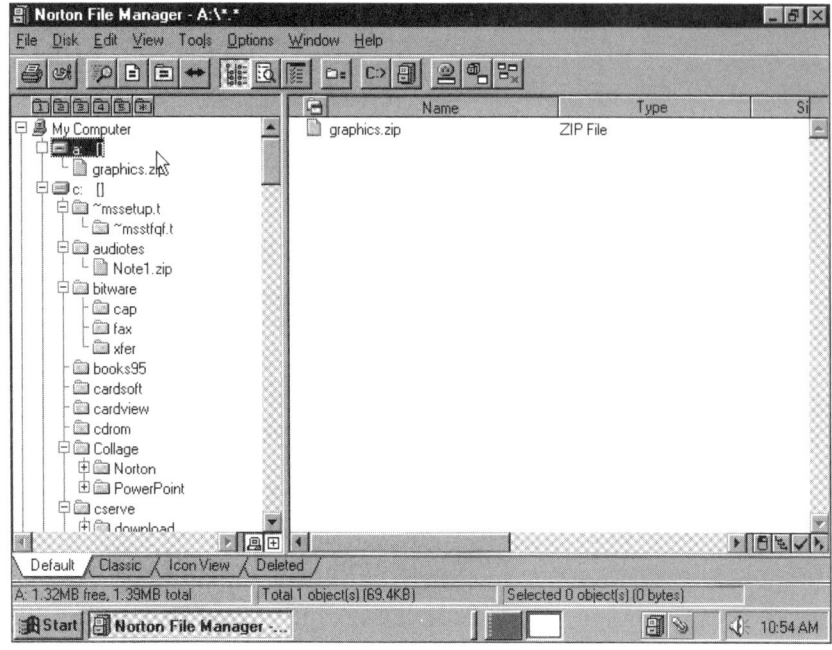

FIGURE 3.14 THE ORIGINAL FILE.

Now move the mouse pointer to the down-arrow in the vertical scroll bar that separates the directory tree and the file list windows. Click the arrow to scroll the display down to **MSPUB**, if necessary. (You may not need to scroll the display at all, depending on how few directories you have on your system.)

Move the mouse pointer to **GRAPHICS.ZIP** in the file list window. Press and hold the mouse pointer and drag the file to **MSPUB**. A small icon will appear as you drag the file. When the file is positioned over **MSPUB** accurately, a dotted rectangle shows you where the target of the copy will be. When the dotted rectangle surrounds **MSPUB**, you can release the mouse button and Norton File Manager will copy the file.

A small status box appears on the screen, asking you to confirm that you want to copy the selected file to **MSPUB**. Click **Yes**. The File

Manager copies the file to the new directory, and the directory tree is immediately updated (see Figure 3.15).

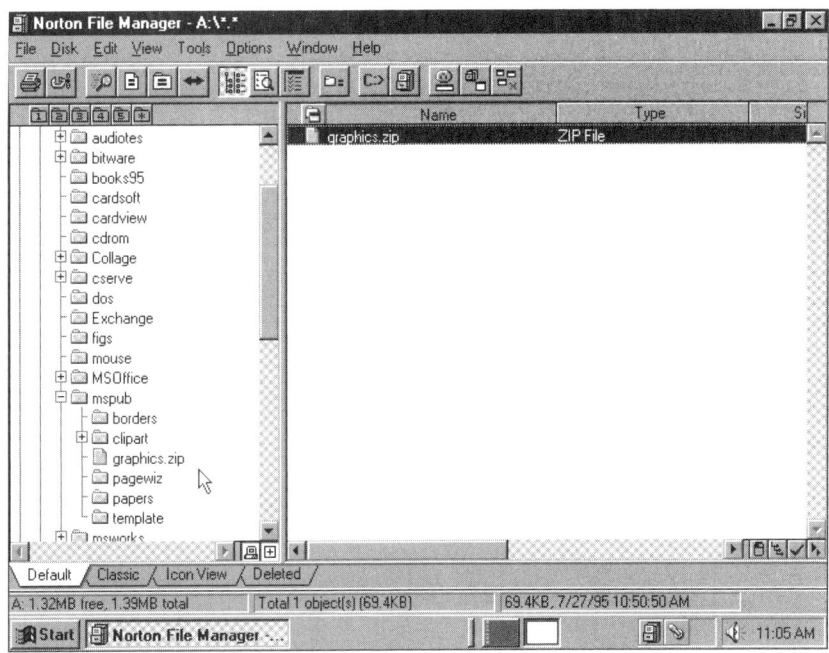

FIGURE 3.15 THE COPIED FILE.

Deleting a File

Deleting a file is a similar process. You can delete one or many files. If you want to select a number of files, use the selection methods discussed earlier in this chapter. Suppose that you've decided that you don't want the **GRAPHICS.ZIP** in **MSPUB** after all. You're going to delete it.

Select **GRAPHICS.ZIP** and press **Del**. The Delete dialog box appears, as shown in Figure 3.16. The filename is already highlighted. The **Wipe Delete** option erases the file data by zeroing out all the data. You cannot recover an accidentally deleted file if you've selected the **Wipe Delete** option, so unless you're dead certain you won't be needing the file again, leave this option unchecked.

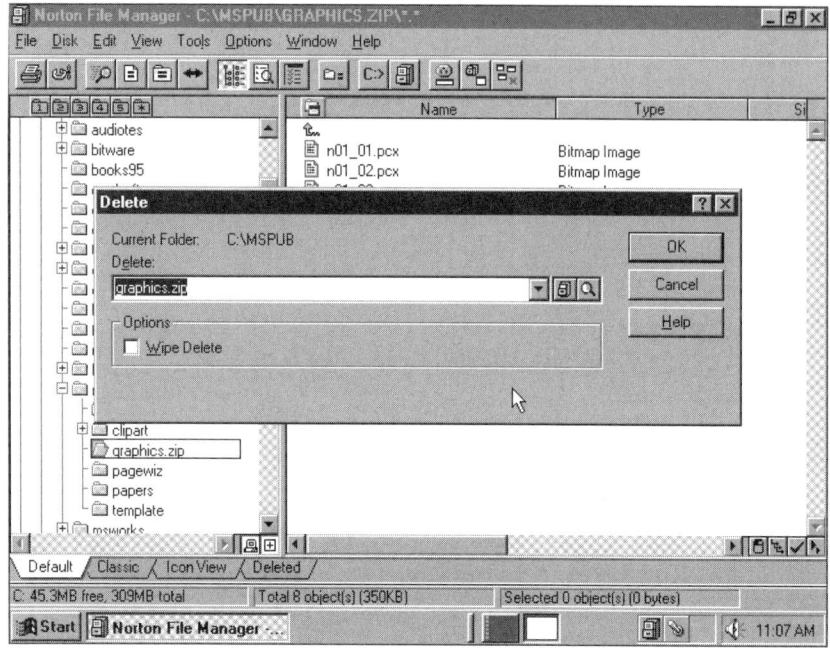

FIGURE 3.16 DELETING A FILE.

When you're ready to delete the file, click **OK**. Norton File Manager will give you another chance to back out by asking whether you're sure you want to delete the selected file. Click **Yes**, and the file is deleted.

| NOTE | If you still see a filename or icon in the directory tree after you know you've deleted it, open the Window menu and choose **Refresh**. This tells the File Manager to take another look at the screen and update any changes that have been made. That'll get rid of the file's ghost. |

Exiting the File Manager

When you've finished your quick run-through of tasks, get out of the File Manager quickly by clicking the **close** box in the upper-right corner of the window. You can also open the File menu and choose **Exit** if you prefer that approach.

THE NEXT STOP

In this chapter, you've learned some of the basic operations you'll use in working routinely with disks, files, and folders. More in-depth information on using the Control Center and the File Manager is covered in Part Two, "Navigation at Its Finest," and Part Three, "The File Manager Extraordinaire."

Chapter 4 begins Part Two with an up-close look at the workings of the Control Center.

Part Two

Navigation at Its Finest: The Control Center

Chapter 4: A Control Center Overview

Chapter 5: Customizing the Screen Display

Chapter 6: Alternate Reality or Alternate Desktop?

Chapter 7: Working with Folders

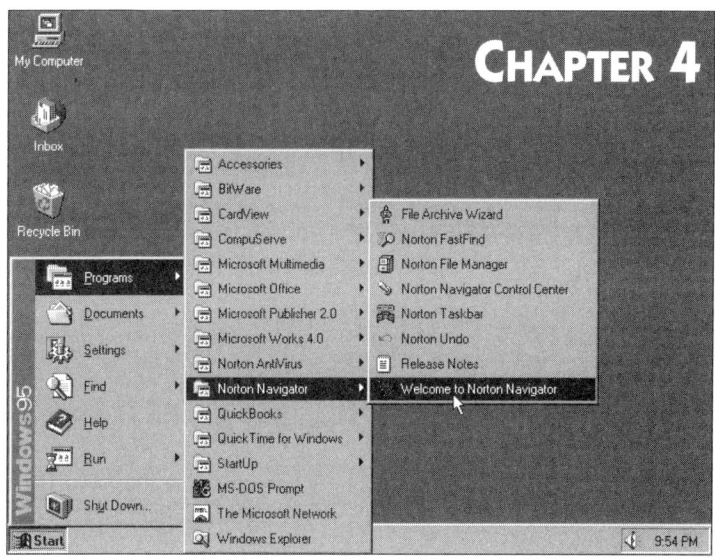

CHAPTER 4

A CONTROL CENTER OVERVIEW

This chapter opens Part Two of the book with an up-close look at the Control Center. Whereas a major part of the focus of Norton Navigator's task-oriented features is spotlighted on the File Manager, the Control Center is the launching pad for many of Norton's ease-of-use and streamlining functions.

What Is the Control Center?

The Norton Navigator Control Center is the hub of Norton Navigator. From the *Control Center*, you can access many of the Norton features, including the following:

- Quick Menus
- The Folder Navigator
- Explorer Extensions
- SmartFolders
- FileAssist
- LFN Enabler
- Indexing
- Undo

Additionally, you can change settings for the Taskbar in the Control Center so that the Taskbar is loaded automatically when you start your computer.

The Control Center makes it easy for you to move in and out of the various Norton utilities from a common vantage point. Most of the features listed in the Control Center help you use your programs more easily, quickly, or intuitively. These items add commands to popup menus, enable you to use long descriptive filenames for your files, create indexed folders on a certain topic you can access quickly, and add many other enhancements.

DISPLAYING THE CONTROL CENTER

You can display the Control Center in one of two ways. Starting at the Windows 95 desktop, you can open the Start menu, choose **Programs**, choose **Norton Navigator**, and then choose **Norton Navigator Control Center**, as shown in Figure 4.1.

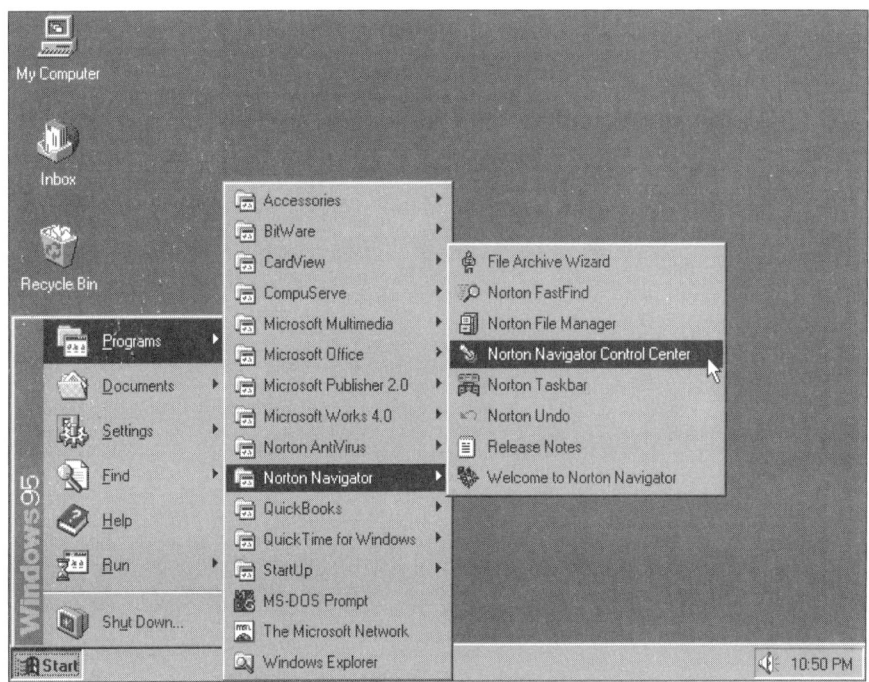

FIGURE 4.1 STARTING THE CONTROL CENTER.

If you plan to use other Norton Navigator features in addition to the Control Center or if you plan to come and go with the Control Center feature, you may prefer to load the Norton Taskbar. To start the Norton Taskbar, begin with the Windows 95 Start menu and click **Programs**, **Norton Navigator**, and then **Norton Taskbar**. The Norton Navigator opening screen appears and disappears, and then the Taskbar appears on the bottom of your screen.

To start the Control Center from the Taskbar, click the **Control Center** icon (to the left of the **File Manager** icon) on the right side of the Taskbar (see Figure 4.2). After a moment, the Norton Navigator Control Center window appears, as shown in Figure 4.3.

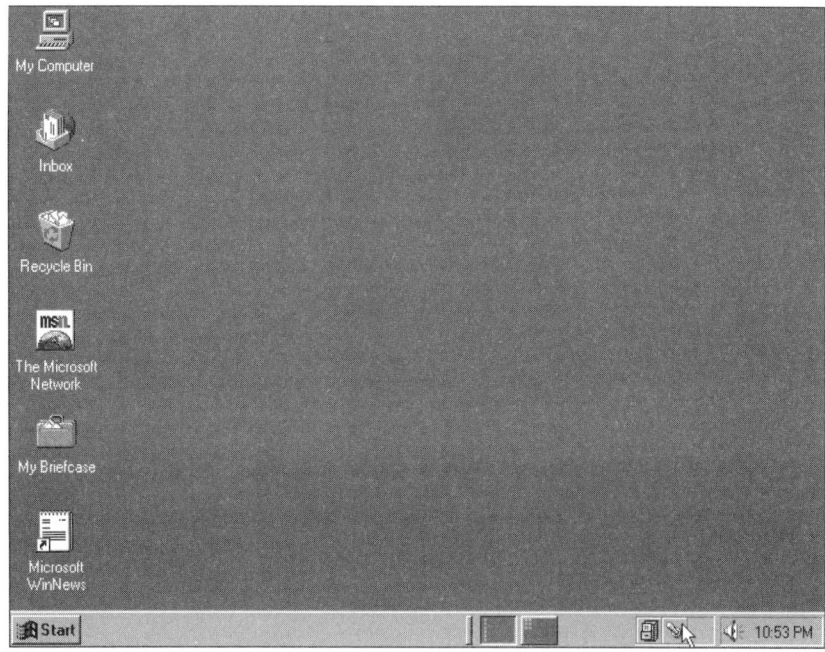

FIGURE 4.2 STARTING THE CONTROL CENTER FROM THE NORTON TASKBAR.

Chapter 4 A Control Center Overview

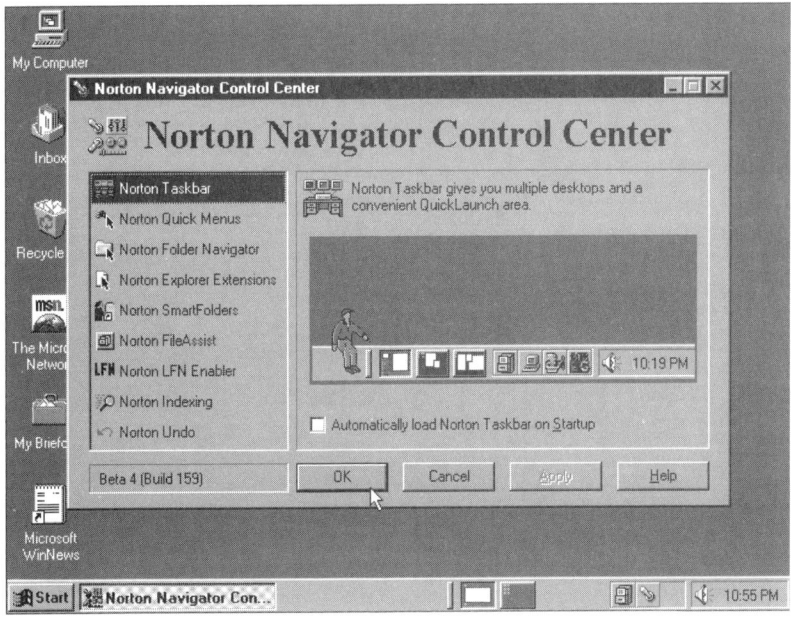

Figure 4.3 The Norton Navigator Control Center.

Exploring Control Center Options

The Control Center includes a number of different options—some of these you'll use religiously; others you may never use. This section gives you a look at each of the elements available in the Control Center so that you can decide for yourself how they can help you with your computing tasks.

Norton Taskbar

When you first display the Control Center, the **Norton Taskbar** option is selected by default. The opening screen of the Control Center contains the only Taskbar choice you've got: to automatically load Norton Taskbar on startup—or not (see Figure 4.4).

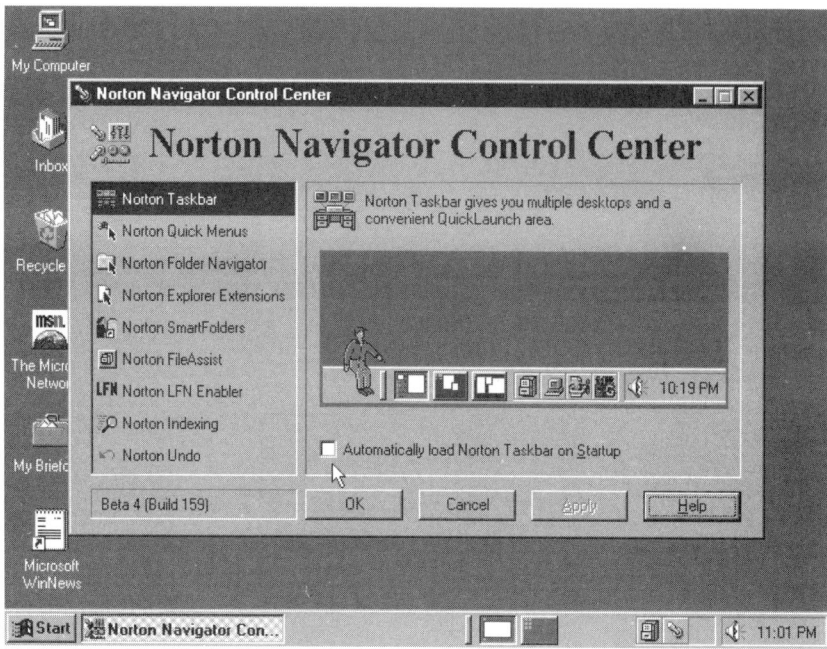

FIGURE 4.4 THE TASKBAR CHOICES INCLUDE ONLY ONE OPTION—WHETHER OR NOT TO LOAD THE TASKBAR AUTOMATICALLY AT STARTUP.

When you first start the program, this setting is not enabled, meaning that Norton is not loaded automatically when you start your computer. If you want the Norton Taskbar to be added over your Windows taskbar when you start your system, click the checkbox.

CHAPTER 4 A CONTROL CENTER OVERVIEW 87

Norton Quick Menus

When you click **Norton Quick Menus**, the display in the Control Center changes (see Figure 4.5). The Norton Quick Menus enable you to add new features to the Windows 95 Start menu, making it easy to navigate and use.

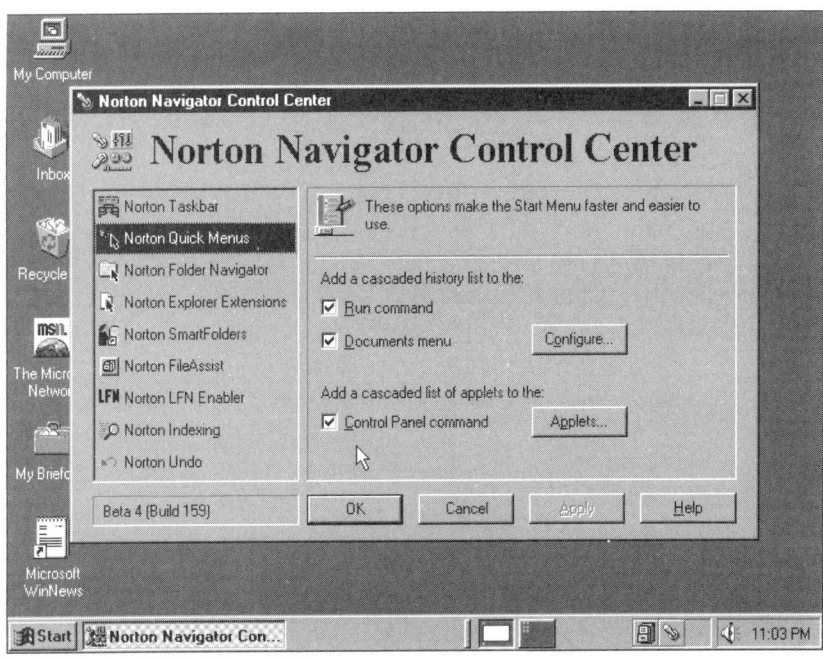

FIGURE 4.5 THE NORTON QUICK MENUS SCREEN IN THE CONTROL CENTER.

88 Inside Norton Navigator

You can add what Norton refers to as a *cascaded history list* to both the **Run** command and the **Documents** command in the Start menu. This means that when you choose the **Run** command, a popup list of the most recently selected commands (that's where the history comes in) is displayed, as shown in Figure 4.6.

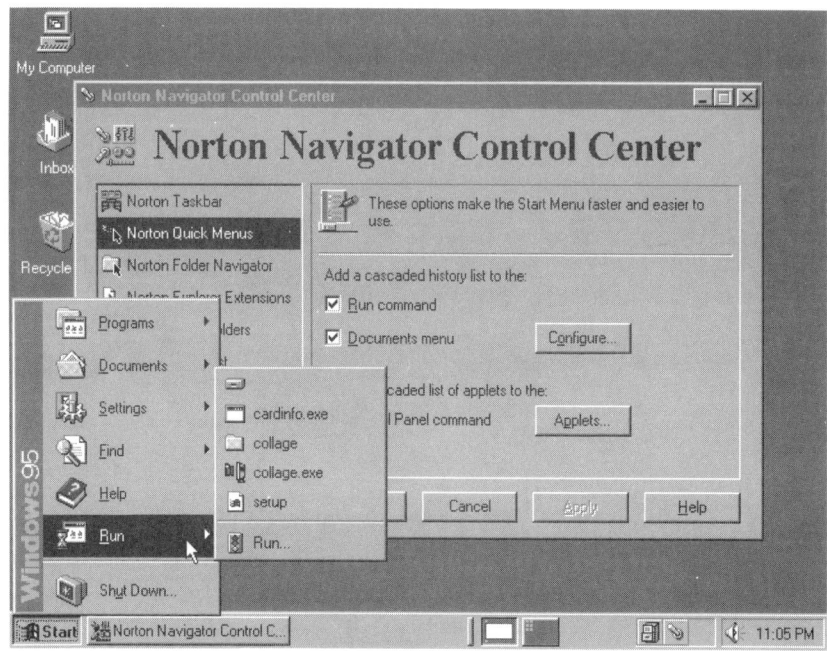

FIGURE 4.6 SHOWING THE RUN COMMAND'S HISTORY LIST.

Likewise, you can add a history list to the Documents menu—and you can determine how many documents you want to show, clear past documents, and start fresh by clicking the **Configure** button and entering your settings in the Document History Configuration dialog box. After you enter your settings, click **OK**.

Also in the Quick Menus window, you can add *applets*—miniapplications—to the Windows Control Panel. When you click the **Applets** button, the Control Panel Applets dialog box appears. You can then click the applets you want (or click selected applets to deselect them, if necessary). When you're finished, click **OK** to return to the Quick Menu window in the Control Center.

Norton Folder Navigator

Clicking **Norton Folder Navigator** displays the screen shown in Figure 4.7. This is a simple feature—it just adds the Navigation command when you click on a folder or drag a file using the right mouse button. By default, both these features are *enabled*, meaning they are turned on.

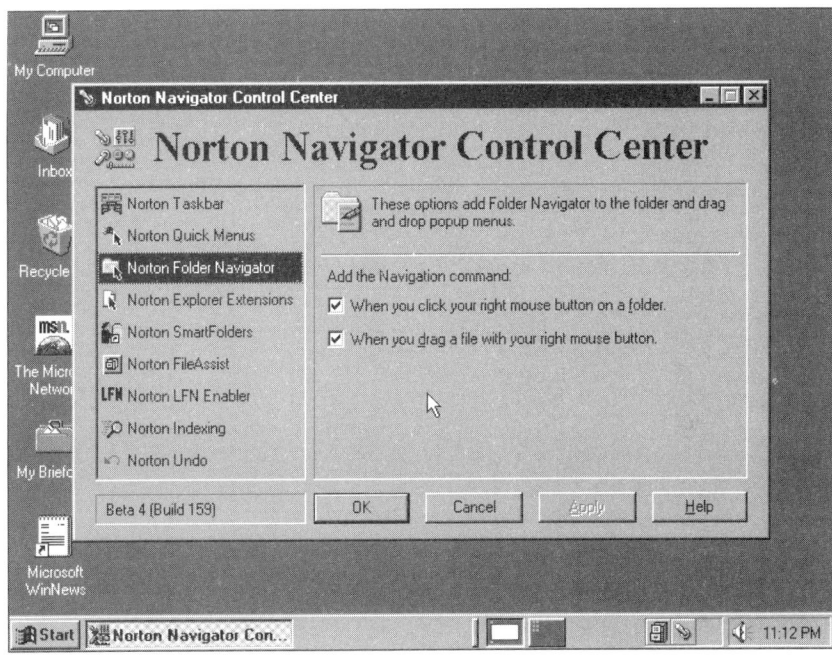

FIGURE 4.7 THE NORTON FOLDER NAVIGATOR.

Let's take a look at this in action.

Suppose that you are working on the desktop. Double-click your **My Computer** icon. The My Computer group window opens on the screen. Now, position the mouse pointer on the drive that represents your hard drive; then click the right mouse button. A Quick Menu appears. Move the pointer down to the **Navigator** command; a popup list of programs appears to the right of the menu. Now you can navigate to the program you want to open or the file you want to see, without ever going into the File Manager or using the Start menu (see Figure 4.8).

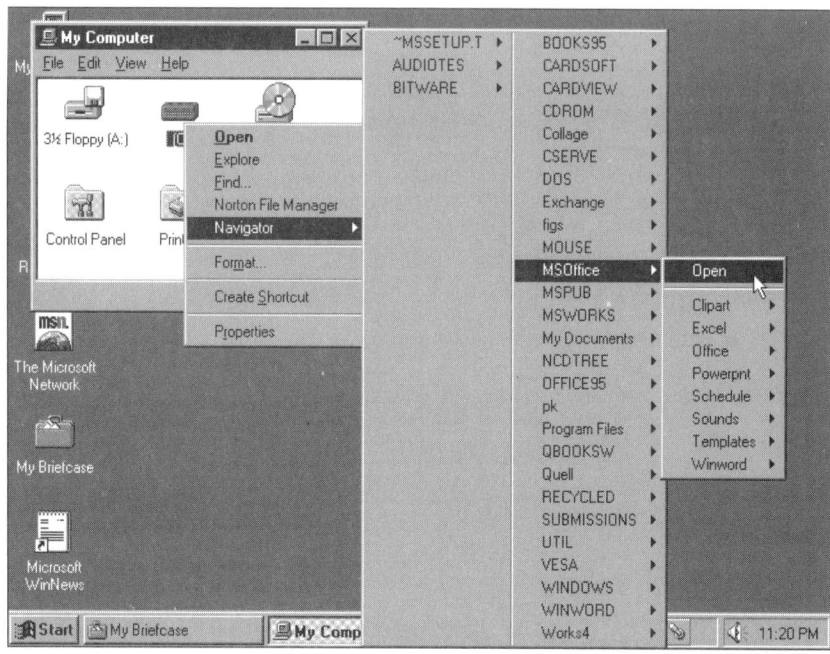

FIGURE 4.8 NAVIGATING WITH THE NAVIGATOR COMMAND.

Norton Explorer Extensions

When you choose **Norton Explorer Extensions**, the Control Center display changes to look like the one shown in Figure 4.9. This feature adds file-management commands to the popup menus added by the Windows Explorer to your files, folders, and drives. You can pick and choose the ones that you need most, thereby limiting the number of commands in the menus to the ones you will truly use.

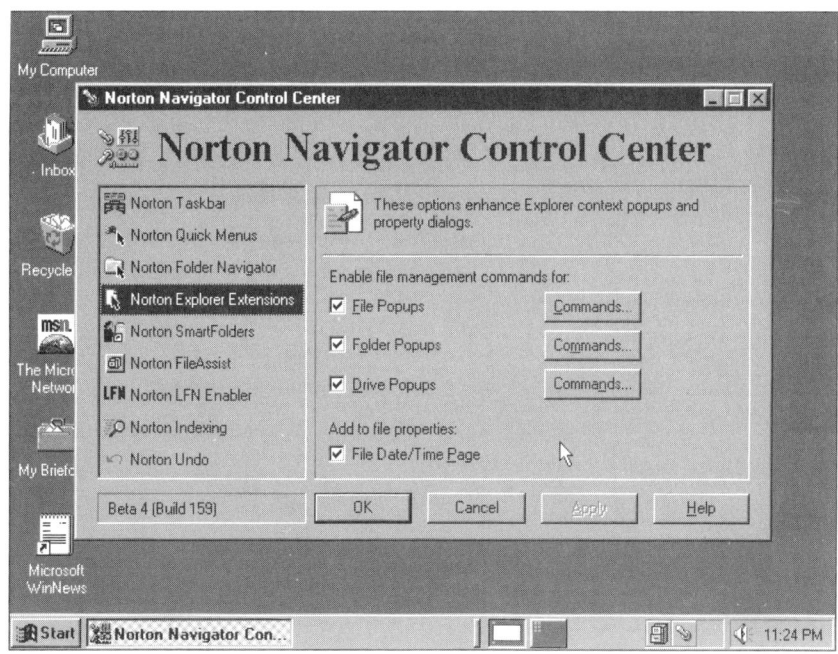

FIGURE 4.9 ADDING NORTON EXPLORER EXTENSIONS.

When you first display the Norton Explorer Extensions screen, all four options on the page—File Popups, Folder Popups, Drive Popups, and File Date/Time Page—are enabled.

You can control which commands are added to these items—or whether any are added at all—by clicking the **Commands** button to the right of the first three options. For example, to see what commands are available for file popups, click the **Commands** button beside **File Popups**. The dialog box shown in Figure 4.10 appears.

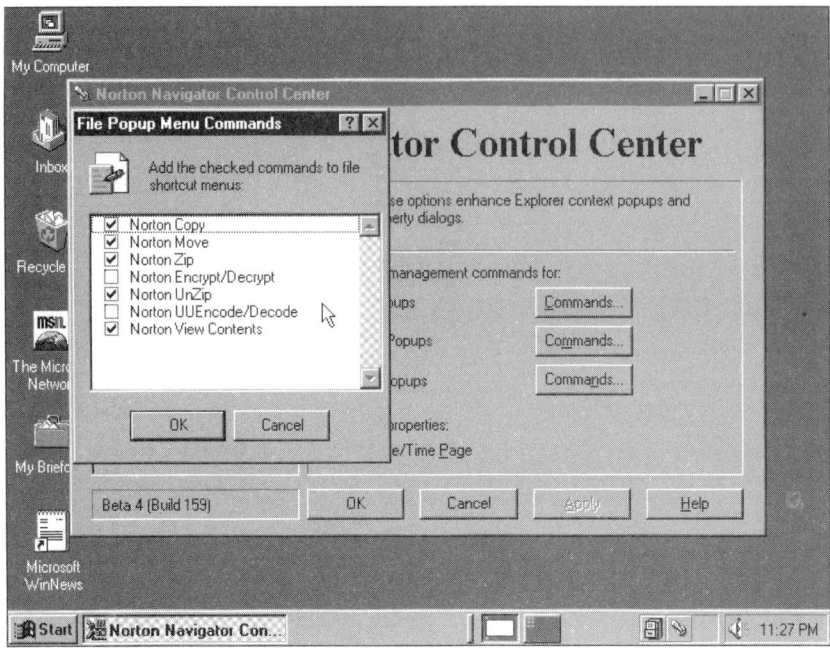

FIGURE 4.10 DISPLAYING THE COMMANDS AVAILABLE FOR FILE POPUPS.

As you can see, a number of these commands are automatically put to use. If you want to remove any of the commands, click its checked box to remove the check mark. If you want to add a command that is not selected, click the box to add the check mark. When you position the mouse pointer on a file and click the right mouse button, you will see the commands you selected in the Norton Explorer Extensions.

In a similar way, you can choose the commands you want to include for folder and drive popups. If you want to do away with the Norton Extensions for any of these three items, simply click the appropriate checkbox to remove the check mark; this disables the feature.

The final option in the Norton Explorer Extensions section of the Control Center is **File Date/Time Page**. This option adds the date and time to the file properties information. Having this information readily available can be useful when you are looking for the current version of a file.

Norton SmartFolders

When you click **Norton SmartFolders**, the Control Center changes to display the window shown in Figure 4.11. Norton SmartFolders are specialized, "intelligent" folders that contain shortcuts to often-used or favorite files. You might, for example, create a SmartFolder to contain all the **.PUB** files on your hard disk.

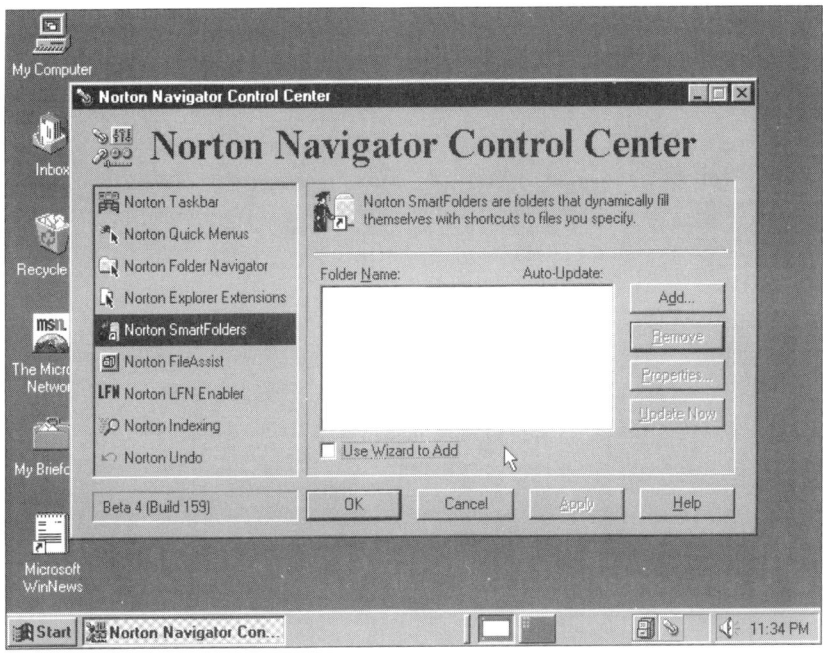

FIGURE 4.11 THE STARTING SMARTFOLDER SCREEN.

You create a SmartFolder using Wizard technology. Norton walks you through the process of creating a SmartFolder by asking you a series of questions, such as the type of file you want to store in the SmartFolder and where the files are found.

To create a SmartFolder (we'll use the .PUB example), follow these steps:

1. Click the **Use Wizard** to Add checkbox; then click the Add button. The **Add** New SmartFolder dialog box appears, displaying the first screen of the Wizard.

2. Enter a name that best describes the SmartFolder; then click **Next**. (For this example, we've entered **Publications**.)

3. In **Track files of Type**, enter search information for the type of files you're looking for. For this example, we entered ***.PUB**.

SHORTCUT

You can search for a File Set by clicking the folder icon to the right of the Track files of Type box. This displays the File Sets dialog box, in which you can choose an entire set of files, such as **[Bitmap Image]** or **[Help File]**. All files of the type you select are then included in the SmartFolder.

4. In the **Located in** box, choose the location for the files you want to include. Click the folder icon to the right of the box. The Location Sets dialog box appears, as shown in Figure 4.12. For this example, click **[All Drives Except Floppies]**, which will cause only the hard disk to be searched.

5. In the final SmartFolder Wizard screen, leave the **Track files with these modification dates** setting as is. Click **Finish** to create the SmartFolder.

Chapter 4 A Control Center Overview

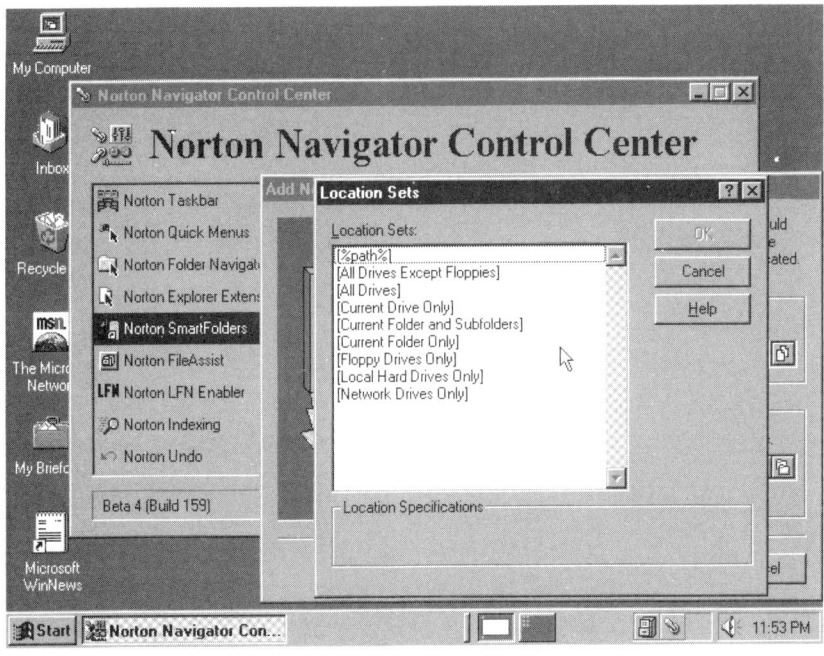

Figure 4.12 Choosing a location for the SmartFolder files.

SHORTCUT If your SmartFolder will include a large number of files, you can limit the number included in the SmartFolder by checking the checkbox in the lower portion of the Wizard window.

Norton Navigator then adds the new SmartFolder to the Control Center screen. When you return to the Windows 95 desktop, the SmartFolder will also appear there.

Norton FileAssist

When you click the **Norton FileAssist** feature, the Control Center displays the window shown in Figure 4.13. FileAssist adds commands you select to the Open, Save As, and Browse dialog boxes in your other Windows applications.

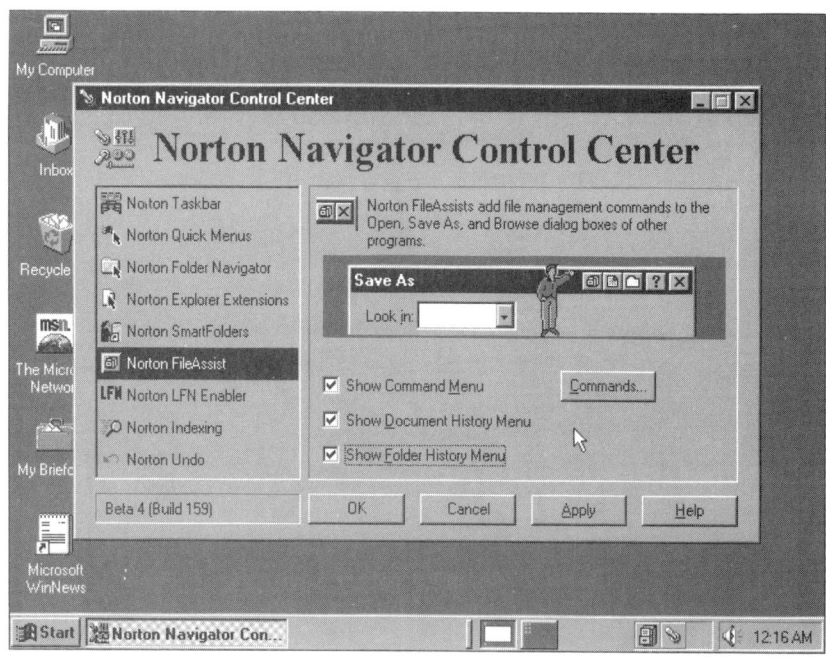

FIGURE 4.13 THE FILEASSIST WINDOW IN THE CONTROL CENTER.

When you first display FileAssist, all three options—**Show Command Menu**, **Show Document History Menu**, and **Show Folder History Menu**—are selected. You can choose additional commands for these menus by clicking the **Commands** button and choosing the items you want from the Properties for Norton FileAssist dialog box (see Figure 4.14).

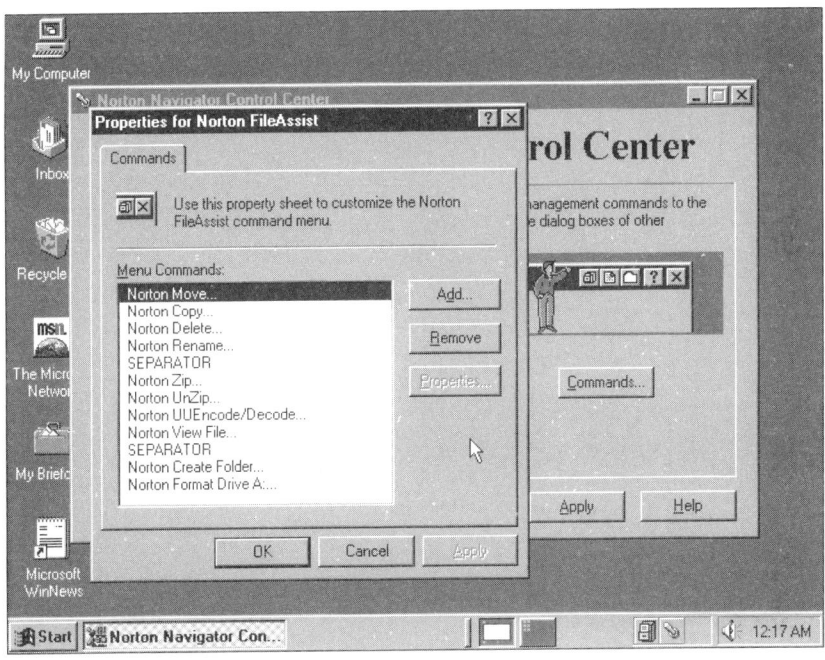

FIGURE 4.14 CHOOSING THE COMMANDS YOU WANT TO USE IN FILEASSIST.

When you use another Windows application—such as Microsoft Word, shown in Figure 4.15—and display the Open, Save As, or Browse dialog box, the FileAssist icons appear in the upper-right corner of the window.

98 Inside Norton Navigator

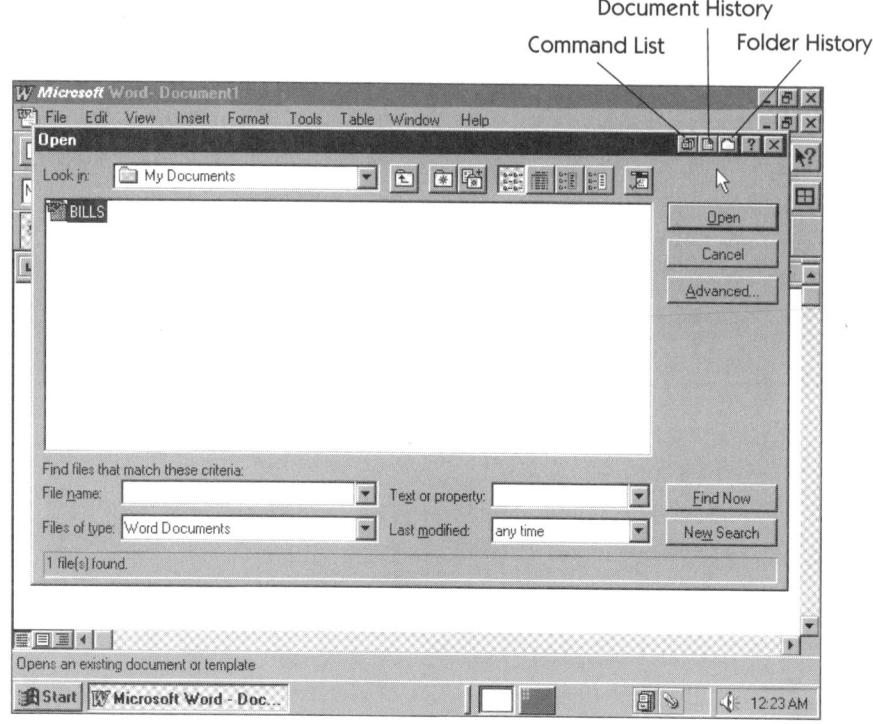

FIGURE 4.15 FILEASSIST ADDS ICONS TO OTHER WINDOWS PROGRAMS.

Norton LFN Enabler

Using the Norton LFN Enabler is simple: just click the option in the Control Center and the window changes to show one option (see Figure 4.16).

CHAPTER 4 A CONTROL CENTER OVERVIEW

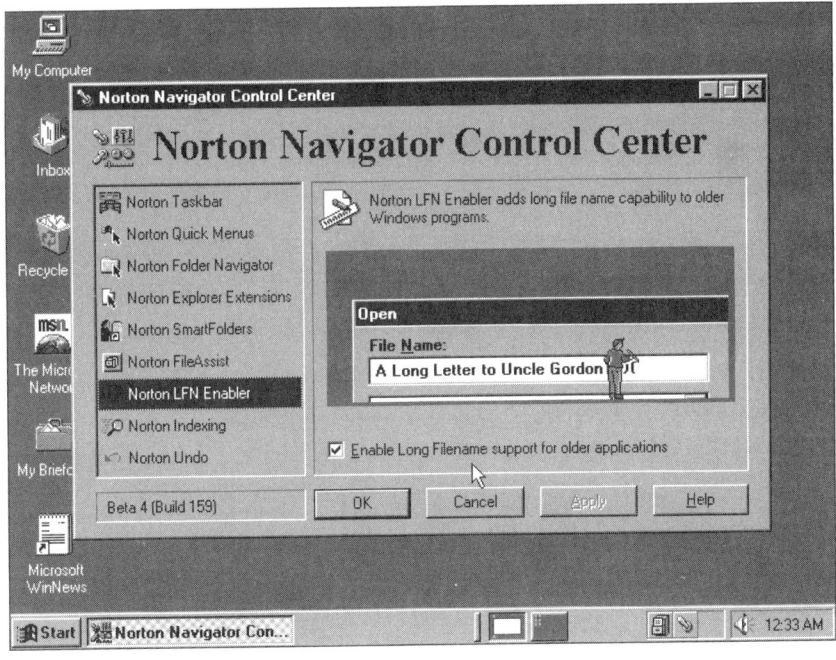

FIGURE 4.16 THE NORTON LFN ENABLER OPTION.

The LFN Enabler is all about adding long, descriptive file name capability to pre–Windows 95 Windows programs. This means that all your old Windows 3.1 applications will be able to run with long file names, making files easier to find and remember. To turn on LFN support, just make sure the **Enable Long Filename support for older applications** checkbox is marked.

Norton Indexing

Norton Navigator gives you the option of indexing files so that you can locate the files you want quickly. The new indexing capability of Norton Navigator is said to perform file searches as much as to 10 times faster than previous versions of Norton Utilities.

You use Wizard technology to create the index you'll use in Norton Indexing. Make sure the **Use Wizard to Add** checkbox is selected; then click **Add**. The Wizard displays its opening screen, asking for a name that will describe the index. Type a name for the index and click **Next**.

The next Wizard page asks you to choose the type of file you want to index. You can either enter a file type (wildcard characters are OK), or you can click the folder icons to choose a File Set of files.

In the **Located in** area, choose the location for the files you want to index. Again, you can type the location or use either the **File Manager** icon or the folders icon to specify the folders and subfolders you want to index.

If you want to include all subfolders in the index, click the **Include subfolders automatically** checkbox.

Click **Finish**. Norton composes the index and displays the index—with the name you specified—in the Norton Index window of the Control Center.

Norton Undo

Norton Undo is the final feature in the Control Center. This option also involves one simple selection (see Figure 4.17). Ordinarily, Norton Undo tracks all Norton File Manager tasks, but you can have it keep track of all Windows 95 operations. Simply make sure the **Track all Windows 95 file operations** checkbox is selected.

CHAPTER 4 A CONTROL CENTER OVERVIEW

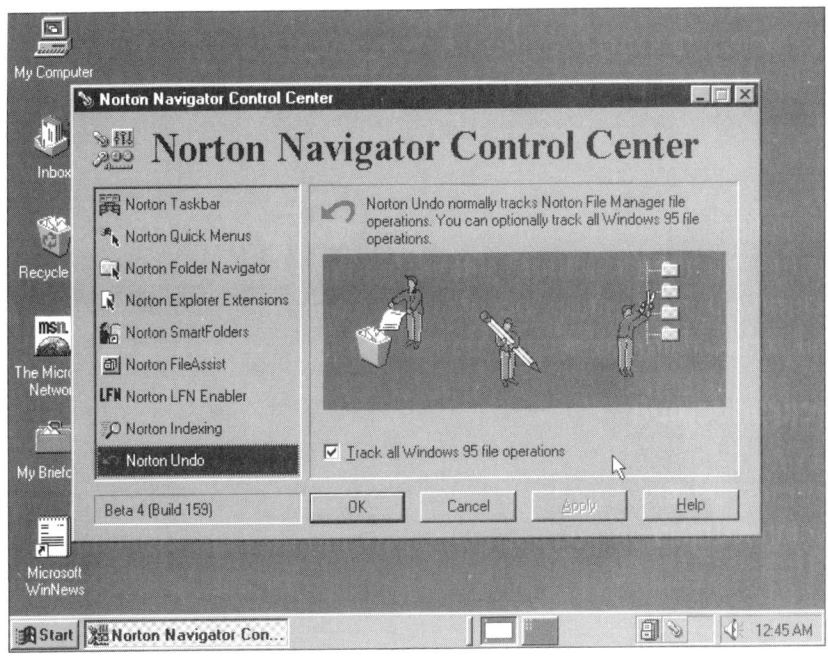

FIGURE 4.17 DISPLAYING THE NORTON UNDO OPTION IN THE CONTROL CENTER.

CLOSING THE CONTROL CENTER

When you're finished working in the Control Center, you can close it one of two ways:

+ You can click **OK** to accept changes you've made in the Control Center.
+ You can click **Cancel** to abandon any changes you've made.
+ You can click the close box to close the Control Center window.

THE NEXT STEP

This chapter has introduced you to the basics of working with the Control Center. You've learned how to display the Control Center, how to display and work with each of the options, and how to close the Control Center once you're finished with your modifications.

The next chapter shows you how to use the Control Center features in more detail to customize the screen display using the Taskbar, Quick Launch, and Quick Menus.

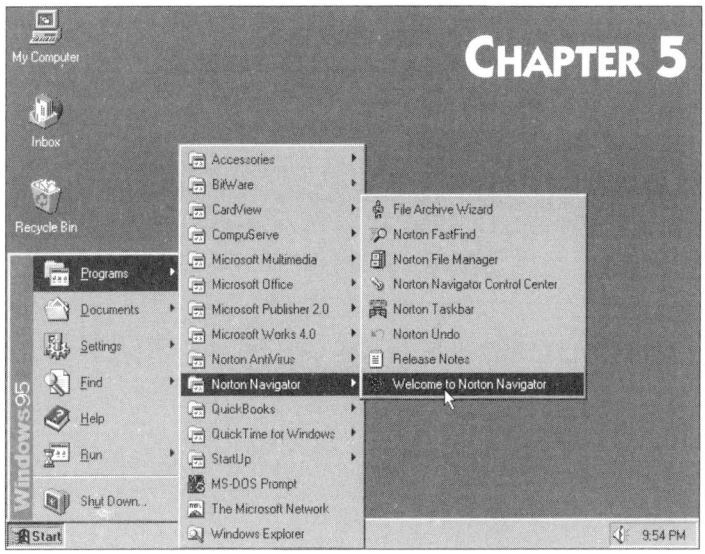

CHAPTER 5

CUSTOMIZING THE SCREEN DISPLAY

In Chapter 4, you learned about the Control Center and discovered how to modify many of the settings in utilities that speed up your computing tasks and help you work with files and folders more efficiently. This chapter focuses on what you see first—the screen display—as you begin working with the Taskbar and Taskbar elements.

Working with the Taskbar

The Norton Taskbar is similar to the Windows 95 Taskbar, except that the Norton Taskbar expands the functionality a step or two beyond Windows. With the Norton Taskbar, not only can you move between open applications—as you can with the Windows Taskbar—but you can also choose different applications and run your favorite programs with a simple click of the mouse button.

Displaying the Taskbar

You can display the Taskbar manually by selecting it yourself, or you can have the Taskbar load automatically when you start Windows.

The first time you load the Taskbar, begin by displaying the Windows 95 Start menu; then choose **Programs**; then **Norton Navigator**; and finally, **Norton Taskbar**, as shown in Figure 5.1.

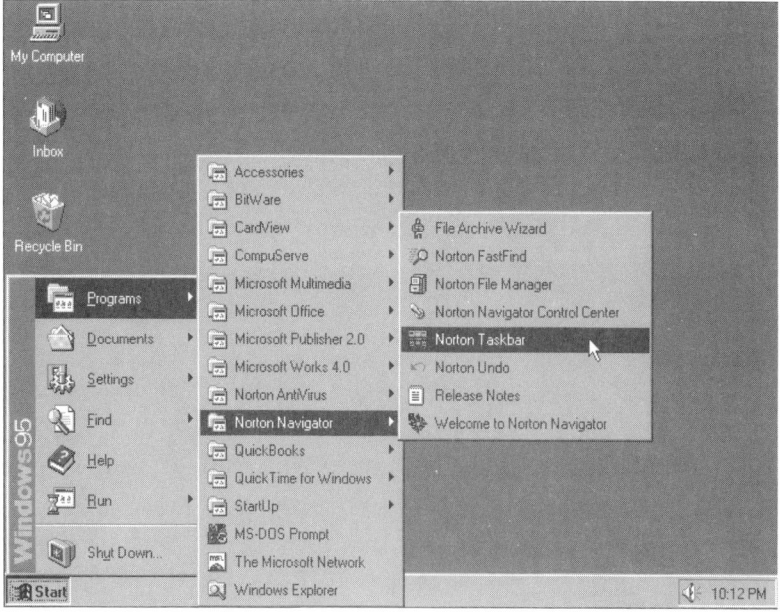

Figure 5.1 Choosing to display the Norton Taskbar.

As soon as you click the option, you see the Norton Navigator opening screen, followed by the Norton Taskbar, along the bottom of your screen.

Understanding Taskbar Elements

The Norton Taskbar is shown in Figure 5.2. At the far left side of the Taskbar, you see the familiar Windows Start menu. Halfway across the Taskbar, you see two small windows—these are the desktops you now have on your system. The first desktop is the Windows desktop; the second is the Norton Navigator desktop.

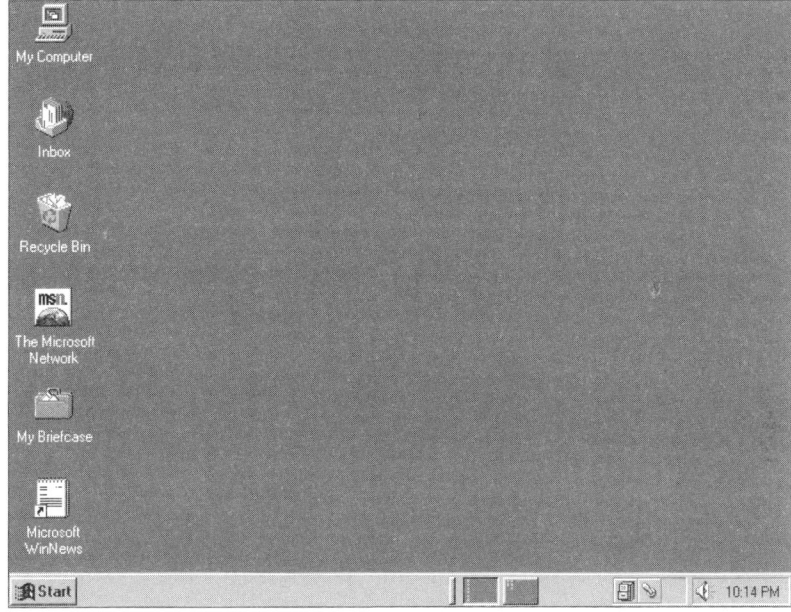

FIGURE 5.2 TASKBAR ELEMENTS.

NOTE With Norton Navigator, you can create more than one desktop—or surface area on which folders and files are stored. You can use different desktops to organize and store folders related to particular projects or functions.

ROAD MAP

For more about creating and working with additional desktops, see Chapter 6, "Alternate Reality or Alternate Desktop?"

To the right of the desktop display area, you see the **File Manager** icon. If you click this icon, the Norton File Manager appears. You can perform whatever file, folder, or disk-management commands suit your purposes—then exit the File Manager and return to the Taskbar.

Next to the **File Manager** icon is the **Control Center** icon. Clicking this icon causes the Norton Navigator Control Center to appear. Again, you can perform the operations you're interested in, and when you finish you are returned to the Taskbar display.

Changing Taskbar Properties

As with everything else in Norton Navigator, you have the option of changing the Taskbar settings. These settings control some of the default decisions made when the Taskbar is loaded: do you always want the Taskbar visible? Do you want the **close** box displayed? You can make your own decisions about the Taskbar by positioning the mouse pointer on the bar and clicking the right mouse button. A popup menu appears, with the option **Properties** at the bottom. Position the pointer on the option and click the mouse button. The dialog box shown in figure 5.3 then appears.

As you can see from the figure, Taskbar is set up to be displayed continually at the bottom of your screen even when other windows or menus would overlap it. If you don't feel strongly about the effervescent presence of the Taskbar, you can click the **Always on top** option to disable it (the check mark disappears). It's a small difference, either way.

Chapter 5 Customizing the Screen Display

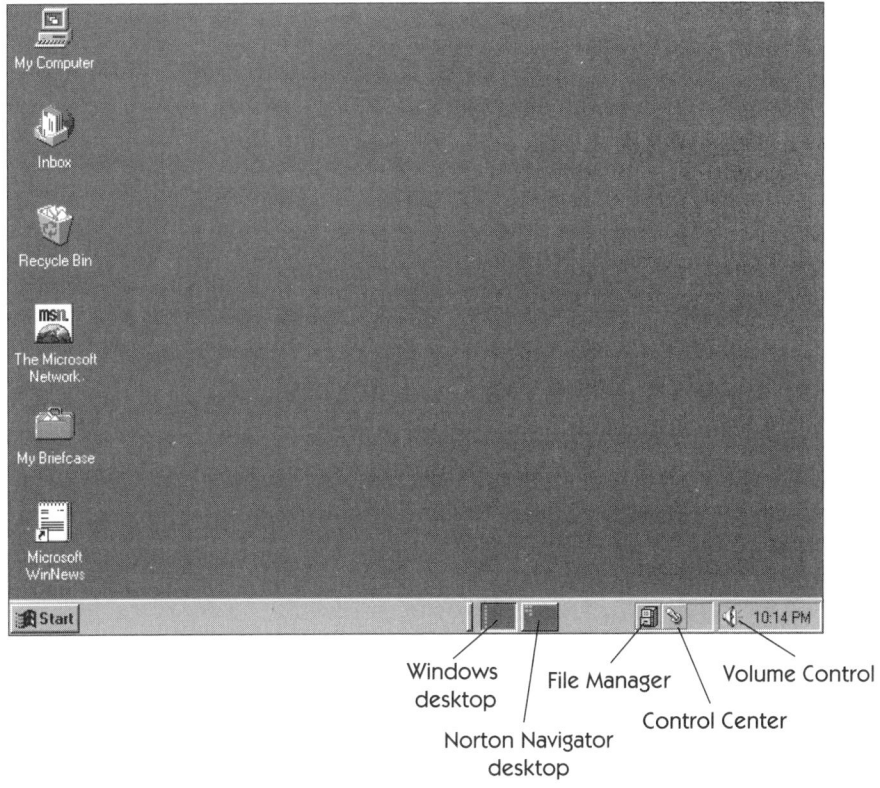

Figure 5.3 Changing Taskbar properties.

The **Auto hide** feature "puts away" the Taskbar, in case you're the type of person who's forever putting away pens and stray Post-Its. You just can't stand to have a cluttered desk. When you click **Auto hide**, the illustration in the Taskbar Properties window shows you how the screen will look without a Taskbar.

SHORTCUT If you want to see what a change will look like immediately but don't want to close the Taskbar Properties dialog box yet, click **Apply** to see the change. If you don't like the change, you can turn the feature back on.

The Taskbar is still there, but it has been reduced to a small gray line at the bottom of the screen (see Figure 5.4). Whenever you move the mouse into the Taskbar area, the full Taskbar appears so that you can select the items you need.

FIGURE 5.4 HIDING THE TASKBAR.

The next option in the Taskbar Options page of the Taskbar Properties dialog box enables you to reduce the size of the Start menu. The **Show small icons in Start menu** option removes the Windows 95 label that runs vertically the length of the menu. Smaller icons are displayed, thus giving you more room on-screen for other cascading menus (see Figure 5.5).

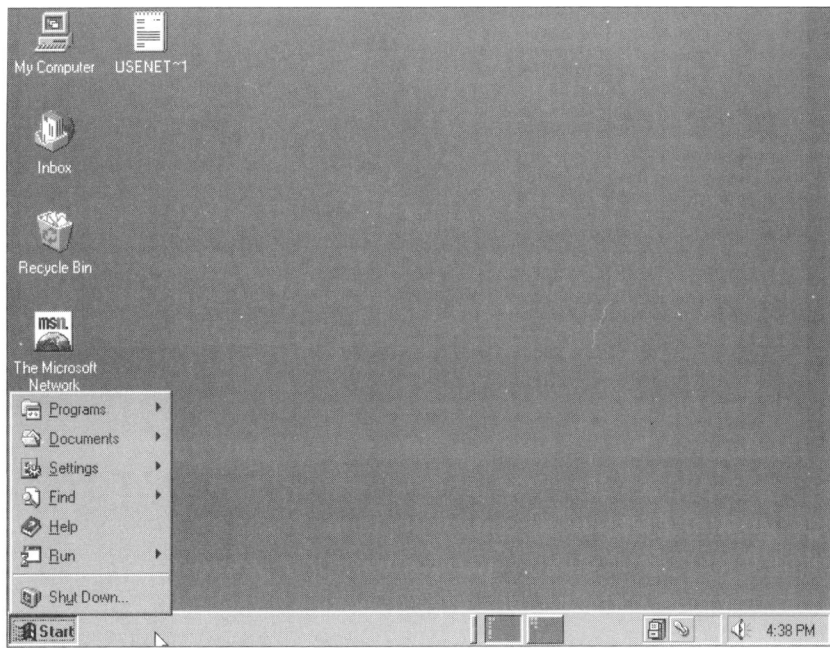

FIGURE 5.5 LIGHTENING THE LOAD ON THE START MENU.

The **Show Clock** option lets you decide whether you want the clock displayed. And why wouldn't you? (Unless you don't want to be reminded how little time you have until that deadline...)

Getting Taskbar Help

Another option lets you display help topics about using the Taskbar. Position the mouse pointer on the Taskbar and click the right mouse button. When the popup menu appears, click **Norton Taskbar** at the top of the menu. Next, click **Using Norton Taskbar**. The Norton Help Topics dialog box appears. Click the **Norton Taskbar** book icon to display the subtopics available (see Figure 5.6).

110   Inside Norton Navigator

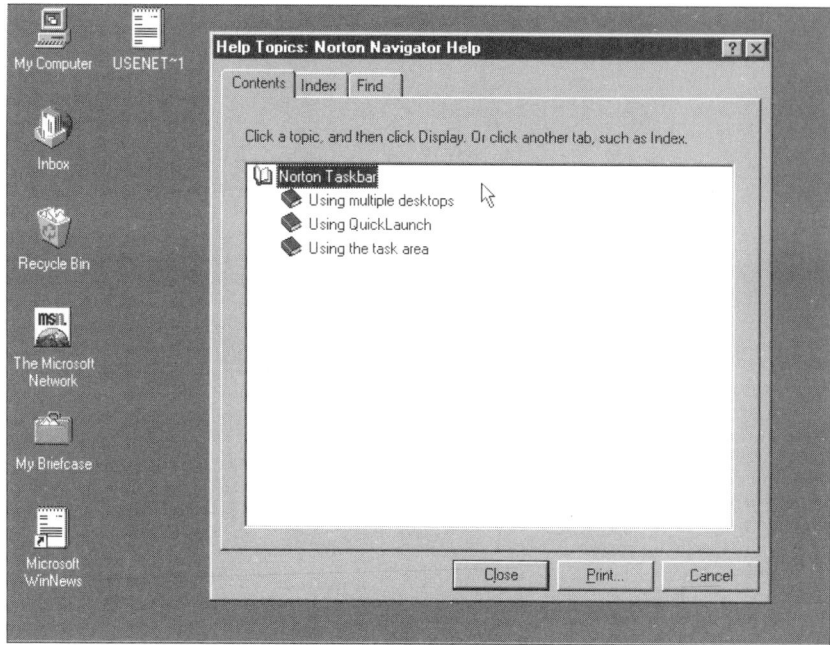

FIGURE 5.6 DISPLAYING TASKBAR HELP.

You can also use the **Index** and **Find** tabs to access different methods of getting the help you seek.

To find out more about getting help with Norton Navigator, see Chapter 2, "A Norton Navigator Overview."

ROAD MAP

QUICKLAUNCHING APPLICATIONS

Windows 95 does make it easy for find the programs you use often. After all, they're listed right there in the Programs submenu. You may also have program shortcuts on your desktop; you can click **Quickbooks** every day when you update your checkbook register, and you can click

Microsoft Word when you're ready to write the report you've been promising your boss.

But in the world of fast everything, Windows 95 isn't fast enough. Shortcuts aren't short enough. You need something that is almost instantaneous. You need QuickLaunch.

Adding Items to the QuickLaunch Area

Norton Navigator lets you add shortcut icons—as well as files and folders you want to get to quickly—to the QuickLaunch area of the Taskbar. When you first load the Taskbar, the QuickLaunch area is that blank space between the **Control Center** icon and the **Volume** icon.

To add items to the QuickLaunch area, start by displaying the folder that contains the item you want to use. If you want to add a folder or file to the QuickLaunch area, display the folder or an icon and then drag it to the Taskbar. If you want to add a program to the QuickLaunch area, display the program icon in a group window and then drag it to the QuickLaunch area.

NOTE
Although it may seem like a logical way to move an icon to the QuickLaunch area, you cannot drag an icon from the Start, Programs, or Documents menu; when you select the icon, Windows 95 activates the program or document. To drag an icon to the QuickLaunch area, display the item's folder or group window first.

Let's try an example. Double-click **My Computer**; then double-click the drive for your hard disk (in this case, **C**). Find a program folder that contains a program you want to add (here, we've chosen Books95—the Microsoft Bookshelf '95 product) and double-click the folder to open it. Now, find the icon you want to add to QuickLaunch and drag it to the QuickLaunch area. Figure 5.7 shows the **Bookshelf** icon added to the QuickLaunch area.

FIGURE 5.7 DRAGGING AN ICON TO THE QUICKLAUNCH AREA.

NOTE

Notice that the Taskbar now occupies twice the space it did before. The Taskbar expands to accommodate open windows and display the necessary QuickLaunch items.

Remember that you are not limited to adding only programs to the QuickLaunch area; you can also add files and folders you use frequently.

QuickLaunching

When you're ready to use the program, folder, or file you added to the QuickLaunch area, simply position the mouse pointer on the item and click the left mouse button. Figure 5.8 shows the opening screen of Bookshelf '95, started from the Norton Taskbar QuickLaunch area.

CHAPTER 5 CUSTOMIZING THE SCREEN DISPLAY   113

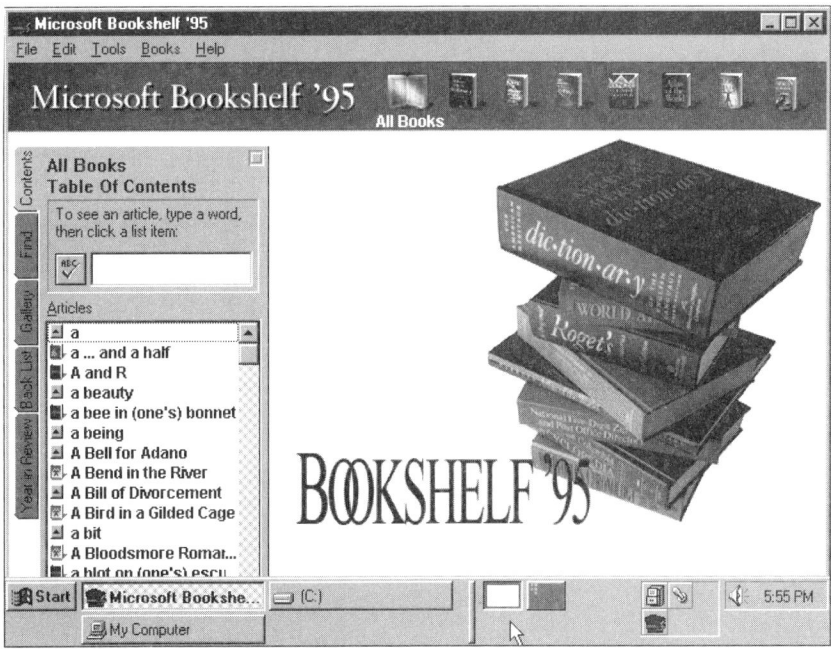

FIGURE 5.8 QUICKLAUNCHING BOOKSHELF '95.

NOTE

Your Taskbar didn't come up automatically over the program you QuickLaunched? There's a simple workaround. Remember the **Properties** command? Position the mouse pointer on the Taskbar and click the right mouse button. Choose **Properties**. When the Taskbar Properties dialog box appears, make sure that both **Always on top** and **Auto hide** are selected. Click **OK**. When you return to the program, the Taskbar will disappear when you move the pointer upward on the screen but will reappear over your program when you move the pointer down to the Taskbar area.

CHANGING THE START MENU WITH QUICK MENUS

Another way you can use Norton Navigator to make your up-front work easier is by adding Quick Menus to the Start menu options.

What's possible? You can display a list of the last several items you've activated using the **Run** command. With Windows 95, you must click the **Run** command and then type the command you want to run. When Norton Navigator gets involved, you can choose the item you want to run from a displayed list. If there's a utility you run often, having a list of the most recent utilities you've run cuts down on the time it takes to find and select the program.

Likewise, you can add a history list to the Documents submenu that displays the documents you've worked with most recently. Windows 95 sticks all the most recently used documents in alphabetical order on the Documents submenu. Norton Navigator, on the other hand, organizes the different files by application—so the Documents submenu is a list of programs you've used recently (such as Microsoft Works), and a history list of only Works documents cascades off that option. This arrangement saves you considerable time hunting for files and trying to remember which program you used to create which file.

Finally, with Quick Menus, you can add to or remove the applets available when you select the Control Panel command. When you choose the **Control Panel** in Windows 95, the Control Panel window opens and you must hunt for the item you want. The Norton Quick Menus create a popup submenu of Control Menu applets that you can customize to reflect the applications you want to use.

All these features enable you to bypass menu choices and window opening and closing—you can get right to the item you want and get right to work (which means you can go home sooner).

Adding Quick Menus

Start by displaying the Norton Navigator Control Center. Remember how? Click the **Control Center** icon in the QuickLaunch area. The Norton Navigator Control Center window appears. Click **Norton Quick Menus** (the second option, just below the Norton Taskbar). The right half of the window changes to show you the Quick Menu options, as shown in Figure 5.9.

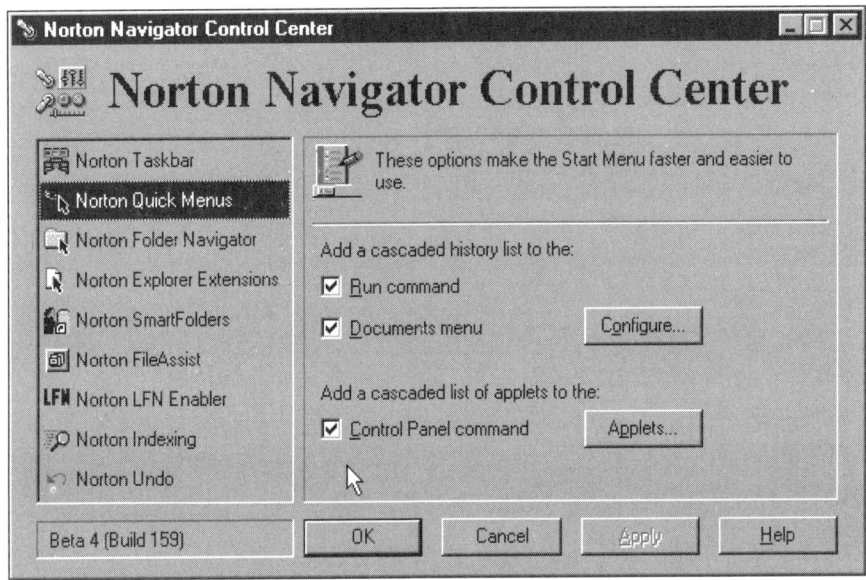

FIGURE 5.9 ADDING QUICK MENUS TO THE WINDOWS 95 START MENU.

The figure shows all three options already activated. If you do not want a history list attached to either the **Run** command or the Documents menu, click the checkboxes to deselect them.

Setting Up the Documents History List

If you want to change the settings for the history list displayed with the Documents submenu, click the **Configure** button. The popup dialog box shown in Figure 5.10 appears on the screen.

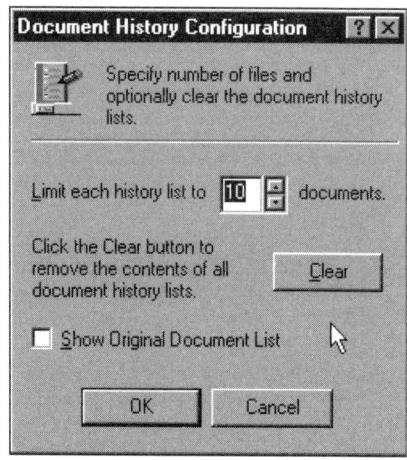

FIGURE 5.10 CHANGING THE DOCUMENT SUBMENU'S DISPLAY.

In the Document History Configuration dialog box, you have three basic choices:

✦ Choose the number of documents you want to be displayed in each history list. The current setting is 10 documents, but you can choose to have as many as 26 documents displayed or reduce the number to zero.

✦ You can clear the current list and start again by clicking the **Clear** button.

✦ You can remove the current list and display the original document list by clicking the **Show Original Document List** checkbox.

After you enter your settings, you may want to display the Documents menu just to see what's going on. Figure 5.11 shows the displayed Documents menu. Notice that immediately to the right of the Documents menu is a listing of the various programs you've used. As you select a program (in this case, **Microsoft Works 4.0 Word Processor**), the Documents history list appears.

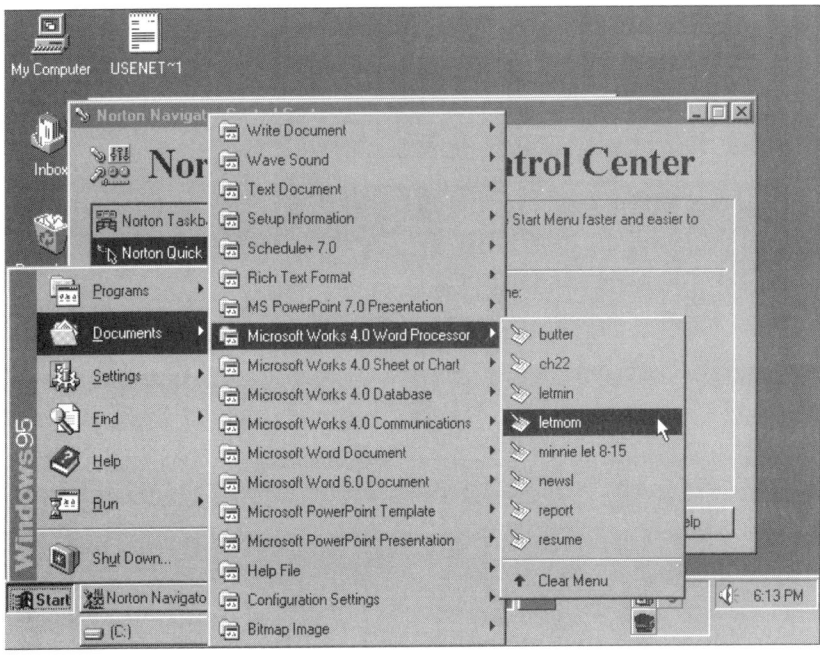

FIGURE 5.11 THE DOCUMENTS MENU IS LISTED FIRST BY PROGRAM AND THEN BY DOCUMENT.

SHORTCUT

At the bottom of the Documents history list is the **Clear Menu** option. You can clear the documents in the list by choosing this option—there's no need to access the Control Panel to do it (unless you're already there).

An Applet a Day...

Another Quick Menu feature lets you change the items that are displayed when you select the **Control Panel** command. Click the **Applets** button to see what Norton has in store for you (see Figure 5.12).

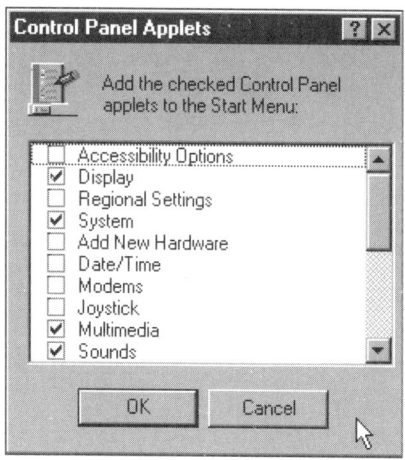

FIGURE 5.12 ADDING APPLETS TO THE CONTROL PANEL.

NOTE An *applet* is not a small apple—rather, this short, supposedly cute phrase means, essentially, "small application." An applet performs a certain task or runs a specific utility. For example, the Date/Time applet enables you to set the date and time on your computer.

For the most part, you may be happy with the applets Norton has chosen for you. If you want to choose a different applet, simply click beside the one you want. A check mark will appear, indicating that the applet is now selected. Likewise, if you want to remove an applet that is currently selected, click the checkbox to remove the check mark. When you' have the applets set the way you want them, click **OK** to return to the Control Center.

Back to the real world

After you've chosen all necessary Quick Menu options, click **OK** to return to the Windows 95 desktop and the Norton Taskbar. You can check the display of the different items you've enhanced by taking a look at the **Run** command (choose **Start**, and then **Run**) or the Control Panel (choose **Start**, **Settings**, and **Control Panel**).

Better, smarter, and faster. What more could you want from a computer program?

The Next Stop

In Chapter 6, you learn how to do something startling: you can create multiple desktops to store frequently used or sensitive files and programs. Want to keep your kids off the Internet? Create a desktop just for them, with only your parent-approved programs available. Working on so many projects it makes your head swim? Organize them on different desktops to keep your files straight.

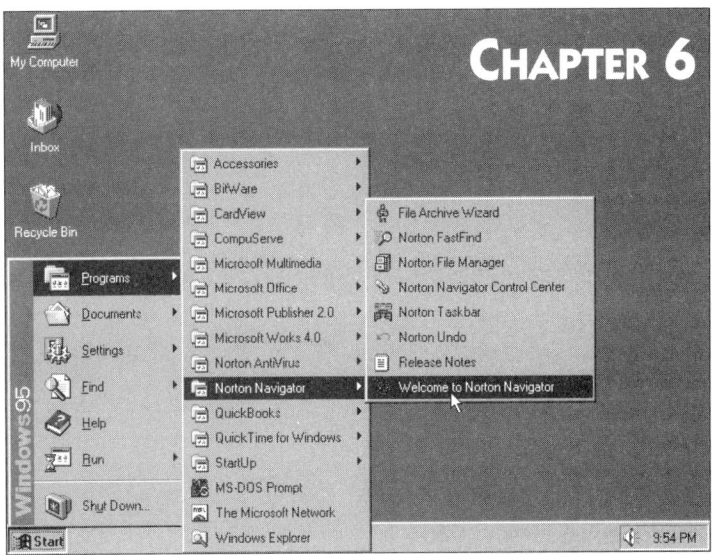

CHAPTER 6

ALTERNATE REALITY OR ALTERNATE DESKTOP?

It's the best of all possible worlds: do your work and keep it, too. Working on 14 gazillion projects at once? Organize them on different desktops. Keep things straight. Combat confusion.

Norton Navigator lets you create entire desktops on which you can store programs, files, and folders.

Understanding Multiple Desktops

If you're used to Windows 95, you may be used to thinking about your files, folders, and desktops in a linear fashion. How can I best organize these windows and folders? How can I keep the desktop from getting so cluttered? How can I find—as easily as possible—the files I use most often?

Norton Navigator's features will help with all these questions. The Control Center, the Quick Menus, and Quick Launch, which we've discussed in the preceding chapters, all help you get your work done faster and keep everything straight in the process.

But the ability to create alternate desktops takes Norton into a whole new arena. It's like having several computers in one, each with a desktop geared toward a particular function, a particular project, or—if more than one person uses your computer—a particular person.

When Will You Use Alternate Desktops?

Once you begin thinking laterally, you begin to see all kinds of possibilities for alternate desktops. Here are just a few:

- You are working on a multimedia project for work that involves using many different programs and files. You have Microsoft PowerPoint to create the presentation; Microsoft Word for the report; Photoshop for the graphics; and clipart and sound clips galore. With all these programs and the files they represent, having a desktop specifically designed to store everything related to that project would be a big relief.

- You have a number of files on your computer that you don't want to risk losing at the hands of another user. If you share your computer with someone else or are working with sensitive files for your eyes only, it's useful to have another desktop where you can put away your important files, folders, and programs.

✦ The kids are forever blowing away your icons. Time to put a stop to that. Create another desktop just for them and put all their favorite programs there: Prodigy, Minesweeper, Myst—who could complain?

NOTE You can change the look of the desktop by choosing a different screen pattern or wallpaper.

CREATING A NEW DESKTOP

The first step in setting up an alternative desktop is to move the pointer to the Taskbar. Click the right mouse button, and the popup menu appears. Move the pointer first to Norton Taskbar and then to New Desktop. Click the mouse button (see Figure 6.1).

FIGURE 6.1 BEGINNING THE PROCESS OF CREATING A NEW DESKTOP.

After you click **New Desktop,** the Create a new desktop dialog box appears, as shown in Figure 6.2. Enter a name for your new desktop. Be sure to name the desktop something that will help you remember its function.

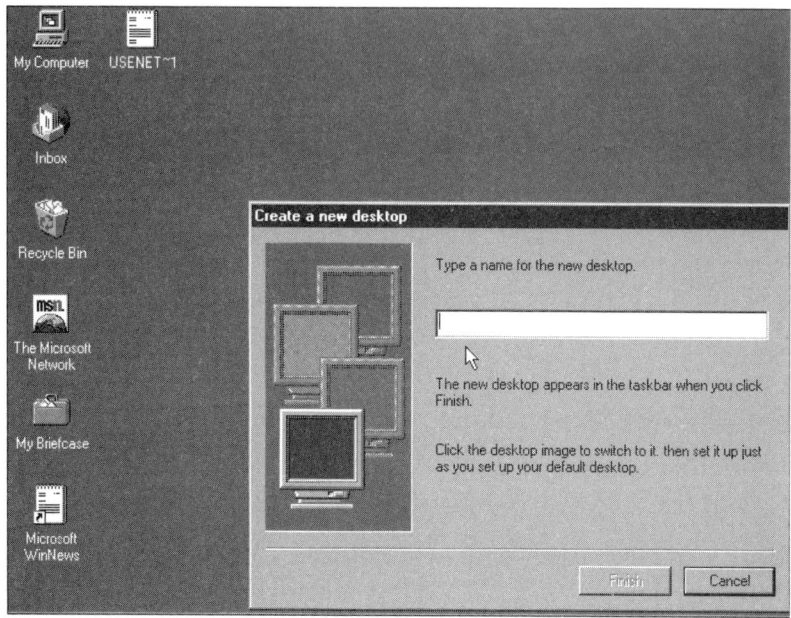

FIGURE 6.2 ENTERING A NAME FOR THE NEW DESKTOP.

Desktop names you don't want to use:

+ Sparky
+ Dumb stuff
+ Kids-stay-outta-here
+ Mistakes
+ Things-I-don't-want-the-boss-to-see

After you click **OK**, the Taskbar is redisplayed and a new desktop icons appears in addition to the Windows 95 desktop and the Norton desktop icons (see Figure 6.3).

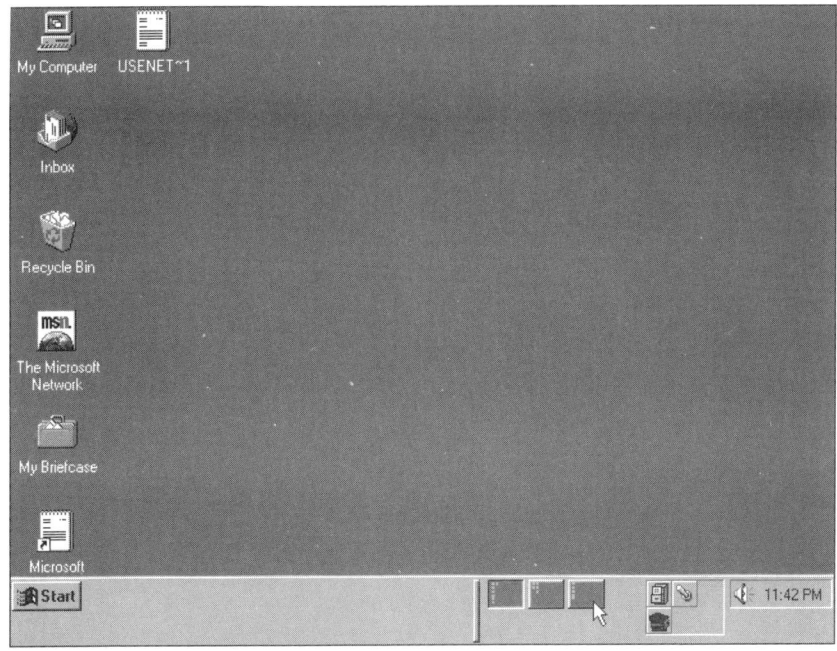

FIGURE 6.3 CHECKING OUT THE NEW DESKTOP ICON.

Changing to a Different Desktop

When you're ready to look at life from a different perspective, click the new desktop icon. Drum roll, please...

What? No big difference?

Not automatically. You have to set up the differences yourself. The only thing displayed on the new desktop are those shortcuts that are staples in Windows—things that cannot be removed, such as My Computer. Figure 6.4 shows the new desktop window, uneventful though it is. We'll spruce it up in a moment.

126   Inside Norton Navigator

FIGURE 6.4 CHANGING TO THE NEW DESKTOP.

Choosing Desktop Backgrounds

Changing the properties of the desktop is really a Windows 95 process, but we'll include it here; if you're setting up new desktops for your system, you won't want a bunch of blue Windows 95 clones. You'll want something different. Something unique. Something that that says, "Go ahead, click me" from the Taskbar at the bottom of your screen.

Start by positioning the mouse pointer in the open area of the new desktop. Click the right mouse button. Another popup menu appears. Move the pointer to **Properties** and click the mouse button. This brings up the Display Properties dialog box, as shown in Figure 6.5.

Chapter 6 Alternate Reality or Alternate Desktop? 127

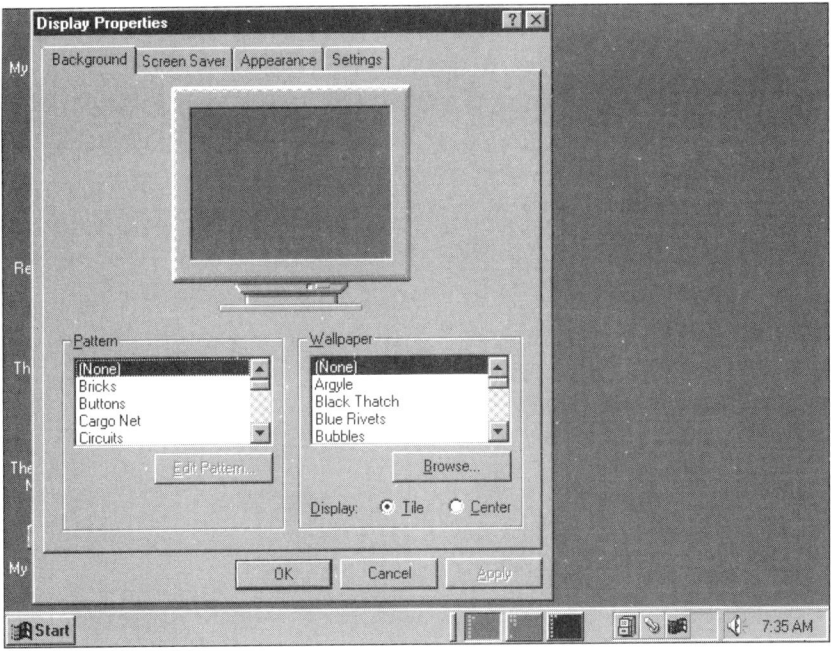

Figure 6.5 Changing the background appearance of the new desktop.

Patterns, Patterns Everywhere

The **Pattern** area of the Display Properties dialog box enables you to choose a background pattern for the screen. You can choose from 20 different patterns (one of which is "no pattern"), and you can edit any one of the patterns to create your own.

If you want to create your own pattern, click the **Edit Pattern** button. The Pattern Editor appears. You can change the pattern by moving the mouse pointer to the **Pattern** side and clicking the mouse button. If you position the pointer in a colored area and click, Windows turns the pixel black. If you want to return the pixel to its former color, click it again.

 **NOTE** The term pixel is computerese for the smallest element—a single dot—in a graphic or character.

Continue making your changes until you have got the pattern you want; then click **Done**. If you've changed the pattern, Windows will ask whether you want to save the changes. Click **Yes** to save them or **No** to discard them.

Wallpapering Desktops

The **Wallpaper** area gives you 24 different wallpaper styles in a variety of patterns and colors. Play around with the samples to find the one you want. Just click one and watch the display change (see Figure 6.6).

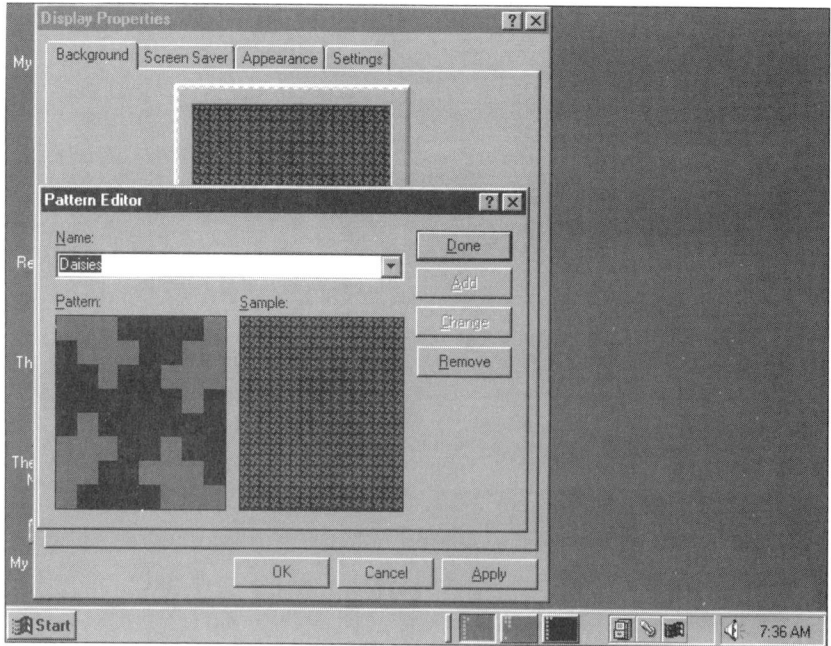

FIGURE 6.6 SELECTING A WALLPAPER.

NOTE When you first begin clicking wallpapers, you'll notice that the sample pops up only in the center of the sample screen. This happens because the **Display** option is set to **Center**. To spread the wallpaper over the entire screen, click **Tile**.

If you want to choose a wallpaper that will stand out against the traditional blue in the Windows and Norton default desktops, try one of these:

- Black Thatch
- Bubbles
- Carved Stone
- Honeycomb
- Red Bricks
- Setup
- Squares
- Tiles

SHORTCUT If you have another wallpaper pattern or design in another folder, you can use the **Browse** button to locate the wallpaper you want.

When you've found the desktop wallpaper you want, click **OK** to return to the desktop.

Choosing a Screen Saver

Another thing you'll want to do for your new desktop is to choose a screen saver for it. When you create another desktop—this is true for your Norton Navigator desktop—there is no screen saver assigned to it. For each desktop you create, you need to add a new screen saver.

Click the **Screen Saver** tab of the Display Properties dialog box. Click the **Screen Saver** down-arrow to choose one of the screen savers on your system. (Unless you've added new screen savers, the Windows 95 defaults are Blank, Flying Windows, or Scrolling Marquee.) Select the one you want. The display automatically begins displaying the new screen saver.

You can click the **Settings** button to change individual items related to the screen saver you've selected. If you've selected **Flying Windows**, for example, you can change the speed and the density of the windows that will come flying at you. If you choose **Scrolling Marquee**, you can select where the message scrolls in from, how fast it appears, the screen's background color, and the text. You also can click Format Text to change the font, size, style, and color of the text.

Help! I'm Locked Out

For those desktops that contain ultrasensitive material or files and folders too important to risk their falling into the wrong paws, you can protect the desktop by adding a password to the screen saver. Once the screen saver starts, no one can display the desktop without entering the assigned password (see Figure 6.7).

CHAPTER 6 ALTERNATE REALITY OR ALTERNATE DESKTOP? 131

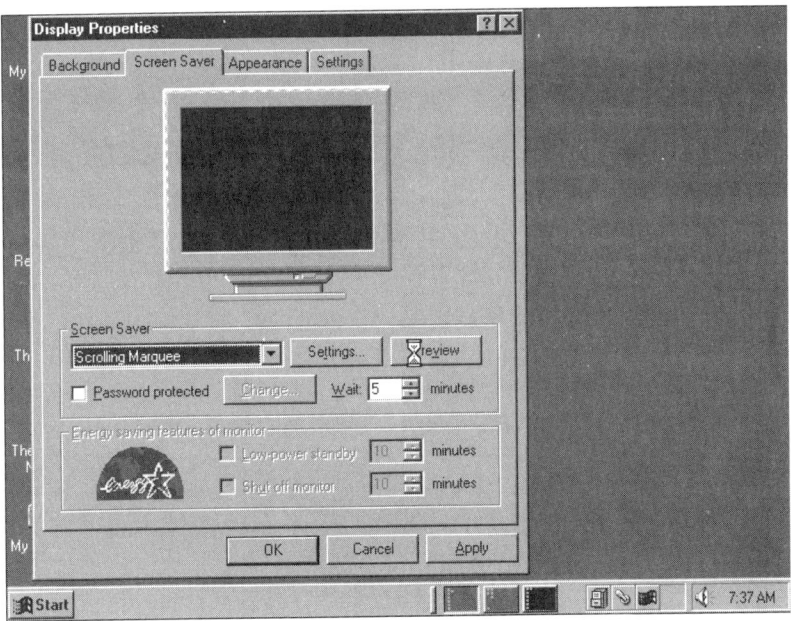

FIGURE 6.7 THE WINDOWS SCREEN SAVER.

To add a password to a desktop, click **Password protected**. A check mark appears in the checkbox and the **Change** button darkens. Click **Change** to display the Change Password dialog box, as shown in Figure 6.8.

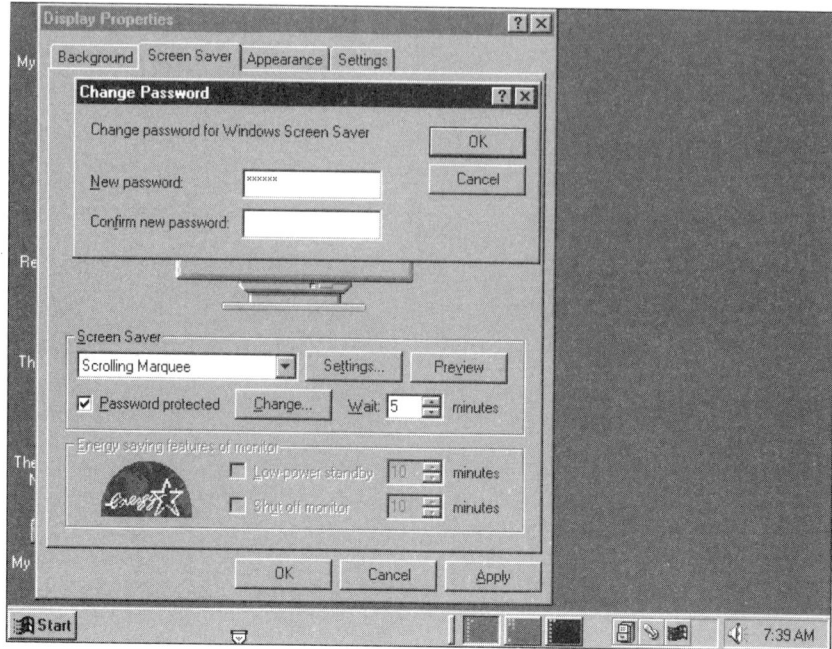

FIGURE 6.8 PASSWORD-PROTECTING YOUR NEW DESKTOP.

Type a password for the desktop in the **New password** box. Notice that the characters do not appear as you type. In the **Confirm new password** box, type the password a second time; then click **OK**.

NOTE It's common sense but bears repeating: Write your password down where it won't be lost. Good places include your Rolodex, inside your computer manual, or even inside this book. Keep your password handy and don't risk carrying it around in your head.

After you click **OK**, Windows tells you that the password has been successfully changed. Click **OK** to return to the Display Properties dialog box.

Later, when you are using your desktop and—after the specified period of time—the screen saver kicks in, you won't be able to get rid of the screen saver without entering your password.

CHAPTER 6 ALTERNATE REALITY OR ALTERNATE DESKTOP?   133

NOTE You may want to modify the **Settings** tab page. You can change the color palette used, the resolution of the desktop display, and specific drivers and configurations for the particular monitor you are using.

When you're finished in the Display Properties dialog box, click **OK**. You are returned to your new desktop, with all the settings you selected in place.

ADDING ITEMS TO THE DESKTOP

Adding items—programs, files, and folders—to your new desktop is simple. Click the right mouse button in the desktop area to display the popup menu and then choose **New**. You have the choice of creating a new **Folder**, or **Shortcut** or any one of the application-specific document types you've been working with recently (see Figure 6.9).

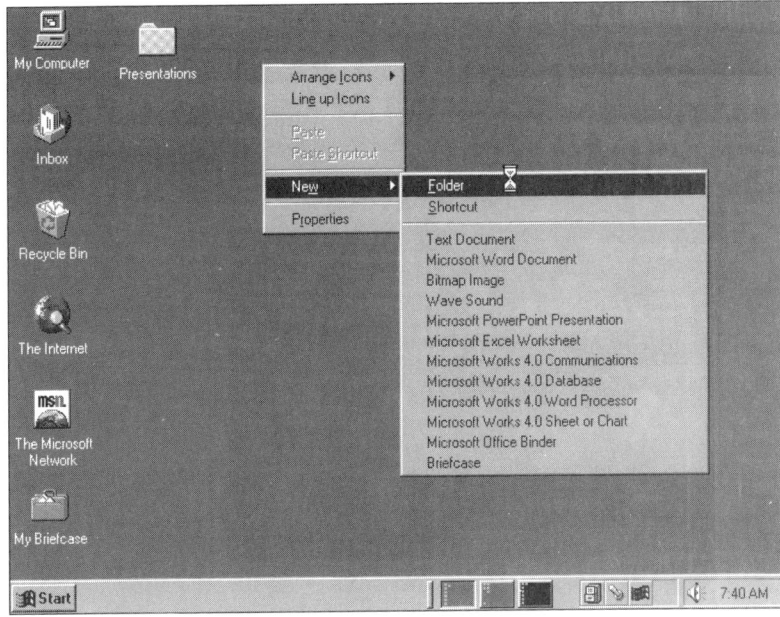

FIGURE 6.9 ADDING ITEMS TO THE DESKTOP.

134 Inside Norton Navigator

To add a new folder, choose—you guessed it—**Folder**. A new folder appears on the desktop with the words "New Folder" immediately beneath it. Click in the folder name area. When the name is highlighted, type the new name for your folder.

If you want to add an existing folder from another desktop to the new desktop, change to the other desktop—where the folder currently resides—and drag it to the new window icon in the Taskbar. In Figure 6.10, the **Collage** folder is being dragged to the new desktop (the desktop on the right in the Taskbar). Notice that the pointer changes to show that an item is being dragged.

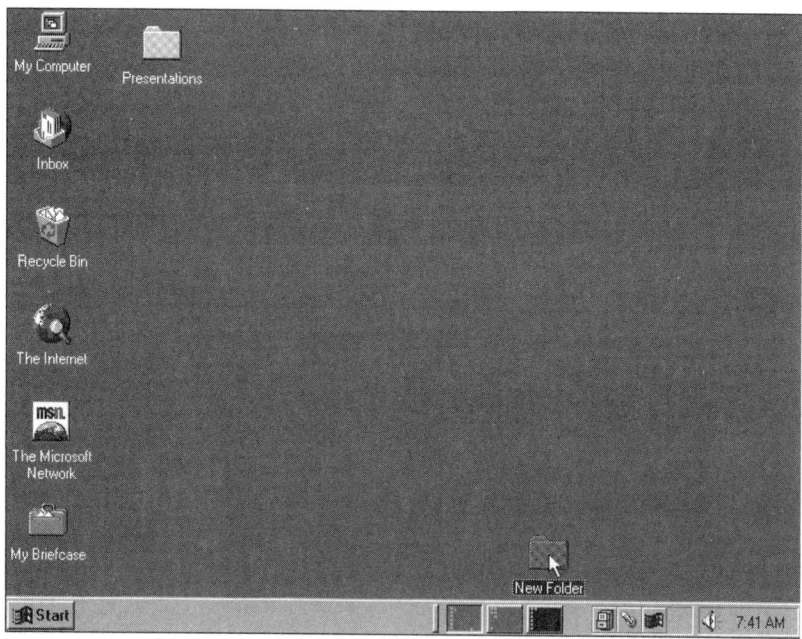

FIGURE 6.10 DRAGGING A FOLDER TO THE NEW DESKTOP.

When you release the mouse button, Norton Navigator copies the folder to the new desktop. You can see the new folder in the miniature desktop window. When you move to the new desktop by clicking it in the Taskbar, the item you dragged is in place (see Figure 6.11).

CHAPTER 6 ALTERNATE REALITY OR ALTERNATE DESKTOP?   135

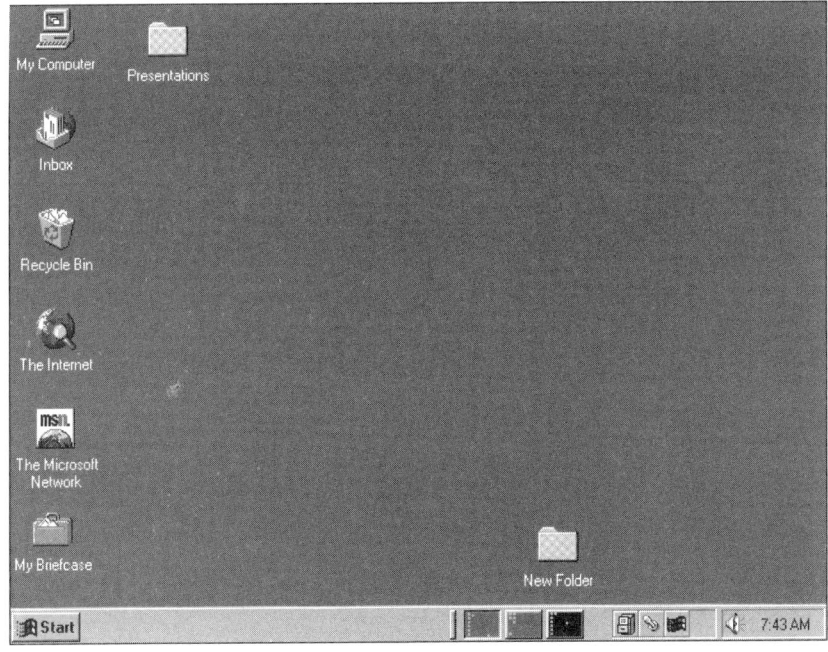

FIGURE 6.11 DRAGGING A FOLDER TO THE NEW DESKTOP.

NOTE Not on my screen, it isn't...If you dragged folders to the new desktop icon and now, they aren't there, position the mouse pointer on the desktop icon in the Taskbar and click the right mouse button. When the popup menu appears, click Refresh. This will update the screen and should display your missing folders.

Adding a New Shortcut

When you want to add your own shortcuts to the new desktop, the task is easy. Position the mouse pointer in the desktop area and click the right mouse button. When the popup menu appears, choose **New**; then Choose **Shortcut**. The Create Shortcut dialog box appears, as shown in Figure 6.12.

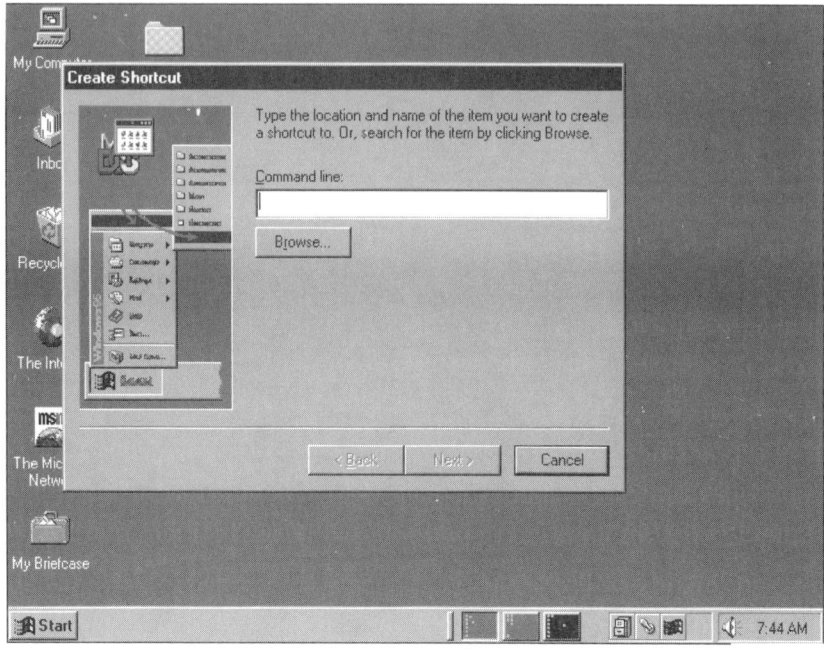

Figure 6.12 Adding a shortcut to folders or programs you use often.

NOTE Like its physical counterpart (as in "taking the shortcut home"), a Norton shortcut is a quicker way to get to a program you want to use. For example, if you use Microsoft Excel every day, you may want to add a desktop shortcut so that you can access the program easily without cascading the Windows menus. (Remember, you can also add the icon to the QuickLaunch area of the Norton Taskbar.)

Enter the name of the file you want to be activated when you click the **Shortcut** icon. If you're not sure about the name of the file, click **Browse** to display the Browse dialog box. You can then navigate through the folders to find the item you want. Figure 6.13 shows the Microsoft Excel icon selected.

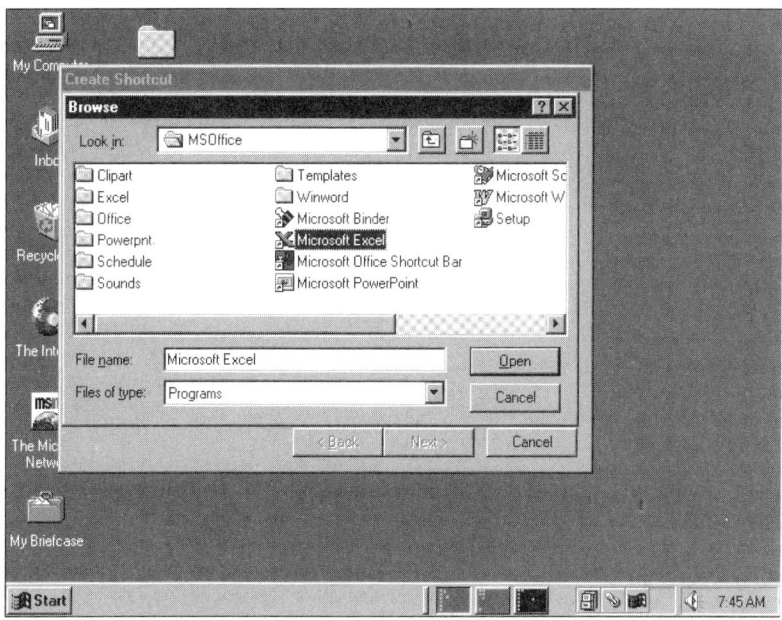

FIGURE 6.13 CHOOSING AN ITEM TO BE LINKED TO THE SHORTCUT.

After you click on the icon and click **OK** in the Browse dialog box, you are returned to the Create Shortcut window. The name of the file has been added in the **Command line** box for you (see Figure 6.14).

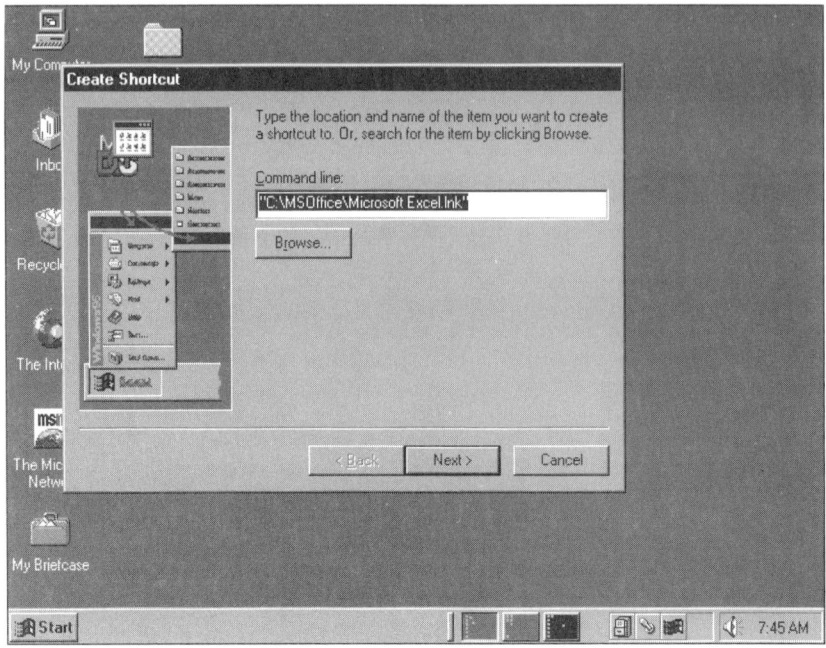

FIGURE 6.14 YOU CLICK THE ICON; THE PROGRAM ADDS THE FILE NAME.

When you click **Next**, the Select a Title for the Program window appears. You can use the entered name (in this case, Microsoft Excel) or enter one of your own choosing. When you've done that, click **Finish**. The new shortcut is created with the name you specified, and now you can start the program with a quick double-click (see Figure 6.15).

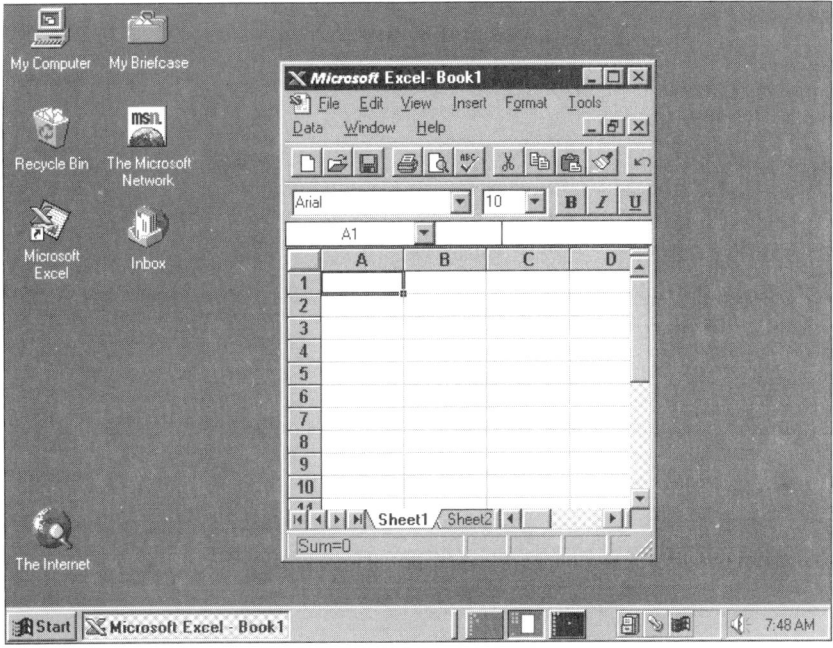

FIGURE 6.15 CHOOSING AN ITEM TO BE LINKED TO THE SHORTCUT.

USING DESKTOPS FROM OTHER PROGRAMS

If you were using an earlier version of PC Tools for Windows or Norton Desktop for Windows, you can import your desktops to Norton Navigator. You use the Desktop Importer program to do this.

THE NEXT STOP

In this chapter, you've learned how to create alternate desktops to help you organize, protect, and unclutter your work. You found out how to customize the look and feel of the desktop so that you can easily distinguish between available desktops in the Taskbar.

Chapter 7 takes a closer look at folders and helps you explore the Folder Navigator and Norton's SmartFolders feature.

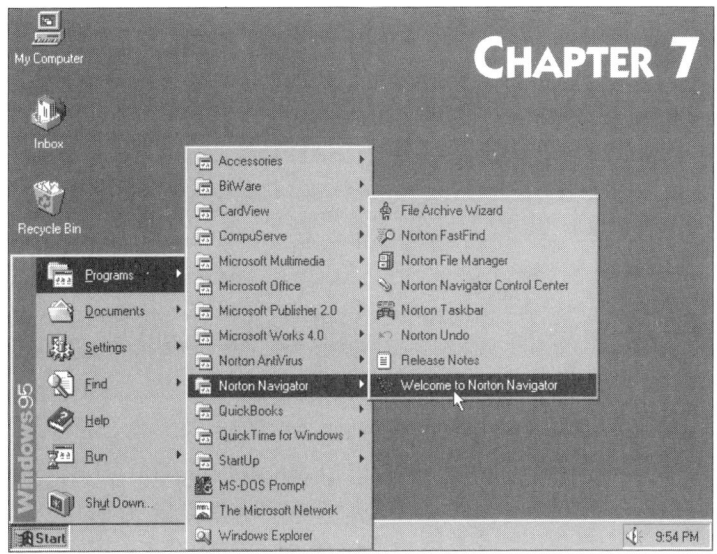

CHAPTER 7

WORKING WITH FOLDERS

Folders have been around for a long time. At the office, you probably use folders to store memos, reports, and financial information. At home, you may use folders to keep your tax things together, hold paid bill stubs, and organize schoolwork.

Folders on your computer continue that basic analogy, but instead of holding physical slips of paper, check stubs, or bill stubs, the folders on your computer desktop store the programs and files you use to accomplish your work.

Norton Navigator includes several features that help you work with folders more efficiently. In this chapter, as part of the "navigation" section of this book, we'll focus on the Norton features that help you move through folders quickly and cleanly. In Chapter 8, you learn to create, rename, and remove folders.

The Folder Navigator adds commands to the folder popup menus (the menus that appear when you click the right mouse button) so that you can move through and work with files quickly without opening a swarm of different folders. Norton also adds the SmartFolders feature, a utility that builds a folder full of shortcuts that will help you organize and locate the files with which you most want to work.

WHAT ARE FOLDERS?

On screen, a computer folder graphically represents a traditional folder, as you might expect (see Figure 7.1). In the My Computer window, two folders are shown: the Control Panel folder and the Printers folder.

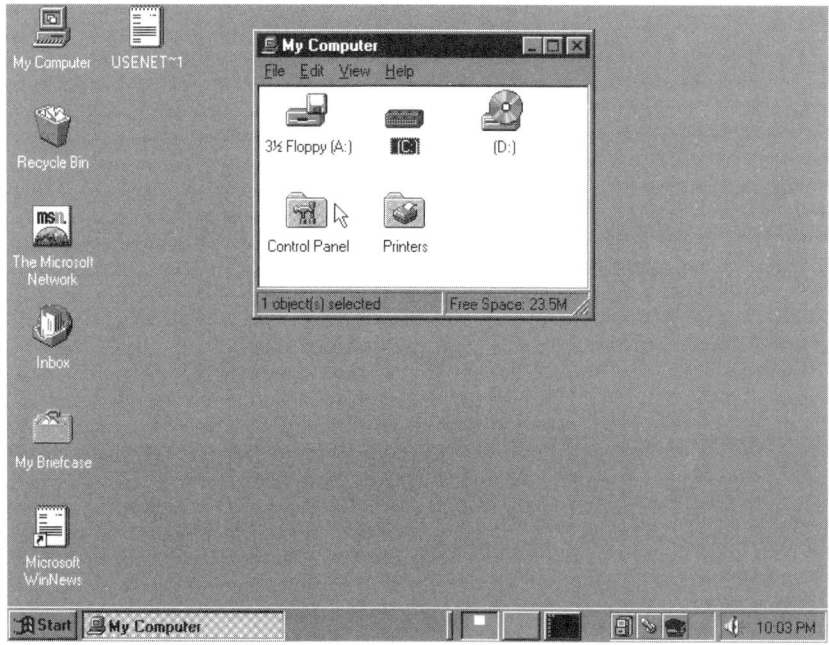

FIGURE 7.1 FOLDERS IN THE MY COMPUTER WINDOW.

When you open either of these folders by double-clicking them, you will see additional items inside the folder. The Control Panel folder is displayed in Figure 7.2.

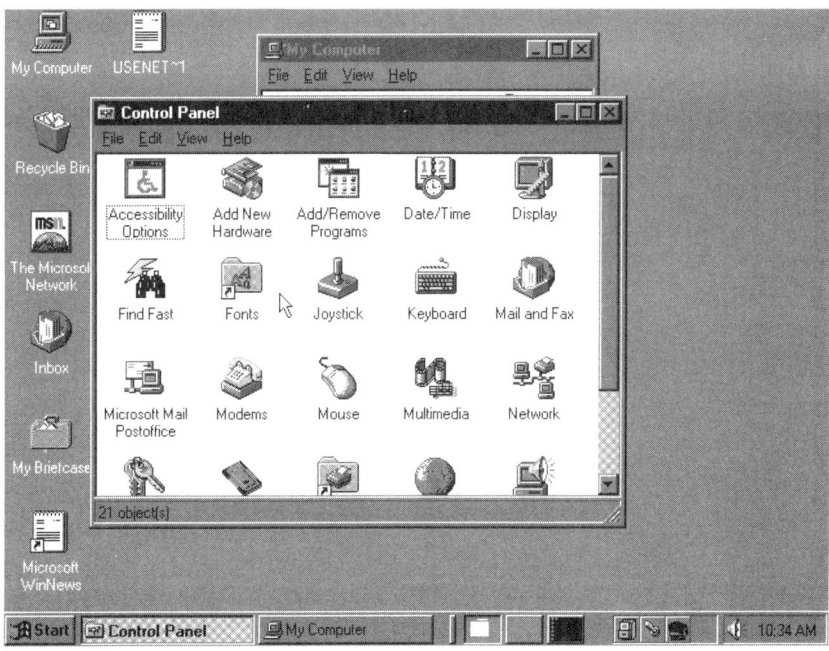

FIGURE 7.2 INSIDE A WINDOW.

As you can see, there are a number of items in this folder (which has now been opened into a window). Some are programs, and others are folders within the current folder. In this example, the **Date/Time** and **Keyboard** icons represent small programs you can use to set the date and time on your computer and change your keyboard settings. You'll also see the Fonts folder and, lower in the window, the Printers folder. When you double-click **Printers**, the folder opens into a window, as shown in Figure 7.3.

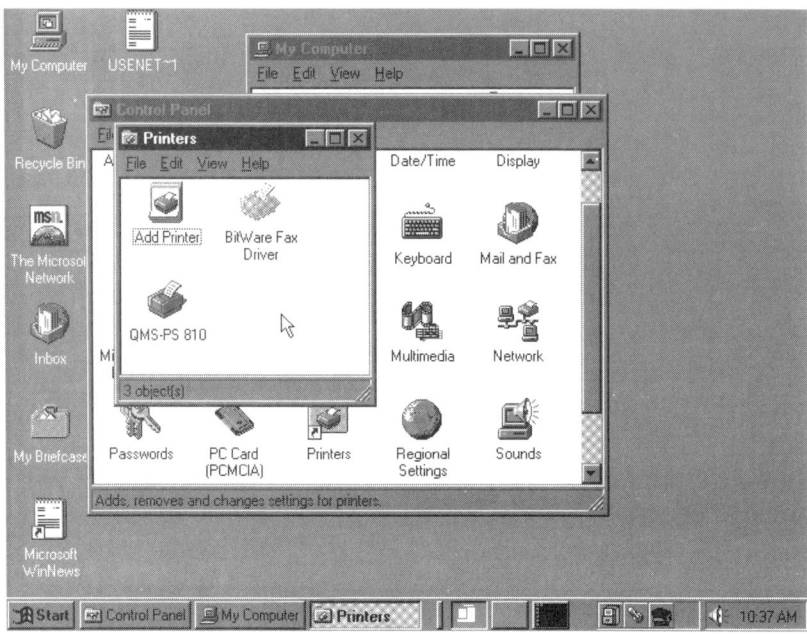

FIGURE 7.3 DISPLAYING A FOLDER WITHIN A FOLDER: PRINTERS.

Not only does Windows store programs and files in folders, but you will also create folders to store the information you work with. (This process is covered in Chapter 8.) The Norton Navigator program itself, for example, is stored in one folder, and its various utilities—Desktops, Indexing, and QuickLaunch—are shown as subfolders of the Norton Navigator folder (see Figure 7.4).

Chapter 7 Working with Folders

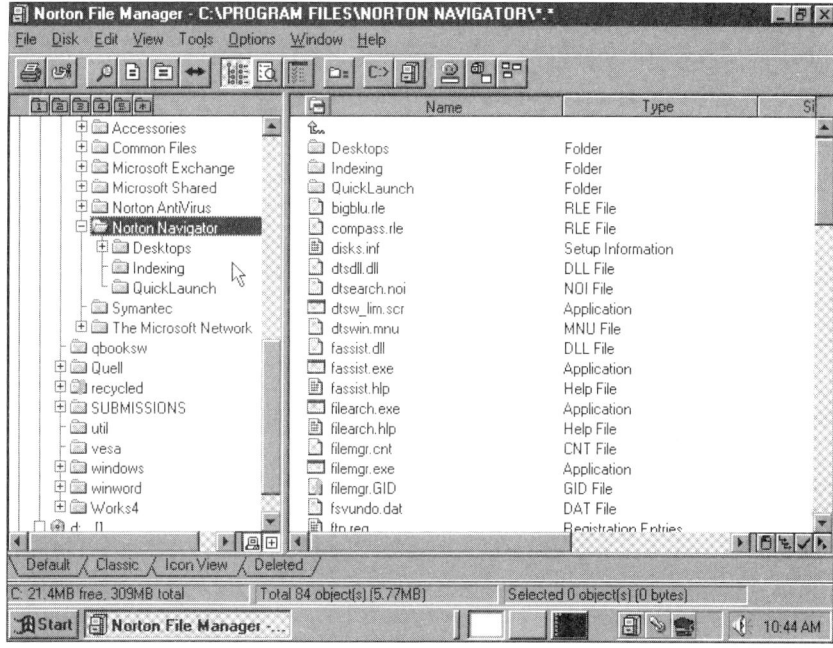

Figure 7.4 Checking out the Norton folder and subfolders.

If you are changing over from Windows 3.11, you may be thrown by the folders analogy at first. You are, after all, accustomed to windows—group windows, program windows—and not to folders. What we used to call *directories* and subdirectories (a holdover from DOS days) we now refer to as *folders* and *subfolders.*

When you're ready to close a folder window, you have four basic choices:

- You can click the **Close** box in the upper-right corner of the window.
- You can open the File menu and choose **Close**.
- You can click the folder icon to the left of the folder name (**Printers**, in this case) and choose **Close** from the displayed menu.
- You can press **Alt+F4**.

For more about working with Windows 95 folders and windows, see *teach yourself... Windows 95*, by Al Stevens.

Using the Folder Navigator

Now that you know the basics of working with folders—what they do and what you do with them—you are ready to see how Norton Navigator enhances the basic folder features of Windows 95.

The first folder enhancement item is located in the Norton Navigator Control Center. It's called Norton Folder Navigator. Turn on the **Folder Navigator** by selecting the option in the Control Center and making sure the choices are checked. Folder Navigator adds navigation capability to your folders automatically.

This means that instead of double-clicking on one folder to open it and then double-clicking on another folder to open that one (as we did in the preceding section), you can simply click the right mouse button and display a cascading menu.

For example, using the My Computer window selected earlier, position the pointer on the Control Panel and click the right mouse button. Choose the icon representing your hard disk (in this case, drive **C**) and double-click it. Move to a folder that you know stores other folders. In this example, we selected the **MSOffice** folder. Double-click the folder to open it. Now position the pointer on a folder and click the right mouse button.

In addition to the commands Windows 95 has conveniently added to folder tasks, there's a new one: Navigator. When you position the pointer on that command, a popup menu appears with options that are related to the folder you selected. In the example shown in Figure 7.5, different types of Excel files are shown in the cascading menus.

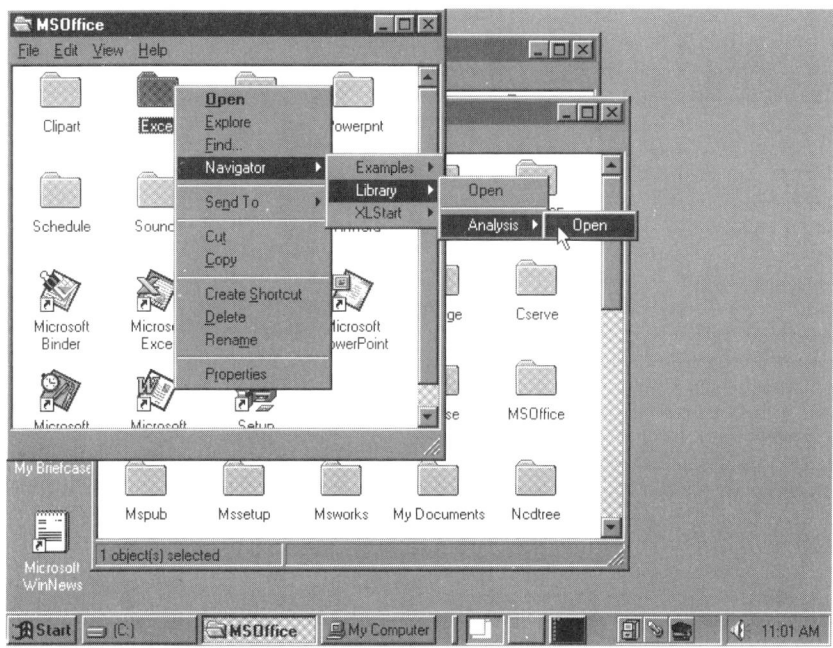

FIGURE 7.5 NAVIGATING EASILY WITH NAVIGATOR.

Even though Windows 95 added many different new commands for copying, moving, sending, and working with folders, there was no command—until now—to make getting to selected files easier.

The Navigator also adds another Navigator command when you move folders from one place to another. Position the mouse pointer on the folder and press and hold the right mouse button. When you release the button, a popup menu appears, listing the other folders in that window (see Figure 7.6). Instead of dragging the folder to another place, you can choose the folder to which you want the selected folder moved. This is especially helpful if you have so many folders that they scroll off the screen.

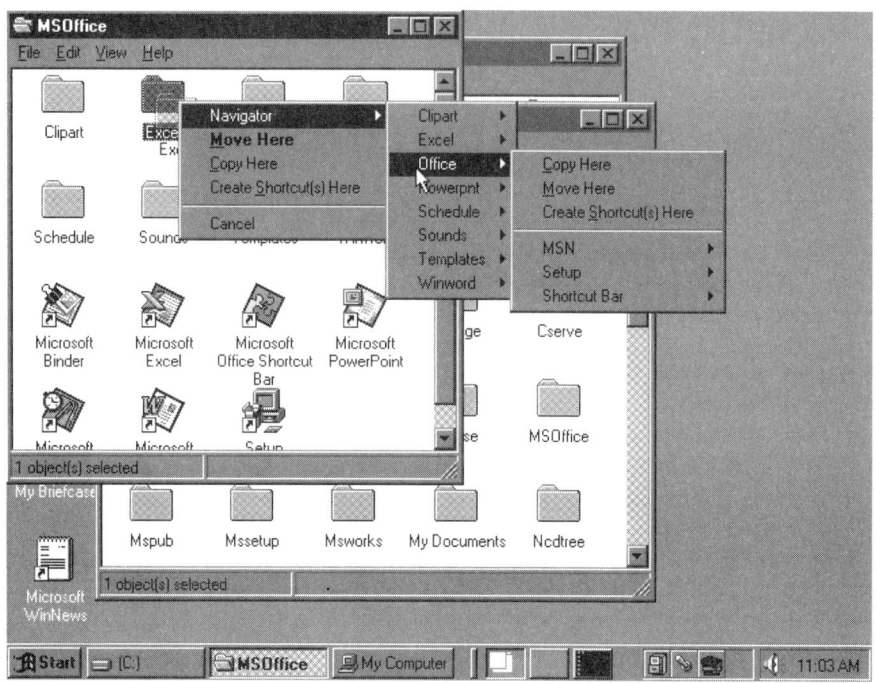

FIGURE 7.6 USING THE FOLDER NAVIGATOR TO MOVE A FOLDER.

If at any time you decide you don't want to use the Navigator command, return to the Control Center, choose **Norton Folder Navigator**, and uncheck the options by clicking them.

CREATING AND USING SMARTFOLDERS

SmartFolders that build on the new features of Windows 95. Earlier versions of Windows didn't include shortcuts—those quick paths to programs and files you use often. A SmartFolder pulls together a collection of shortcuts—files you specify—to create an easily updateable folder of files. As you create and delete files from your system, your SmartFolders are added to or removed from automatically.

What Is a SmartFolder?

In simplest terms, a SmartFolder is a special folder that holds shortcuts to other files. For example, suppose that you do much of your work in Microsoft Word. You're forever using **.DOC** files. You can create a SmartFolder that stores shortcuts to each of the **.DOC** files in the folder you choose. This can save you considerable time and trouble in looking for a file or hunting groups of files you worked on weeks ago.

You can determine when you want Norton Navigator to update the SmartFolder so that files no longer on your system are weeded out and new files are added as necessary.

Creating a SmartFolder

Norton Navigator includes a wizard that helps you create the SmartFolder. First, display the Control Center by clicking the **Control Center** icon in the QuickLaunch area. Next, click **Norton SmartFolders**. The Control Center changes to display the options shown in Figure 7.7.

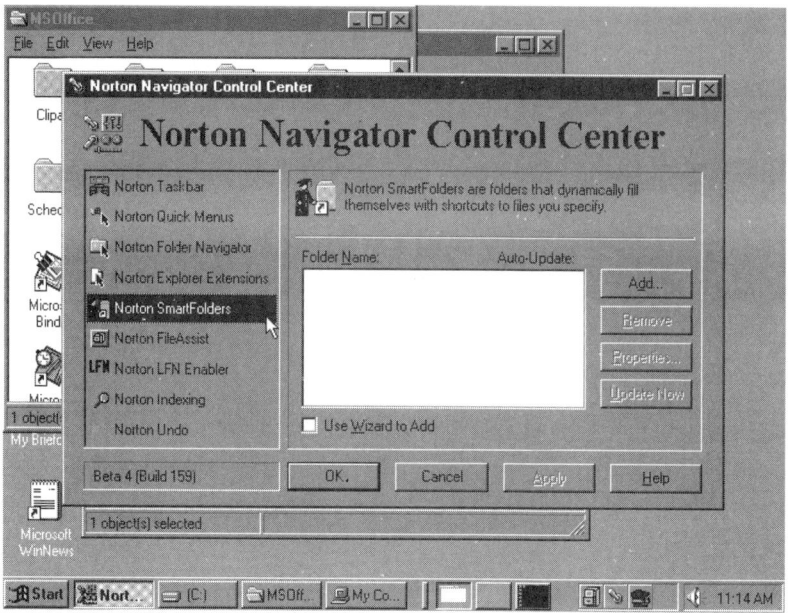

FIGURE 7.7 USING THE FOLDER NAVIGATOR TO MOVE A FOLDER.

To begin creating your first SmartFolder, click the Use **Wizard to Add** checkbox. Then click **Add**. The Add New SmartFolder dialog box appears, as shown in Figure 7.8. You are asked for a name for the SmartFolder. Choose something that reflects the files you'll be storing there—in this case, we choose **Word documents**. Click **Next**.

CHAPTER 7 WORKING WITH FOLDERS   151

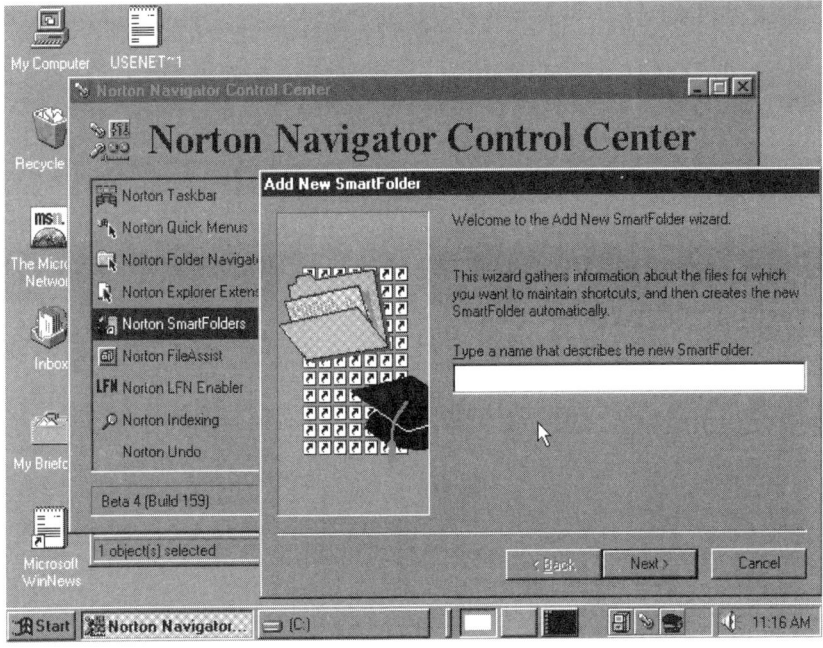

FIGURE 7.8 USING A WIZARD TO CREATE A SMARTFOLDER.

The second screen of the Add New SmartFolder wizard asks you to specify the kind of files you want Norton Navigator to look for. This is where you enter ***.doc**.

 **NOTE** The asterisk (*) is a wildcard character. It can be substituted for any number of characters or numbers. When you tell Norton Navigator to search for ***.doc**, you are saying, in effect, "Search for any file that ends with **.doc**."

In the **Located in** box, enter the folder you want Norton Navigator to search in. If you're not sure where you want to look, click the **File Manager** icon. The Browse for Folder dialog box appears, and you can navigate through the drives and folders to find the folder you want. In the screen shown in Figure 7.9, we've selected **Winword** as the folder. Click **OK** when you've selected the folder you want to search.

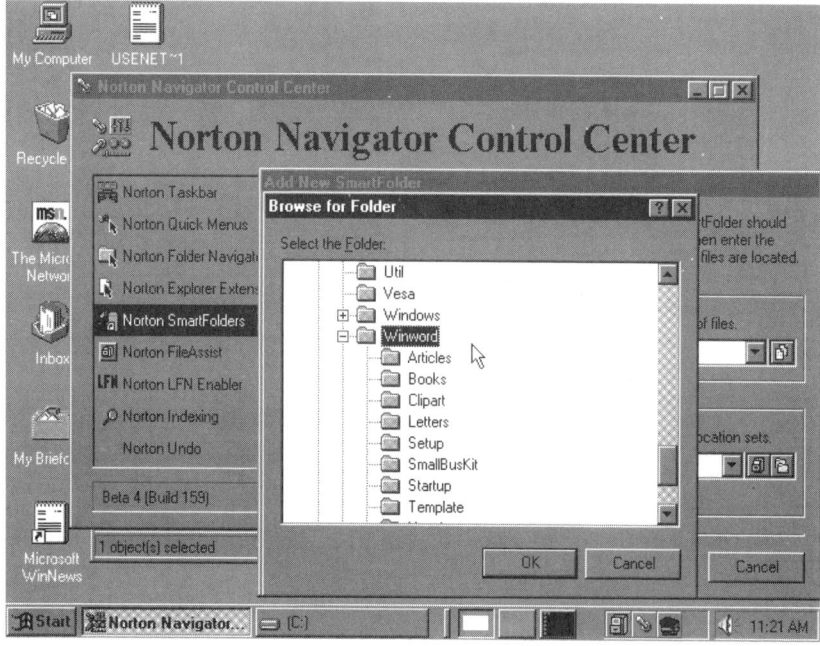

FIGURE 7.9 THE BROWSE FOR FOLDER DIALOG BOX LETS YOU CHOOSE THE FOLDER YOU WANT TO SEARCH.

CHAPTER 7 WORKING WITH FOLDERS   153

SHORTCUT

If you want to search all folders on the hard drive, click the drive icon when Browse for Folder first appears.

Norton Navigator enters the drive and folder (this is called the *path*) in the **Located in** box. Now you can click the **Search Subfolders Automatically** checkbox if you want to search all folders stored in the current folder. If you don't, leave the option blank. Click **Next**.

The final screen lets you specify files of a certain age to be included in the search. You can click the down-arrow beside the **Ignore** option to display your choices. Norton allows you to choose any of the following:

✦ **Ignore** (the default, meaning that no date is specified)
✦ **On**
✦ **Before**
✦ **After**
✦ **Between**
✦ **Last**
✦ **Prior to last**

When you click one of the options, a date box appears so that you can enter the date that will further narrow your search.

NOTE

If you're not sure whether to specify the data now, remember that you can change the date information later, as well as the search criteria, by clicking **Properties** in the Control Center dialog box.

Additionally, you can click the checkbox toward the bottom of the window if you want to control how many items should be included in your

SmartFolder. When you click the checkbox, the **How many shortcuts to keep?** box appears. Use the arrow keys to change the default number.

When you're finished entering your choices, click **Finish**. The wizard searches the folders you specified and displays the name of the folder in the Control Center screen.

If you want to have Norton update folders for you automatically, click **Properties** in the Control Center window; then click the **Contents** tab. The **Automatically update SmartFolder** in the background will make sure that the file you're working with is always the most current.

Updating a SmartFolder

When you're ready to manually update a SmartFolder, click the **Update Now** button in the Control Center window. Norton does a quick search, automatically updating all the files on your hard disk with any new information.

Using a SmartFolder

You won't see the SmartFolder until you return to the desktop. Norton creates the SmartFolder and then puts it over by the Windows icons on your screen (see Figure 7.10).

To use the SmartFolder, double-click it as you would any other folder; then double-click the shortcut to the file you want to use.

FIGURE 7.10 THE NEWLY CREATED SMARTFOLDER.

Moving SmartFolders

To help keep your work organized, you can deposit SmartFolders inside other folders. You might, for example, want to put the Word documents SmartFolder inside the Winword folder so that you can easily access all those Word documents without searching through different directories to find the one you want.

To change the location of the SmartFolder, display the Norton SmartFolders screen of the Control Center and click the **Properties** button. The Properties for "Word documents" window appears, as shown in Figure 7.11. (Note: Whatever name you've entered for your SmartFolder will appear in place of "Word documents.") Choose the **Name** tag and enter a new location for the SmartFolder in the **Folder Location** box. When you're finished making changes, click **OK**. Norton will move the SmartFolder to the new location you specified.

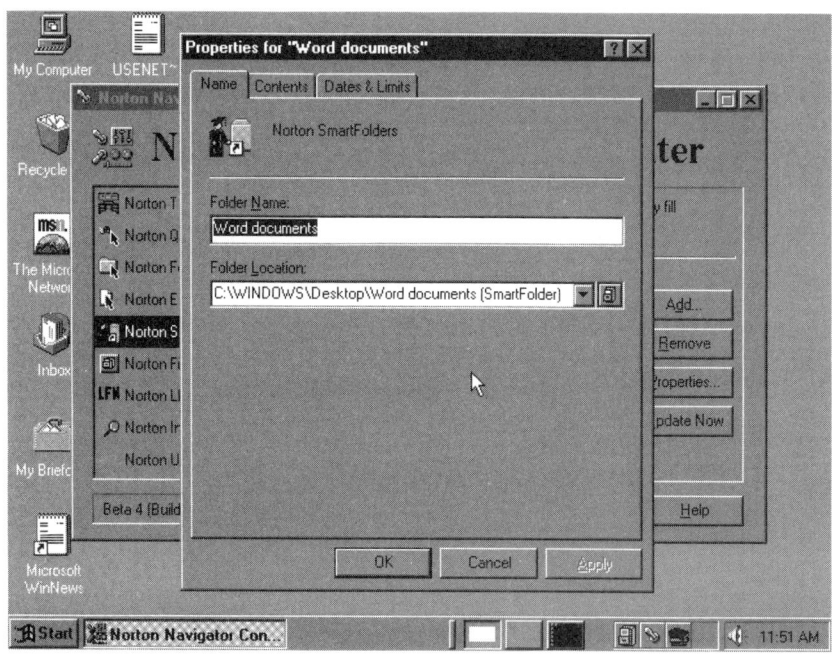

FIGURE 7.11 YOU CAN MOVE SMARTFOLDERS TO DIFFERENT FOLDERS, DESKTOPS, OR DRIVER.

Removing a SmartFolder

As the nature of your work changes and projects come and go, you will want to update and, at some point, remove SmartFolders you no longer need. The process is simple.

Display the Control Center and choose **Norton SmartFolders**. Choose the SmartFolder you want to delete and click the **Remove** button. Norton Navigator displays the Norton SmartFolders message box, alerting you that you're about to delete all the shortcuts in the selected SmartFolder and asking you to confirm the request (see Figure 7.12). To remove the SmartFolder, click **OK**; to keep it, click **Cancel**.

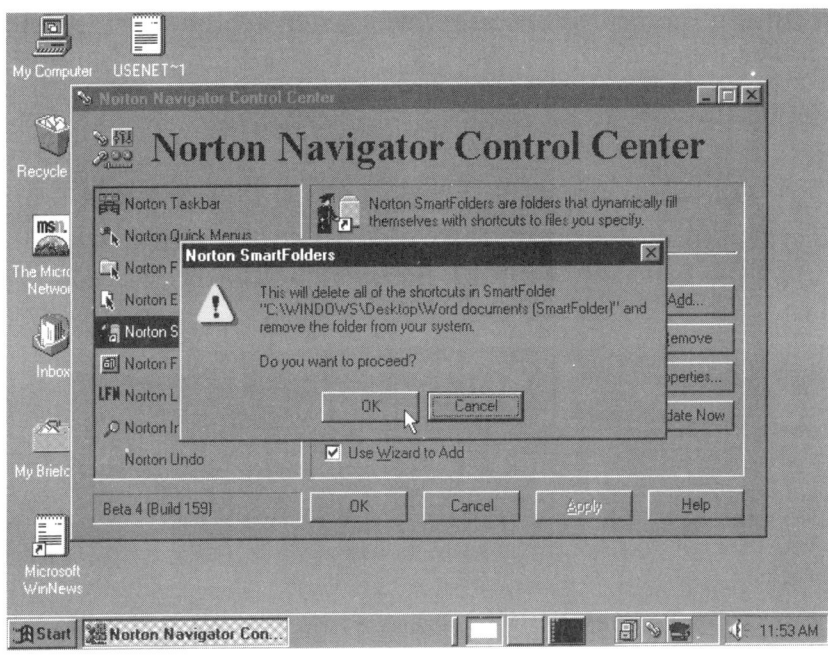

FIGURE 7.12 NORTON NAVIGATOR WARNS YOU THAT YOU'RE ABOUT TO DELETE THE SMARTFOLDER YOU CREATED AND ASKS FOR CONFIRMATION.

The Next Stop

In this chapter, you learned about two of the basic folder navigation techniques Norton Navigator incorporates to make working with folders and files easier. We explored the folder features from a navigation standpoint—how do you get from here to there?

This chapter completes Part Two, on the various ways you can use Norton Navigator to enhance your computing tasks. Chapter 8 begins Part Three, which focuses on a closer, more procedural look at the nuts and bolts of computing: working with files, disks, and folders and performing a myriad of file and disk operations with the File Manager "extraordinaire."

PART THREE

THE FILE MANAGER EXTRAORDINAIRE

Chapter 8: File Manager Basics

Chapter 9: Working with Files

Chapter 10: Working with Disks

Chapter 11: Special File Procedures: Searching, Sorting, and Indexing

Chapter 12: Mapping FTP Internet Sites

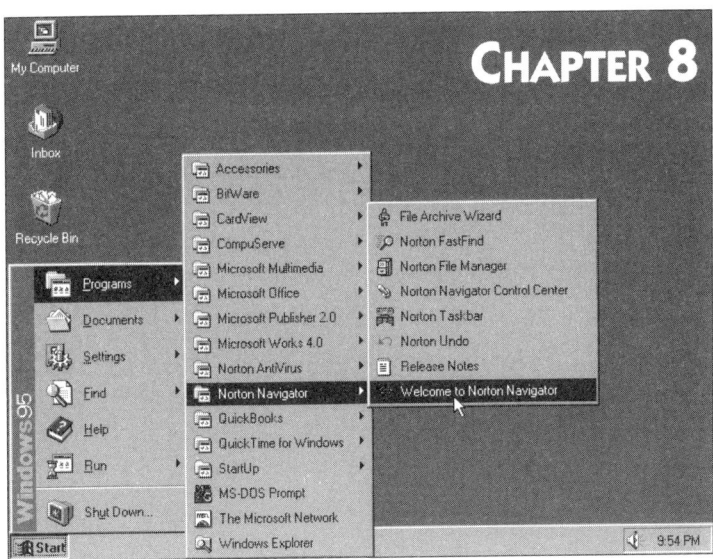

CHAPTER 8

FILE MANAGER BASICS

If you've been using Windows—in any of its generations—you are most probably accustomed to some sort of file-management utility. Each earlier Windows version had its own version of a file-management feature that it called the File Manager (no direct relation), an aspect of the program that was often blasted by new users as being difficult to understand and use. Windows 95 replaced the old File Manager with the Windows Explorer—a utility that's getting better press but remains somewhat lacking in its feature list.

Not so with Norton's File Manager. You'll find everything you need to grab and organize your files, folders, and disks. You can easily create, open, move, delete, and rename folders. You can zip and unzip files. You can display almost anything any way you want to. Perhaps more than any other feature, Norton's File Manager makes the entire program shine.

The way you organize and work with your programs and files is an important part of your computing life. This chapter introduces you to the basics of the File Manager—the *Norton* File Manager—which adds powerful features, lightning-fast operation, and easy-to-use and easy-to-understand commands to necessary, if sometimes uninteresting, tasks.

DISPLAYING THE FILE MANAGER

You can display the File Manager in one of two ways. If you currently have Norton Navigator loaded and are working with the Taskbar, you can click the **Norton File Manager** icon in the QuickLaunch area to start the program (see Figure 8.1).

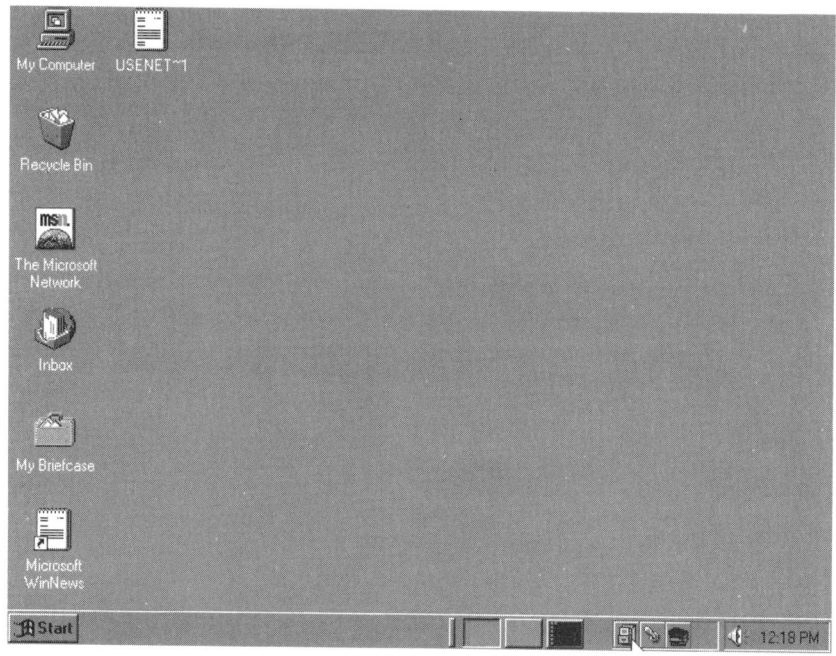

FIGURE 8.1 STARTING THE FILE MANAGER FROM THE TASKBAR.

If you don't have Norton loaded and don't particularly want the Taskbar on the screen, you can start the File Manager independently. Open the Windows 95 Start menu and click **Programs**. Scan the list for Norton Navigator and position the pointer there. When the submenu appears, click **Norton File Manager**, as shown in Figure 8.2.

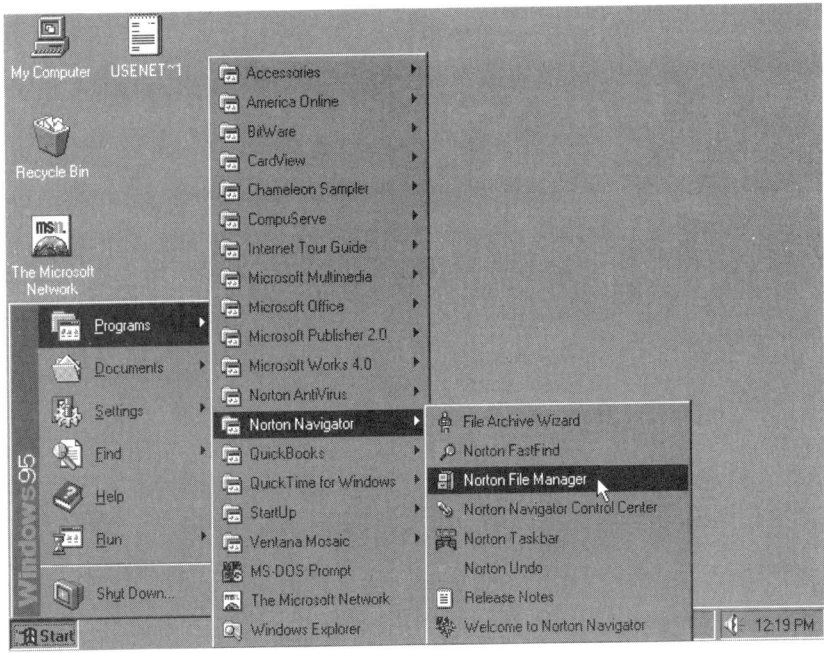

FIGURE 8.2 CHOOSING NORTON FILE MANAGER FROM THE WINDOWS MENUS.

UNDERSTANDING THE FILE MANAGER WINDOW

After a moment, the File Manager window appears on the screen. If your File Manager doesn't appear maximized—that is, the window doesn't fill the entire screen—click the Maximize button in the upper right corner of the window to enlarge the File Manager to its fullest size. (Note: The **Maximize** button is the button between the **Minimize** button and the **Close** button.)

Figure 8.3 shows the File Manager window as it first appears. At the top of the window, you see the familiar title bar. We'll discuss the other elements in the coming sections.

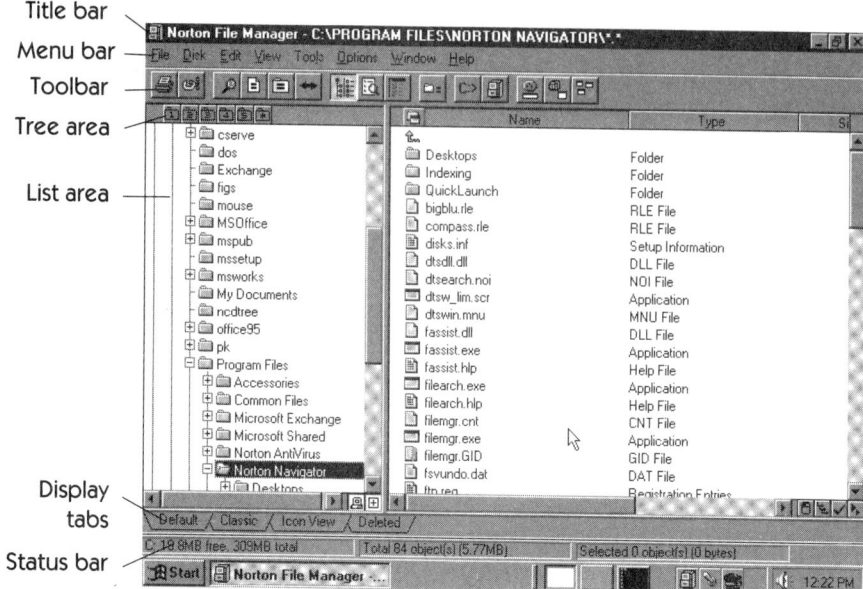

FIGURE 8.3 THE FILE MANAGER SCREEN.

The Menus

Menus are standard in today's computer programs. You know what to do with a menu—point and click. Each menu houses commands that are central to a particular task or topic. Table 8.1 gives you an overview of the function s of the different File Manager windows.

TABLE 8.1 THE FILE MANAGER MENUS.

Menu	Description
File	Contains all the commands you need to create, move, copy, delete, rename, change, zip, encode, run, and print files. Also includes the **Exit** command so that you can leave File Manager.
Disk	Takes care of all disk tasks, such as copying, labeling, formatting, scanning, mapping, and sharing disks.

Edit	Lets you reverse your most current operations and cut, copy, paste, and select items.
View	Lets you change the way items are displayed in File Manager. You can add or remove file details, display specific files, change the tabs, use an Auto-Viewer, or display tagged files.
Tools	Contains special File Manager commands that let you perform specific functions with files and folders—for example, **FastFind**, **Compare**, **Synchronize**, and **Go to** let you work with files and folders in a manner not supported in other programs.
Options	Lets you change the basic settings of the File Manager and the way elements are displayed on the screen.
Window	Lets you change the way windows are displayed in the File Manager and move between open windows.
Help	Displays the **Help Topics** option so that you can find help on a specific function of the File Manager.

Customizing the Menus

The level of opportunity is amazing—you can customize your own menus in the Norton File Manager. If you want to add different commands, change the way the menus look, or add nested submenus, open the Options menu, choose **Customize**, and select **Menus**.

When the Customize Norton File Manager dialog box appears, start creating a new menu by clicking **Copy**. Then you can insert or delete commands and features as you make choices about the way your menus are displayed. Click **Save** when you're finished.

What About Shortcut Keys?

Every program has shortcut keys—where are they in the Norton File Manager screen? You may be relieved to know that all the basic shortcut keys you are familiar with are in effect. They work in File Manager, although they are not displayed on the screen.

You can add and remove shortcut keys by opening the **Options** menu, choosing **Customize**, selecting **Shortcut Keys**, and then choosing the ones you want to display from the list that appears.

Start by clicking **Copy** so that you don't accidentally write over the existing shortcut keys. Then you can click **Insert** and **Delete** to your heart's content, adding and removing the shortcut keys you'll use with File Manager. Don't forget to click **Save** when you're finished so that File Manager saves the changes you've made.

The Toolbar

The Toolbar probably looks different from anything you've previously encountered; it has new tools you won't have seen in any traditional Windows programs until now.

SHORTCUT

This is the first time we've seen "tools" per se in Norton Navigator. If you're not sure about using the tools in the Toolbar, here's the lowdown: just point and click. If you're not sure what a particular tool does, position the mouse pointer over the tool and leave it there for a second. A small label will appear—this is called a tool tip in Microsoft-speak—to tell you the name of the tool.

Table 8.2 lists the different tools available in the Norton File Manager Toolbar.

TABLE 8.2 THE FILE MANAGER TOOLS.

Tool	Name	Description
	Print File	Displays the Print dialog box

	Zip	Displays the Norton Zip dialog box so that you can zip files
	FastFind	Lets you find files and folders quickly
	Compare Files	Displays the Compare Files dialog box so that you can compare the status, case, and content of two files
	Compare Folders	Displays the Compare Folders dialog box, where you can enter the name of the folder you want to compare for content (choose the first folder before you select Compare Folders)
	Sync Folders	Shows the Synchronize Folders dialog box so that you can make sure two folders include identical contents
	Tree and List	Displays the File Manager in its (default) Tree and List display
	Search Results	Shows the Search Results window
	Tagged List	Displays a window containing only those files that have been tagged
	Branch Size	Figures and displays the branch sizes of all folders in the file list
	MS DOS Prompt	Displays a DOS window

	File Manager	Opens another File Manager window and tiles it automatically on the screen
	FTP Log Window	Opens an FTP log window at the bottom of the screen so that you can keep an eye on Internet file transfer while you work
	Auto-Viewer	Displays the binary contents of a file in its own popup window
	Close Viewers	Closes all viewers currently open in File Manager

Changing the Toolbar

You can change the tools in the Toolbar to include other tools you might use more often. Open the Options menu and choose **Customize**. When the cascading menu appears, choose **Toolbar**. The Customize Norton File Manager dialog box appears. Create a new Toolbar by clicking **Copy** and typing a new name for the new toolbar (or use the default Toolbar #1 that appears).

To remove tools you don't want to use, click them in the toolbar in the center of the dialog box and click the **Delete** button. To add tools, scroll through the tools in the **Commands** box. When you find one you want to add, click **Insert**.

After you add and remove tools, click the **Save** button to save the toolbar. If you want to make the new toolbar the default that is displayed automatically in the Norton File Manager, click the **Default** button.

To change the look of the tools in the Toolbar, click **Style** in the Customize Norton File Manager dialog box.

WORKING WITH THE TREE AND LIST DISPLAY

In the **Tree and List display** area, you see a collection of disks, folders, and files. The **Tree** area is the area on the left; the **List** area is the area on the right.

At the top of the **Tree** area, you see six small folder icons numbered 1 through *. These icons represent the level of subfolders available on your system. Let's take a moment and experiment with changing the **Tree** display.

Changing the Tree Display

Moving among folders is a big part of using the File Manager. Start by clicking folder **1** in the **Tree** area. Notice what happens. The **Tree** list appears to collapse, and all subfolders beneath that first level disappear (see Figure 8.4).

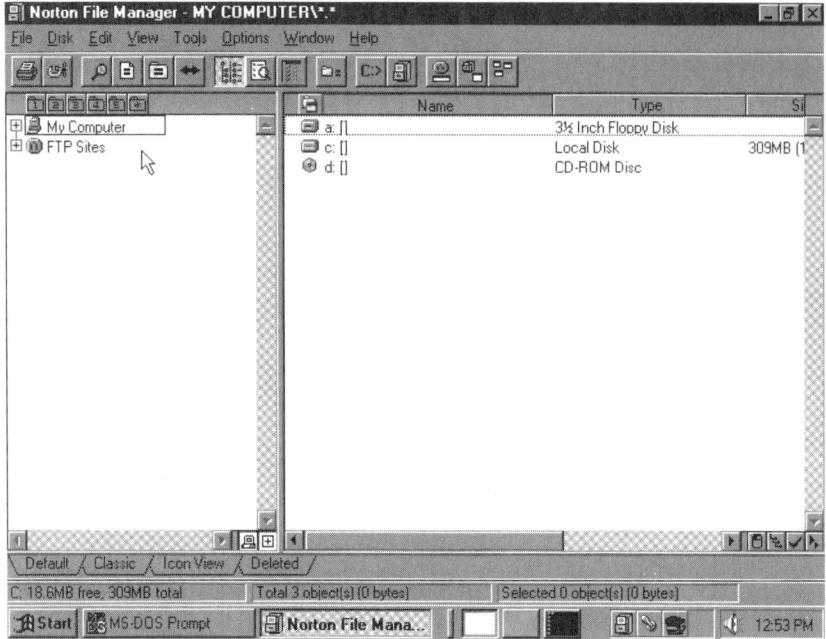

FIGURE 8.4 THE FILE MANAGER SCREEN.

Now, when you click folder **2**, you notice a change. Beneath My Computer, you can see the drives on your system. You may have a floppy disk drive (usually **a:**), a hard disk drive (usually **c:**), and perhaps a CD-ROM drive (**d:** or higher). All of these items appear beneath the My Computer category in the **Tree** area.

NOTE If you don't see all the drives on your system in the **Tree** area, click the **Show All Drives** button. (This button is in the lower-right corner of the **Tree** area—it looks like a miniature computer.)

Let's go another level further. Click folder **3**. Now you see a big change. This action, in effect, displays all the first-level folders on your hard drive. Consider Figure 8.5.

CHAPTER 8 FILE MANAGER BASICS

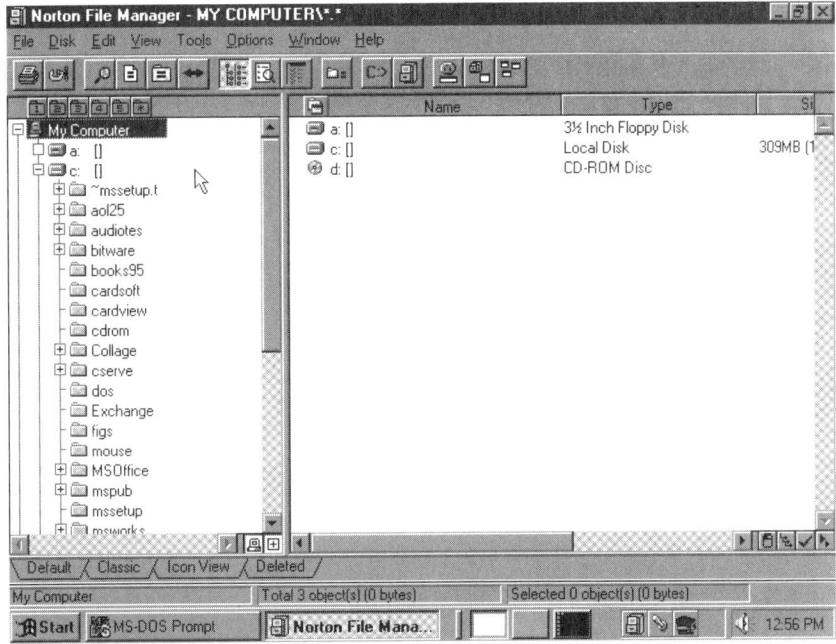

FIGURE 8.5 CHANGING THE DISPLAY OF FOLDERS IN THE **TREE** AREA.

NOTE Notice that the **List** area is not changing as we modify the display in the **Tree** area. This is because we are not choosing a different folder—the highlight is still on My Computer, so the contents of My Computer are being continually shown in the **List** area.

You'll notice some symbols in the small squares to the left of the folders in the **Tree** area. Here's what they mean:

[ ] means that there are no subfolders on this drive or in this folder.

[-] means that all subfolders of this drive or folder are currently being displayed.

[+] means that this folder or drive contains additional subfolders not currently being displayed.

NOTE If you don't like the small icons or—for whatever reason—want to hide the fact that some directories have subfolders available, you can turn off the display of the symbols by clicking the **Indicate Expandable Branches** button (where the vertical and horizontal scroll bars meet in the lower portion of the **Tree** area). This button turns off the display of [+] and [-], blanking all the folder boxes. To turn the feature back on, click the button again.

Methods of Navigating through the Tree Area

If the folder you want to see doesn't appear in the Tree list, it may be off the screen. (Notice that the folders are listed in alphabetical order.) To reach folders that are off the screen, use the vertical scroll bar in the center of the **Tree** and **List** areas. Just click the down-arrow until you locate the folder you want.

Another method of reaching your intended folder is to begin typing the name. A small popup box appears, as you can see in Figure 8.6. As you type the name, a rectangle moves to the name that Norton File Manager recognizes as the one you're typing. Press **Enter** or click the name to select it as the folder to move to.

CHAPTER 8 FILE MANAGER BASICS   173

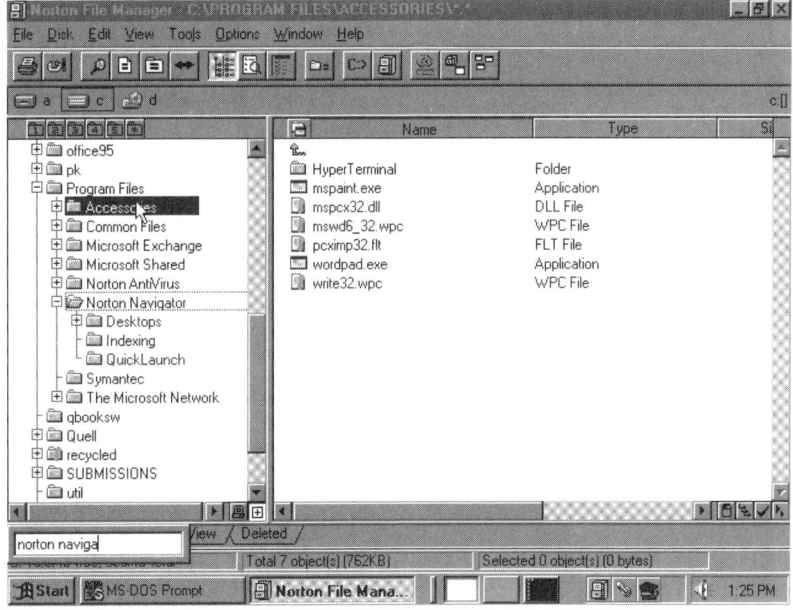

FIGURE 8.6 MOVING TO A FOLDER BY TYPING THE NAME.

Adding Folders to the Tree Area

Inevitably, you'll need to add new folders to store new project files and programs. The File Manager makes this an easy task.

First, move to the folder—or drive—where you want to create the new folder. For example, if you are working in the Winword folder and want to create a subfolder called Memos, click the **Winword** folder. If you want to create a new folder immediately off your hard drive, click the hard drive icon at the top of the **Tree** display.

Open the File menu and choose **New**. A cascading menu shows that you can choose to create a new **Folder** or a new Shortcut (see Figure 8.7). Click **Folder**. The Create Folder popup box appears. Type a name for the new folder, as shown in Figure 8.8, and click **OK**. Norton File Manager adds the folder to the **Tree** list.

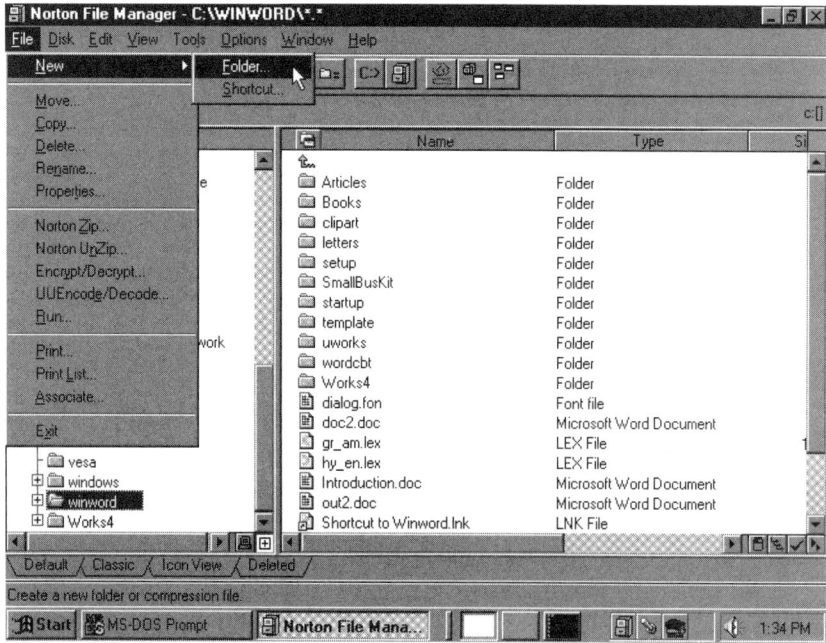

FIGURE 8.7 CREATING A NEW FOLDER.

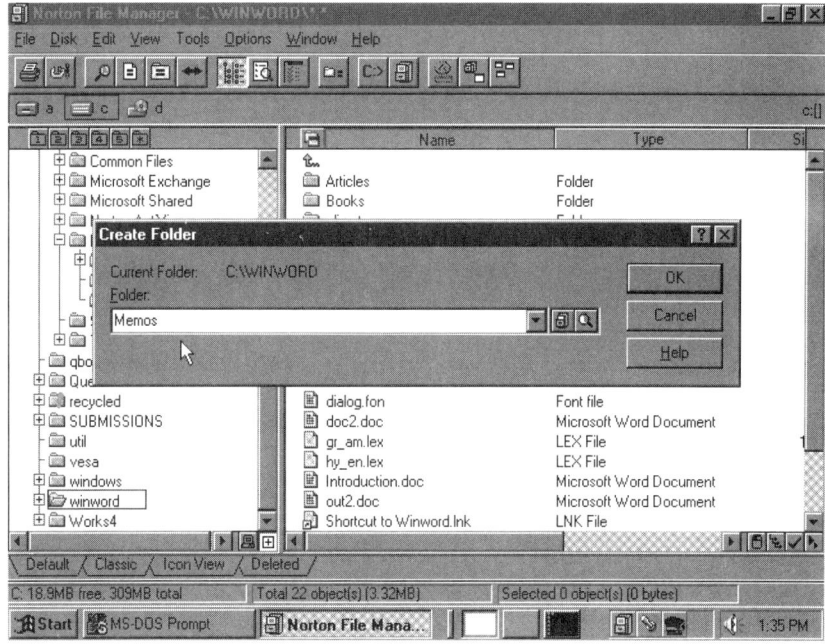

FIGURE 8.8 TYPING A NAME FOR THE NEW FOLDER.

NOTE If you later want to change the name of the folder you've just created, you can simply click it, open the File menu, and choose **Rename**. The Rename dialog box appears so that you can type a new name and click **OK** to rename the folder.

Using the List Display

Now that you know how to move through the **Tree** area, you need to know some of the ways you can use the **List** area. Depending on how many folders deep your currently selected folder is, you may have folders and files in your **List** area—or you may have just files. You will be copying, moving, and renaming the files and folders displayed in the List area. Figure 8.9 shows a folder in that contains both subfolders and files.

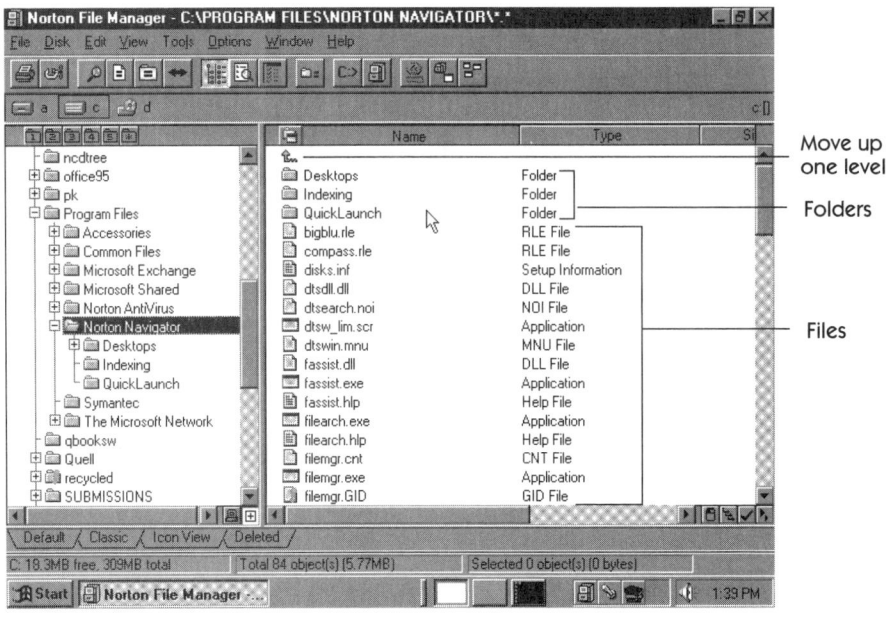

FIGURE 8.9 THE LIST AREA SHOWS FOLDERS AND FILES IN THE CURRENTLY SELECTED FOLDER

To select a file, simply click it. You can then perform any number of operations, such as copying, moving, renaming, associating, or printing the file. For more information on simple file-maintenance tasks, see Chapter 9, "Working with Files."

Changing the List Display

As with the **Tree** area, you can change the way things look in the **List** area. The commands are housed in the View menu. When you want to change the information that's displayed in the **List** area, open the View menu and choose **Details**. The File Details dialog box appears, as shown in Figure 8.10.

CHAPTER 8 FILE MANAGER BASICS 177

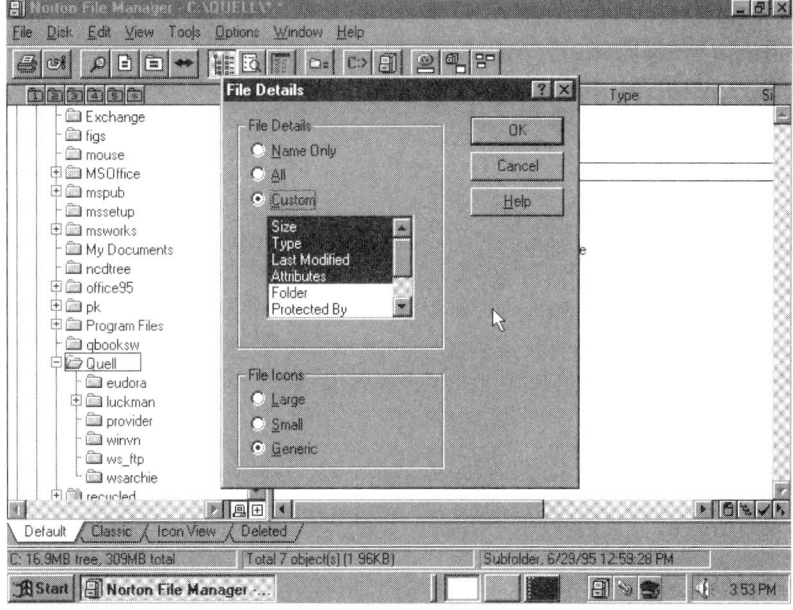

FIGURE 8.10 CHANGING THE WAY THE LIST AREA IS DISPLAYED.

You can choose to modify the display by selecting **Name Only**, **All** (which displays all items available in the Custom list box), or **Custom**, which is selected by default. The choices you have for file information are as follows:

- File size
- File type
- Date last modified
- Attributes
- Folder
- Protected by
- DOS file name
- Date created
- Date last accessed

If you want to display information items related to your files other than the ones already shown, click the item you want to add.

You can also change the size of the file icons displayed from **Generic** to either **Large** or **Small**. When you've made your changes, click **OK** to return to the File Manager display.

USING SMARTTABS

Up to this point in the chapter, we've been working with the File Manager in Default display. At the bottom of the **Tree** area, you'll see the **Default** tab and three other tabs, called SmartTabs. Each tab will display the File Manager in a different view.

What's a SmartTab?

SmartTabs enable you to view the files and folders in the File Manager in a variety of ways. Norton File Manager is equipped with several tabs, but you can create your own views, based on the settings you prefer, and then save them as SmartTabs. You can then display the view you like by simply clicking the SmartTab you created.

A SmartTab "remembers" the following settings:

- Any settings currently in effect those settings controlled by the current SmartTab
- The status of **Show All Drives**
- Whether or not you've selected **Indicate Expandable Branches**
- Whether the **List** area is in **Tag** or **Multiple Select** mode

- The way files and folders are displayed in the **List** area
- Which font is used to display file and folder information
- Any filters applied to the displayed files and folders
- The view that is in effect
- Any sort instructions that have been used to display the current files

ROAD MAP

For more information on how to search for, sort, and filter files, see Chapter 10, "Searching and Sorting Files."

Using the Default SmartTabs

The **Default** SmartTab displays the **Tree** area as folders and folders within folders—symbols are used to the left of the folders to show you which ones have additional subfolders and which ones are fully displayed. In the **List** side, the **Default** tab shows the names of the folders and files and tells what type they are.

The **Classic** SmartTab, on the other hand, displays the **Tree** area a little differently; expandable branches are not indicated, and each folder has an open box (unlike **Default**, which shows boxes only when they have a corresponding symbol). In the **List** side, the **Classic** tab shows the name of the folders and files, the size of the files, the date and time they were last modified, and the file attribute. Figure 8.11 shows the **Classic** display with the file attribute choices shown. (You can display this list by clicking the right mouse button on the **Attr** heading.)

180　Inside Norton Navigator

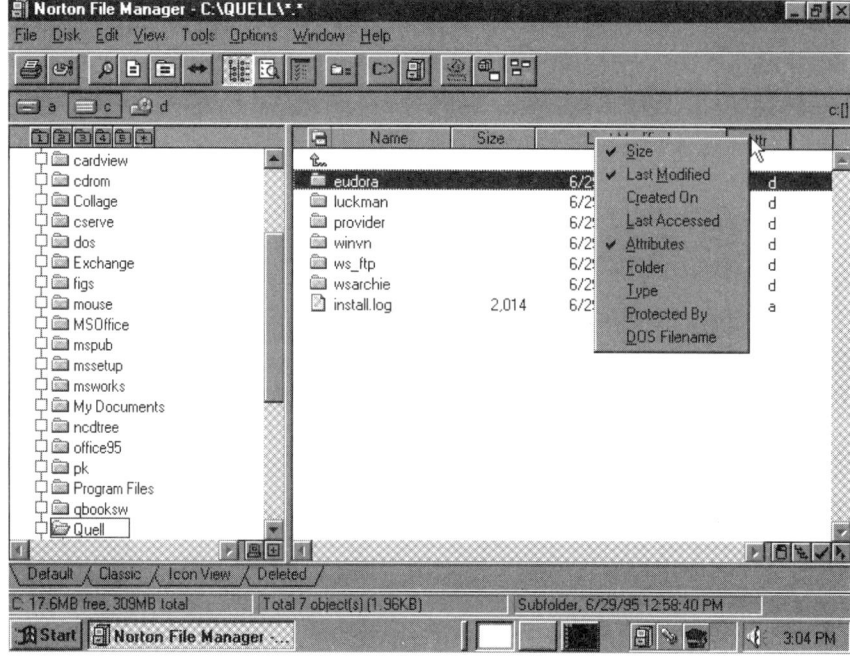

FIGURE 8.11 DISPLAYING THE CLASSIC LOOK.

The **Icon View**, as you might expect, displays all the files as icons. If you're more comfortable with the old Windows-style look (or even the Macintosh), you might like using this display (see Figure 8.12).

CHAPTER 8 FILE MANAGER BASICS 181

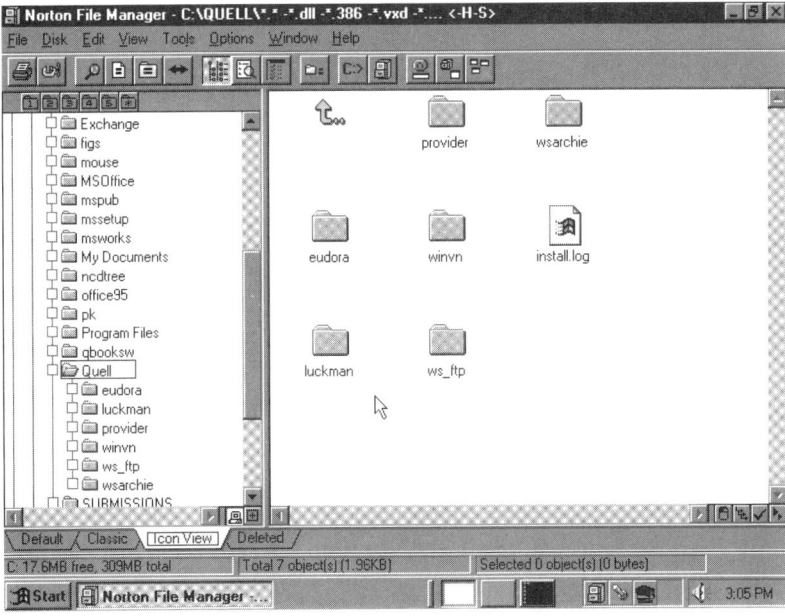

FIGURE 8.12 DISPLAYING THE ICON VIEW.

The final SmartTab, **Deleted**, shows you the files you have recently deleted in the selected folder so that you can, if necessary, undelete them. (Note: Undelete works only if you have displayed the **Deleted** tab or you have turned on the **Show Deleted Files** option in the Filters dialog box. For more about using **Undelete** with files and filters, see Chapter 10.)

Creating a SmartTab

When you learn to display certain types of files—for example, you may want to display only those PowerPoint files you used on the Smith project in September of 1995—you may want to create a SmartTab just for them. That way, you won't have to enter search information each time you want to locate that group of files.

ROAD MAP

For more about searching for specific files and displaying them in the File Manager, see Chapter 10, "Searching and Sorting Files."

To create a SmartTab of your own, start by displaying the files you want with all the settings in effect. For example, if you are searching for specific files, want to make sure **Indicate Expandable Branches** is turned on, want to make sure **Tag Mode** is in effect, and so on, do that first. Get everything set the way you want it.

Then open the View menu and choose **SmartTabs**. The SmartTabs dialog box appears, as shown in Figure 8.13. Next, click **Add**. The Add SmartTab popup box appears. Type a name that describes the view you're adding (you can use up to 32 characters); then click **OK**.

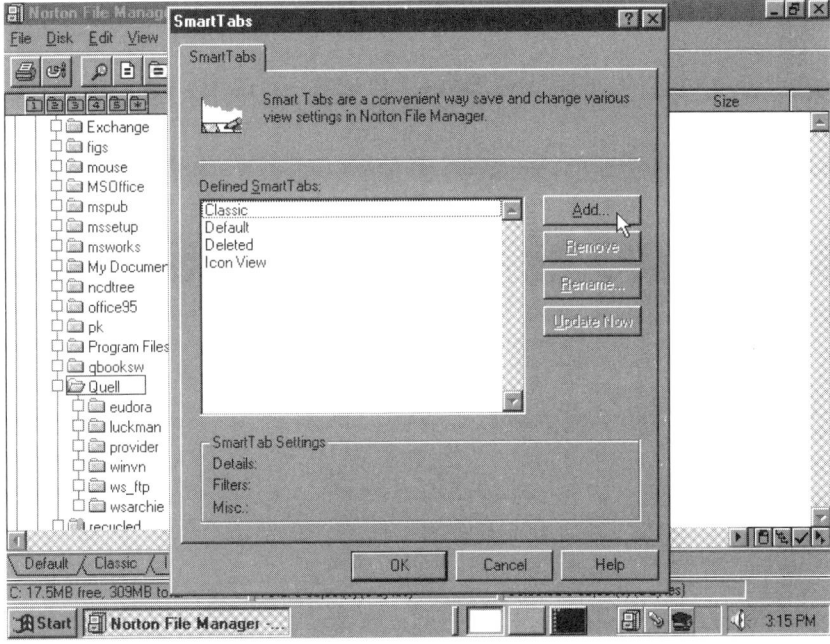

FIGURE 8.13 CREATING A NEW SMARTTAB.

After you click **OK**, Norton File Manager adds the new name to the Defined SmartTabs list in the SmartTabs dialog box. You can now access the new view at any time by clicking the SmartTab you created.

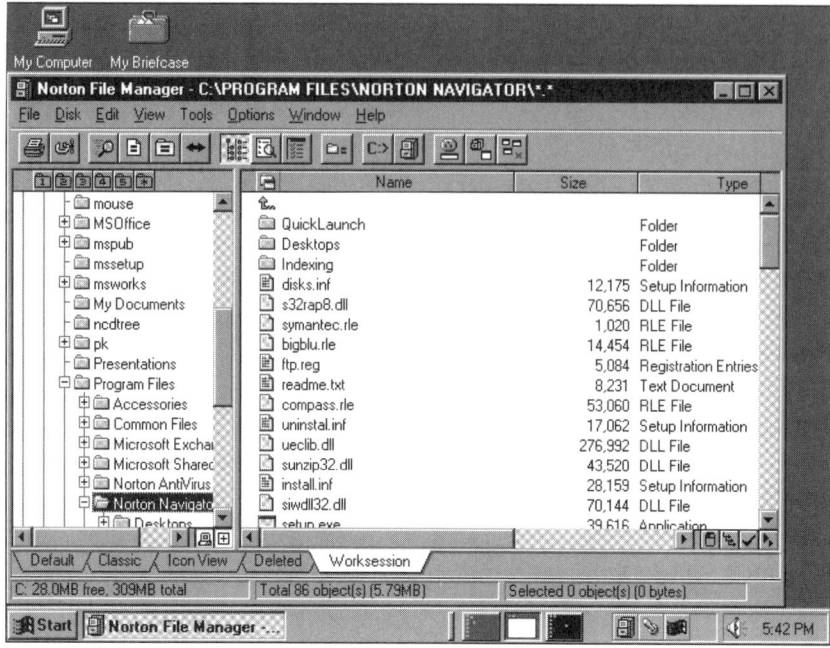

FIGURE 8.14 THE NEW SMARTTAB.

The Next Stop

In this chapter, you've learned a lot about the File Manager. From a basic introduction of the menus and tools to an exploration of the various ways you can view your files, this chapter has set the basis for further File Manager tasks. Chapter 9 takes you through the basics of simple file-maintenance operations—things you'll do often, perhaps daily—such as selecting, copying, moving, and deleting files.

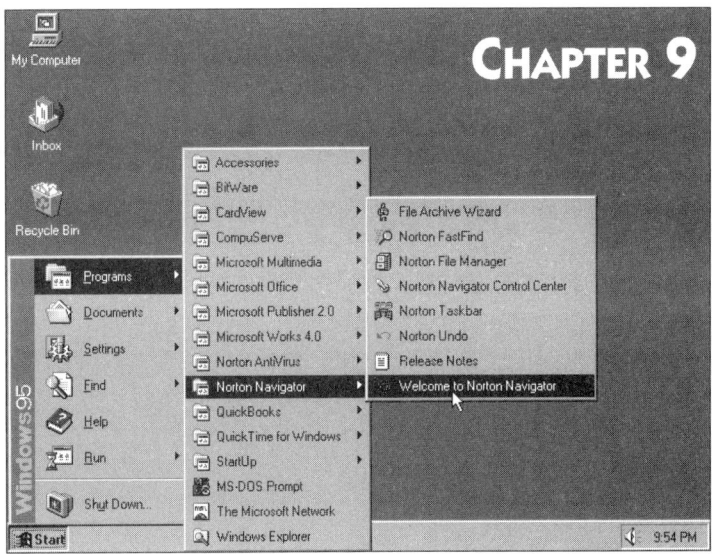

CHAPTER 9

WORKING WITH FILES

A file is perhaps the most basic of all computer elements. It's not a 1 or a 0 for those of us who don't speak binary very well—rather, it's the product of our effort, the result of our labor. The file we create.

Your files include the report you wrote for the board, the letters you compose to Aunt Mildred, the financial forecast that had you in a cold sweat before last Tuesday's budget meeting. You work hard to create these files, and you need to know how to work with them—quickly, efficiently, and safely—in Norton File Manager.

This chapter takes you on a quick tour of the basic file-maintenance tasks you may be familiar with from other programs. Including them here is a safety net, just in case you don't remember how to copy or tag or move selected files.

SELECTING AND TAGGING FILES

The first step in any file operation is to select the file you want to work with. You can easily select a single file, a group of files, or all files in Norton File Manager. Here's the lowdown.

To select a file, click it.

To select a block of files, click the first file, press and hold **Shift**, and click the last file in the block.

To select multiple files that are not contiguous, press and hold **Ctrl** while clicking additional files.

SHORTCUT

You can use **Multiple Select** to choose multiple files without pressing **Ctrl**. Click the first button in the lower-right corner of the **List** window to turn on **Multiple Select**. To turn the feature off, click the button again.

To select all files, open the Edit menu, choose **Select**, and then choose **All Files**. (If you want to select everything in the **List** window, choose **All**. If you want to select only specific files, click **Some**.)

NOTE

Why "tag" when you can "select"? You might want to tag a file (or files) when you think you might be using them again later. For example, if you tag all files that you created after August 31, 1995, you might want to first copy them to a disk as a backup and then use the same tagged files later to search for a report you know you created in there somewhere. You can use the tagged group as a basis for other searches you perform later.

To tag a file, first click the **Tag Mode** button (the check mark button in the lower-right corner of the **List** area); then click the file you want to tag. A check mark appears beside the file (see Figure 9.1).

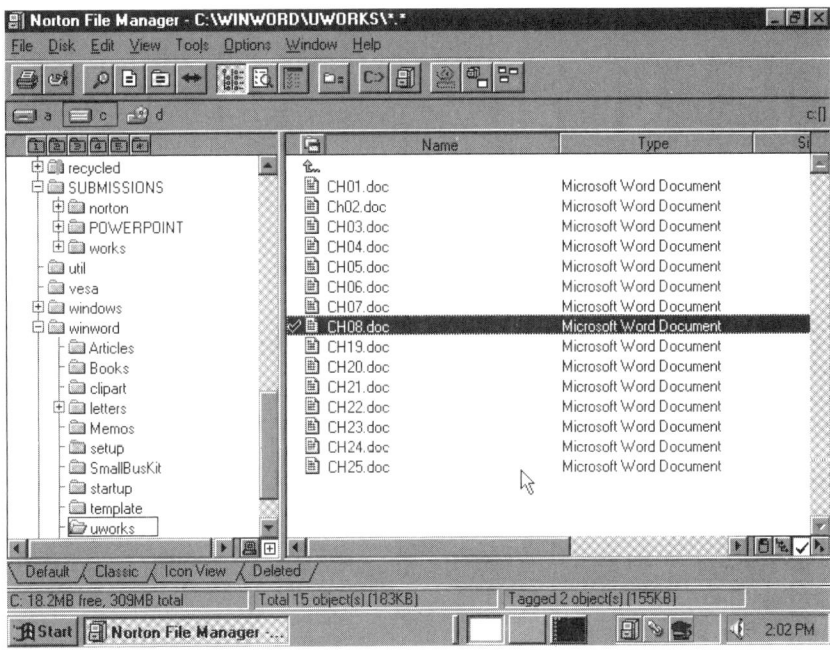

FIGURE 9.1 A TAGGED FILE.

SHORTCUT

Once you tag files, you can display only the files you tagged by opening the **View** menu and choosing **Tagged List**.

To remove the selection, click outside the **List** area.

To deselect files, open the Edit menu, choose **Deselect**, and then choose **All** (if you want all selected files and folders to be deselected) or **Some** (if you want to specify only those files to deselect).

COPYING FILES

To copy a file from a folder on your hard disk to a disk in a floppy drive, select the file and drag it to the appropriate file icon. A rectangle encloses the drive to show you when you're hitting the target. When you drop the file, the Confirm Drag and Drop Action dialog box appears, as shown in Figure 9.2.

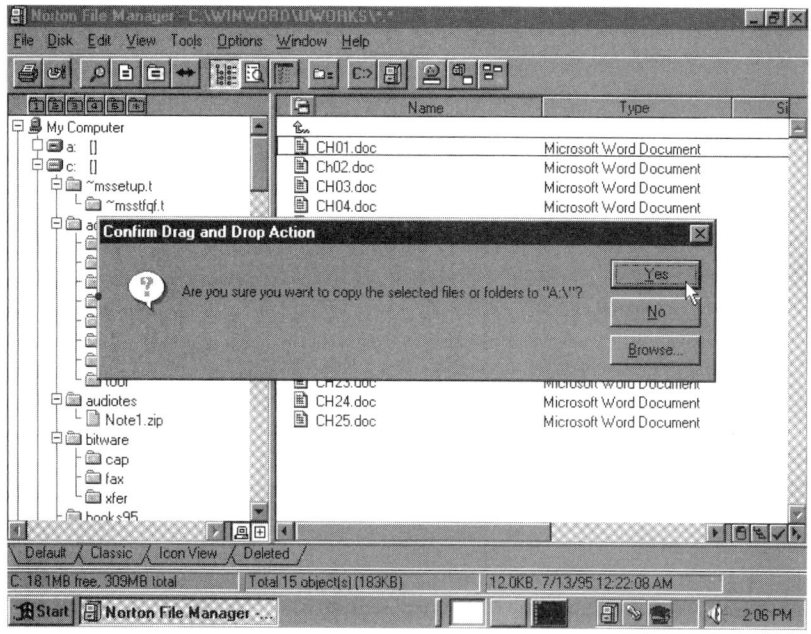

FIGURE 9.2 COPYING A FILE WITH DRAG AND DROP.

To copy a file from one folder to another on the same disk, select the file, open the Edit menu, and choose Copy. Then move to the directory in which you want the file copied, open the Edit menu, and choose Paste.

SHORTCUT

You can easily copy multiple files at once—just highlight or tag them first.

Moving Files

To move a file from one folder to another, select the file and drag it to the new location. The Confirm Drag and Drop Action dialog box appears, asking whether you really want to move the selected file. Click **Yes** to continue the move or **No** to cancel.

Deleting Files

To delete a file you no longer need, highlight the file and press Del. The Delete dialog box appears, and Norton File Manager asks you to confirm that you want to delete the displayed file (see Figure 9.3). Click OK to delete the file or Cancel to stop the deletion.

NOTE

What does **Wipe Delete** mean? There are different levels of deletion in Norton Navigator. If you don't have **Wipe Delete** turned on, you can recover a file you accidentally remove. If you have checked **Wipe Delete**, however, the file has been "wiped clean" and Norton won't be able to salvage it.

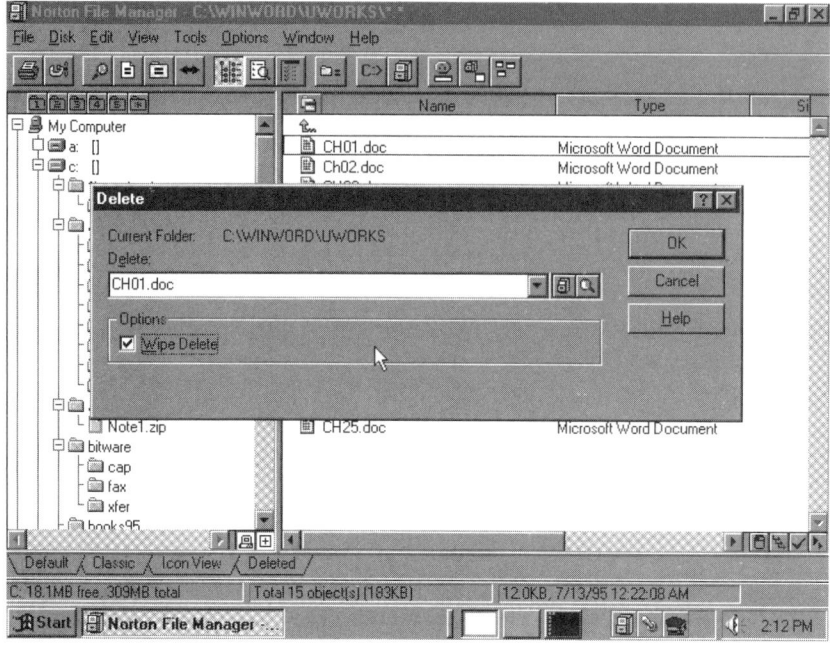

FIGURE 9.3 DELETING A FILE..

RENAMING A FILE

This is so simple that by the time I type it, you will have already done it. Click the file (or folder) you want to rename, open the File menu, choose **Rename**, and type a new name for the item. Click **OK**. End of story.

DISPLAYING FILE PROPERTIES

Being able to get general information about a file—things such as file size, when it was last modified, whether it's a read-only file, and what program created it—is a good thing. There will be times when you need to know whether a file will fit on a disk, whether you have the program you need to run the file, and whether you have the most current version.

Click the file you want to find out about, open the File menu, and choose **Properties**. The Properties dialog box appears, as shown in Figure 9.4.

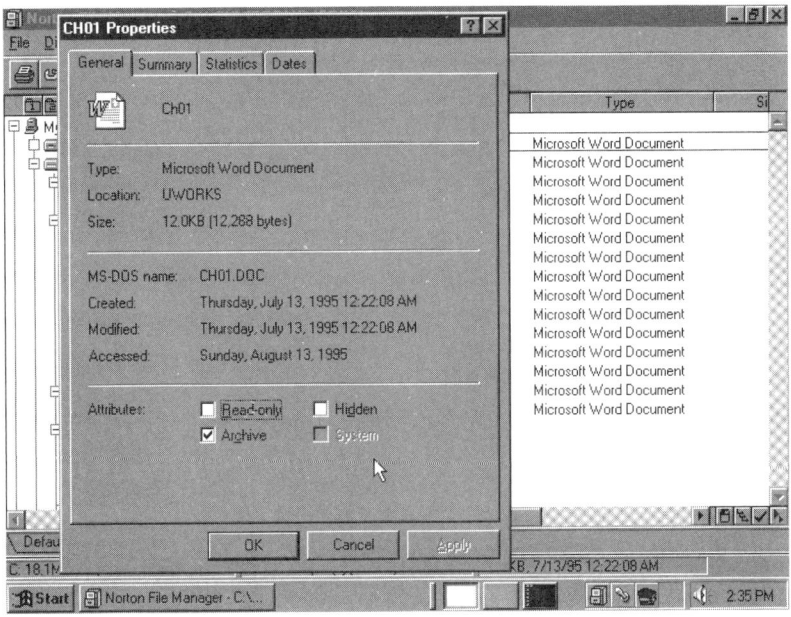

FIGURE 9.4 REVIEWING FILE INFORMATION.

You can choose from **General** information (that's where we started); **Summary** information (such as author and title); **Statistics** (how many lines, words, paragraphs); and **Dates** (when created, when modified). When you've seen all you need to know, click **OK**.

COMPARING FILES

For those times when you two similar files and you have which is the most current, you can use file compare. Select the two files you want to compare and click the Compare Files button in the Toolbar. The Compare Files dialog box appears with both names entered (see Figure 9.5).

192 Inside Norton Navigator

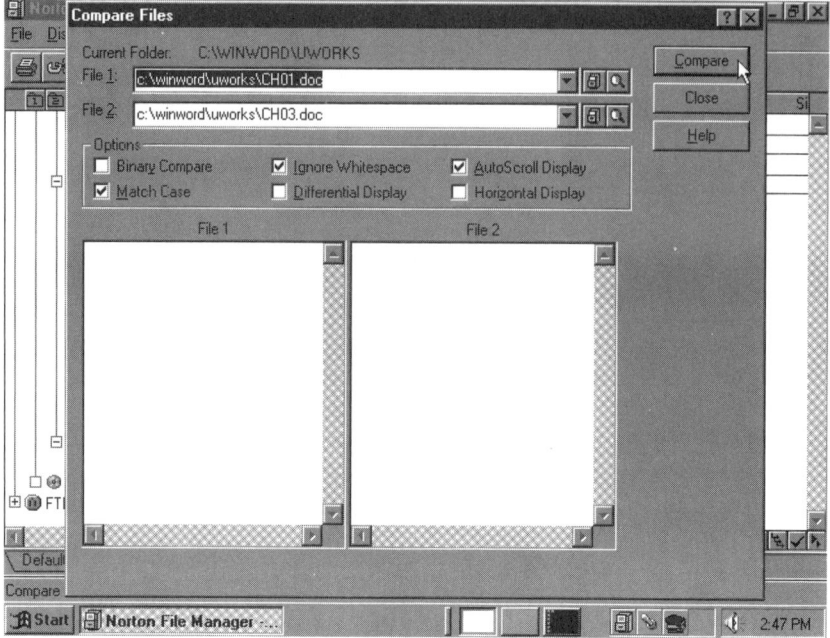

FIGURE 9.5 COMPARING FILES.

Click **Compare** to begin. Norton File Manager analyzes the files line by line and displays the findings in the windows at the bottom of the Compare Files dialog box. Use the scroll bars to navigate through the documents; they both scroll together. As you can see in Figure 9.6, the two files are different.

CHAPTER 9 WORKING WITH FILES   193

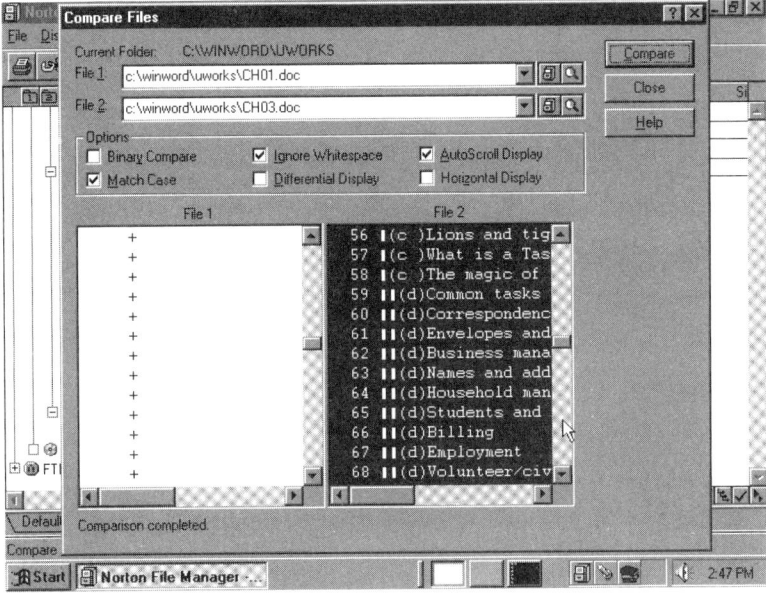

FIGURE 9.6 COMPARING FILES IN THE COMPARE FILES WINDOWS.

NOTE If you are interested in a code-level search, you can select **Binary Compare**, which compares the files on a binary level, which means you'll see numeric codes instead of the text you see in the figure. For the most part, the default settings for Compare Files—**Match Case**, **Ignore Whitespace**, and **AutoScroll** Display—should work fine for traditional text-based comparing.

When you're finished comparing files, click **Close** to return to the File Manager.

ZIPPING AND UNZIPPING FILES

With the advent of larger and larger files (blame it on multimedia) comes the need to compress those files into smaller and smaller spaces. Today's file might be larger than the average disk can hold.

Norton Navigator includes Norton Zip and Norton Unzip, two utilities that, respectively, compress full-size and expand compressed files. Zip enables you to compress one or many files into a single file that will fit on your disk; Unzip allows you to unzip the files as necessary on the other end.

To zip files, start by selecting the files you want to zip. Then click the **Zip** button in the Toolbar or open the File menu and choose **Norton Zip**. The Norton Zip dialog box appears, as shown in Figure 9.7.

Position the cursor in the **To:** text line and type a name for the file. Leave the **.ZIP** at the end of the name. Click **OK**. Norton displays a small icon in the right side of the window, showing you that the files are being zipped.

After the files are zipped, Norton displays them as "electric" green files in both the Tree and List areas. This way, you can always tell which files are zipped by their appearance on the screen.

CHAPTER 9 WORKING WITH FILES

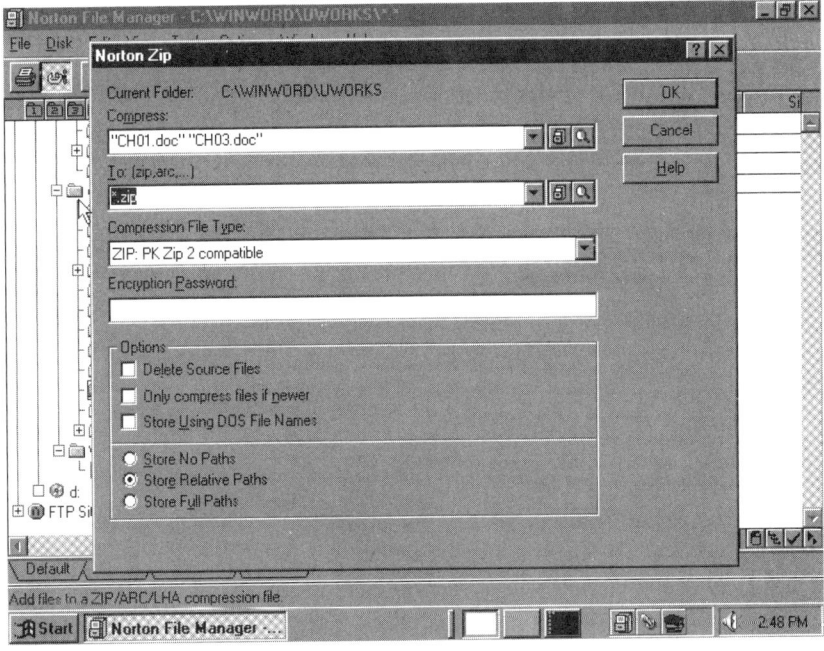

FIGURE 9.7 ZIPPING SELECTED FILES.

SHORTCUT

If you can't remember what you zipped in a file, just click it. Norton displays the zipped file's contents in the List area of the screen.

When you want to unzip files, select the zipped file you want to work with. Then open the File menu and choose **Norton Unzip**. When the Norton Unzip dialog box appears, as shown in Figure 9.8, enter the location you want the files unzipped to in the **To:** box. Then click **OK**. Norton expands the files and puts them in the folder you specified.

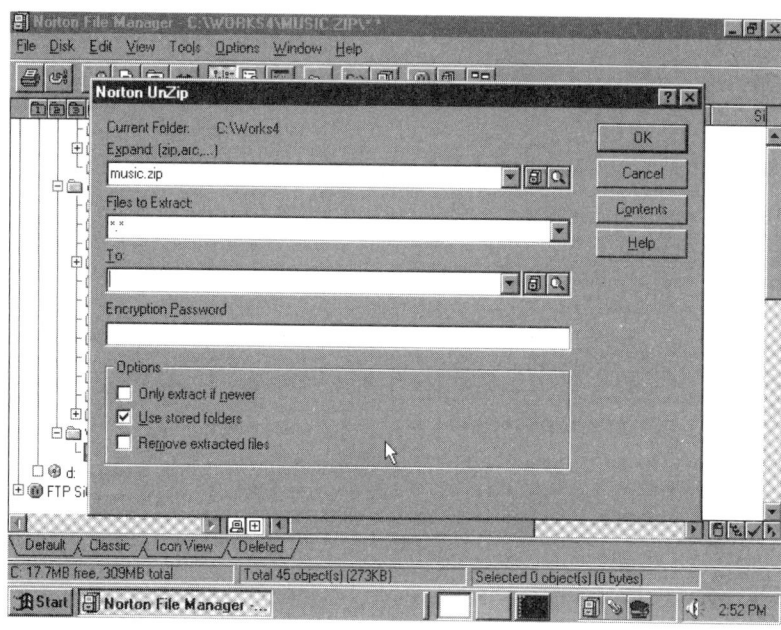

FIGURE 9.8 UNZIPPING ZIPPED FILES.

UNDELETING FILES

Suppose that you've been working on a set of files all day. You just got all the data together and zipped it into a nice file you can deliver to your associate's desk for the tomorrow-morning meeting. As you prepare to drag the file from the List area to the **a:** drive in the Tree area, someone walks up and asks you a question.

When you go back to your work, you have forgotten that you didn't yet copy the file and you delete it. Oops.

The bigger the file, the more intense the panic as you try to figure out how to get the file back. You've been working on that file all day. You could never reenter all that data, gathered over months. Where can you find a backup?

Before you sink too deeply into panic, remember that Norton has an **Undelete** command, and it's simple to use.

Start by clicking the **Deleted SmartTab** at the bottom of the File Manager window. (You always need to start there.) Take a few deep breaths while Norton scans the disk to find recently deleted files. When the file is found, Norton File Manager displays it in the List area (see Figure 9.9).

To undelete the file, simply double-click it. Norton flashes a message on the screen, telling you the status of the undelete procedure and then delivers the saved file back to its original folder.

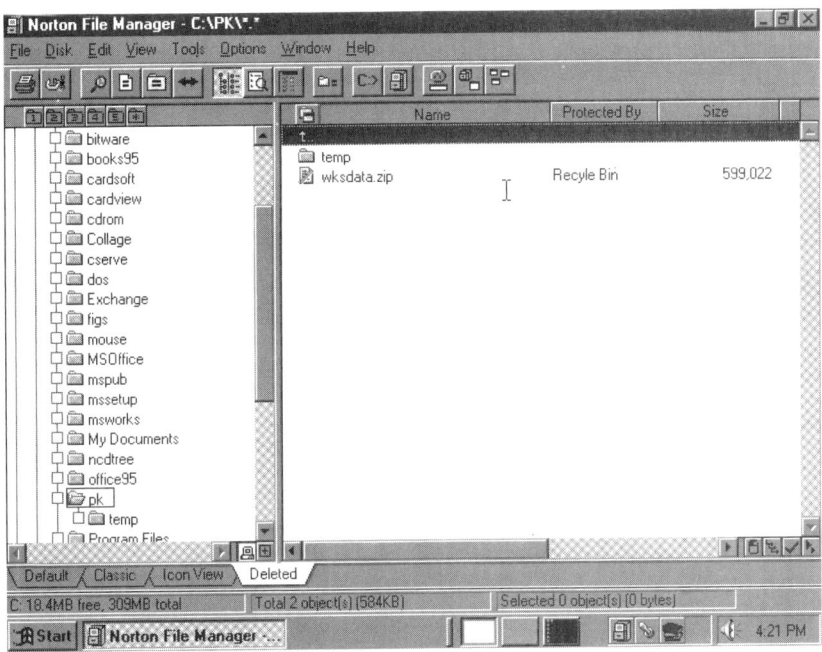

FIGURE 9.9 FINDING THE LOST FILE.

THE NEXT STOP

This chapter has introduced you to the basic file-management tasks you'll perform with Norton File Manager. The next chapter moves things along by exploring the different aspects of working with disks—selecting, changing, formatting, and scanning disks—procedures you'll be likely to use in your everyday experience with Norton File Manager.

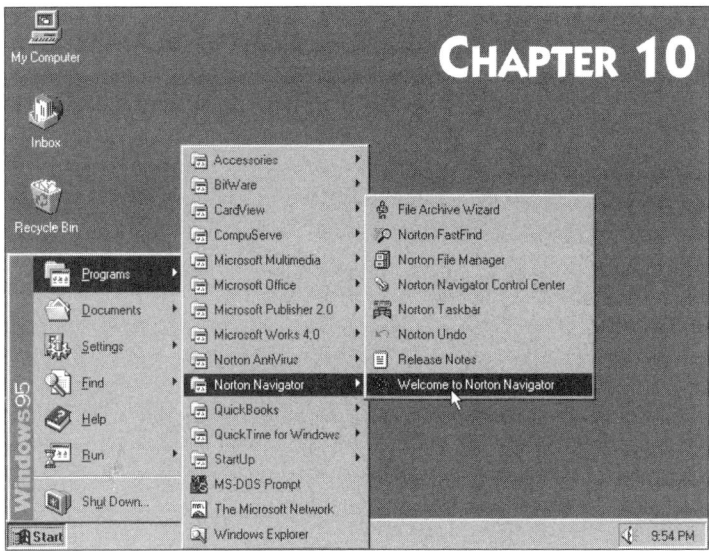

Working with Disks

You store the files so important to your day-in, day-out work on disks—either the diskette variety, which you insert in the waiting disk drive, or the hard disk, which is enclosed in a housing either inside the system unit of your computer or outside, connected by a cable.

Norton Navigator makes it easy for you to work with both types of disks. You need to be able to display what's on a disk, search for files on a disk, change to display a different disk, label disks, format disks, check disks for viruses, and erase disk contents. This chapter explains these basic disk procedures and helps you find the quickest method of performing these routine operations on your own system.

Disk Basics

If you've been working with computers for any length of time, you are probably familiar with disk terminology. A *diskette*, once known as a *floppy disk*, stores a limited amount of information (usually 1.44MB) on a small, 3.5-inch cartridge that slides into the slot in your disk drive.

Two types of diskettes are in use today, although one kind is quickly becoming outdated: the 5.25-inch diskette, which is made of bendable mylar (hence the name "floppy"), is still available for use with older machines but is no longer being sold for new computers. (You can still purchase a stand-alone 5.25-inch disk drive if you need one for compatibility with other computers in your office.)

Your computer's hard disk stores the bulk of your programs and data files—most hard disks store about 250 megabytes of information. Years ago, when the first hard disks were introduced, a 10-megabyte hard drive was seen as a huge incredible expanse of storage space—who could ever fill up all that room? Today, we're into the hundreds—even thousands—of megabytes. Drives capable of storing gigabytes of information—that's a thousand million, or one billion, bytes of data—are becoming the norm.

Simple Disk Procedures

How will you work with the disks on your system?

A number of simple, common disk procedures come to mind. First, and perhaps most often, you will copy files back and forth from your hard disk to your diskette. Suppose you need to take a report home tonight to work on it after the kids are in bed. You copy the report file from a hard drive to the diskette; then you take the diskette home, insert it into the disk drive on your home computer, and copy the file to the hard disk.

When you need to make a copy of an entire disk—perhaps to keep one as a backup in case something happens to the original—you can use Norton Navigator to make the copy.

Another basic disk procedure involves formatting a disk. Before a disk can store data, it must be prepared with a process known as *formatting*. Formatting prepares the disk to store data, dividing the disk into tracks and sectors. It also creates an index-like entry, called a *file allocation table*, that serves as a disk index. When you copy files to the disk, the operating system knows where on the disk the files are stored.

The following sections walk you through basic disk procedures you'll use often in your routine computer tasks.

Before you begin, display the Norton File Manager if you haven't already done so. You can either display the Taskbar and click the Norton File Manager **QuickLaunch** icon or begin at the Start menu, choose **Norton Navigator**, and then choose **Norton File Manager** from the cascading menu.

Selecting Disks

When you first display the Norton File Manager, the contents of your hard disk are displayed in the tree area on the left side of the File Manager. You may need to click the up-arrow at the top of the center scroll bar (between the tree area and the list area in the File Manager window) to scroll the tree display up to the top of the tree.

To find out what disk drives are available on your system, click **My Computer**. The right side of the File Manager, the list area, shows all available drives on your system (see Figure 10.1).

FIGURE 10.1 DISPLAYING DRIVES IN THE FILE MANAGER.

At the top, you see the primary drives on your computer. In most cases, the diskette drive is drive **a:** and the hard disk is drive **b:**. If your computer has a second diskette drive (perhaps a 5.25-inch drive), it may be named **b:**. You may also have a CD-ROM drive or a second hard drive named **d:**.

NOTE

Even though a CD-ROM drive, drive **d:**, is used on the system in the figure, because of the number of folders on drive **c:** (the hard drive), drive **d:** is not visible. To see additional drives that may be displayed at the bottom of your directory tree, click the down-arrow at the bottom of the vertical scroll bar.

To choose a disk other than the one currently displayed in the list area, move the mouse pointer to the drive you want and click the mouse button. The display in the list area changes to show the contents of the drive you've selected. Figure 10.2 shows the contents of the disk in drive **a:**.

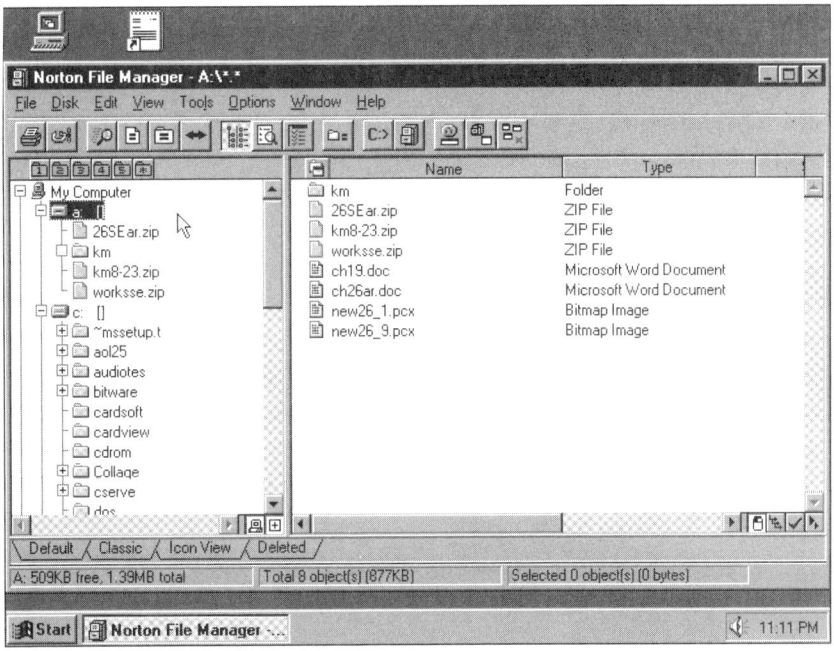

FIGURE 10.2 DISPLAYING THE CONTENTS OF DRIVE **A:**.

If you change disks and the display in the list area doesn't change the way you expected it to, open the Window menu and choose **Refresh**. Norton File Manager updates the screen, and the file list accurately reflects the contents of the disk.

Copying Disks

Copying disks is one of the most common of all disk procedures. You might copy a disk, for example, when you need a backup copy or want a copy to give to a co-worker.

In Norton File Manager, copying a disk is simple. First, insert the disk you want to copy into the diskette drive. Next, open the Disk menu and choose **Copy Disk**. The Copy Disk dialog box appears, as shown in Figure 10.3.

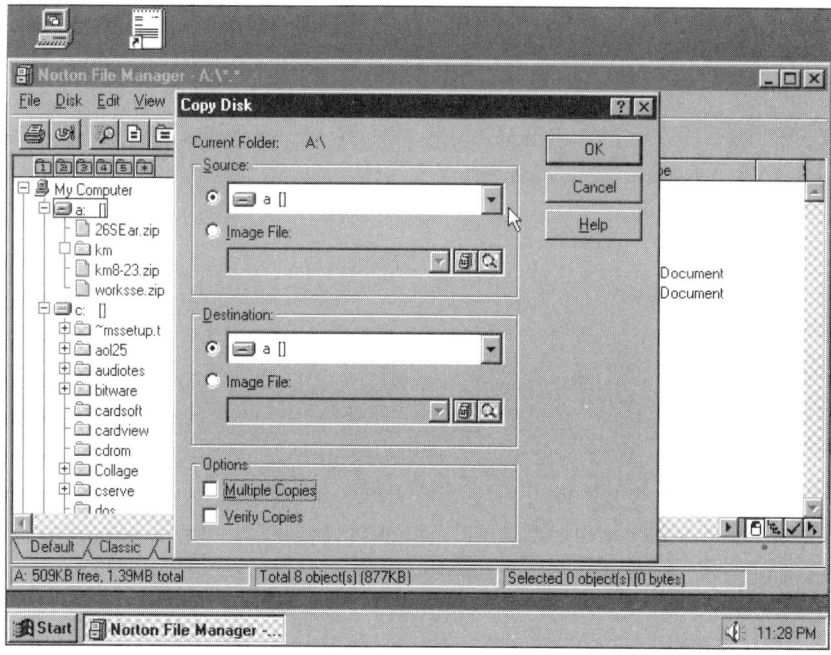

FIGURE 10.3 USING THE COPY DISK DIALOG BOX TO COPY A DISK.

If drive **a:** was selected when you selected **Copy Disk**, drive **a:** is shown as the **Current Folder** in the top of the Copy Disk dialog box. The disk you are copying should be shown as the **Source**. If you need to choose a different disk, do so by clicking the down-arrow and selecting the disk you want to copy from the displayed list.

In the **Destination** box, make sure that the disk you want to copy to is selected. If you are making a copy of a diskette in drive **a:** and you have only one disk drive, make sure that **a:** is entered for both the **Source** and the **Destination**. Norton File Manager will prompt you when you need to remove the source disk in drive **a:** and insert the destination disk.

You can choose to make more than one copy of a disk. This is handy for those times when you need to circulate several copies of a presentation or report or when you need to verify that the copies were made accurately.

The **Multiple Copies** option in the lower-left corner of the dialog box enables you to make as many copies of the source disk as you want. Each time a copy is made, Norton File Manager asks you whether you want to make another copy. Select **Yes** until you are finished making copies; then click **No**.

If you want Norton File Manager to make sure the copy was done correctly, you can click the **Verify Copies** option. Norton File Manager will check the contents of the destination disk against the source disk to ensure that all data was copied the way it appears on the original disk.

When you're ready to start the copy, click **OK**. Norton File Manager will lead you through the process. A Copying Disk dialog box appears on the screen to display the progress of the copy. After Norton File Manager reads the information from the disk, the program prompts you to insert the destination, or target, disk in drive **a:** (see Figure 10.4)

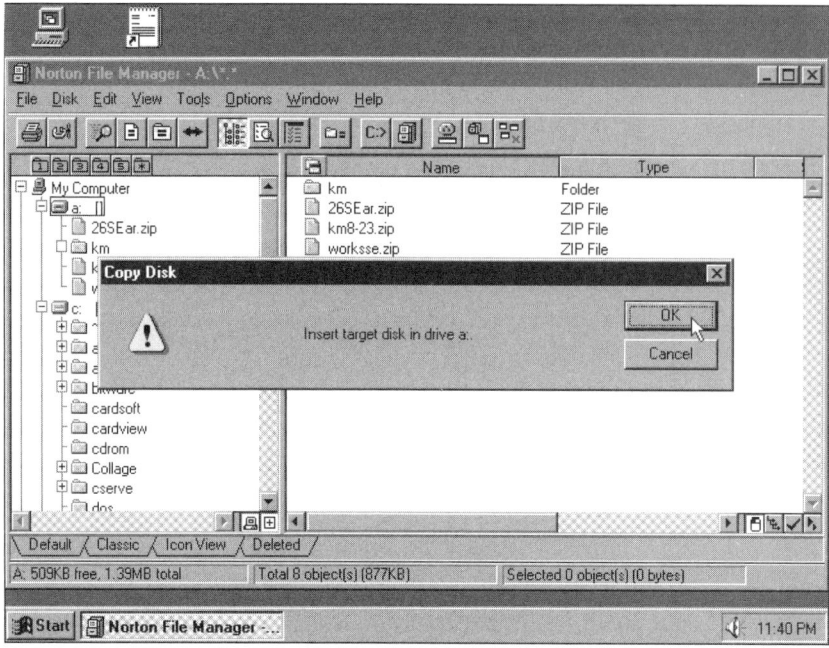

FIGURE 10.4 NORTON FILE MANAGER PROMPTS YOU FOR A DISK.

NOTE

If you want to stop the copy process at any time, click **Cancel**.

Labeling Disks

Why would you want to label a disk? Disk labels provide you with a quick way to identify what you've stored on the disk. If you're working on a PowerPoint presentation for Granger, Inc., you might label the disk **GRANGER**, **GRAN_PRS**, or **GRANGER_PRS**.

To label a disk, insert the disk in drive **a:** and select that drive. Then open the Disk menu and choose **Label Disk**. The Label Disk dialog box appears, as shown in Figure 10.5.

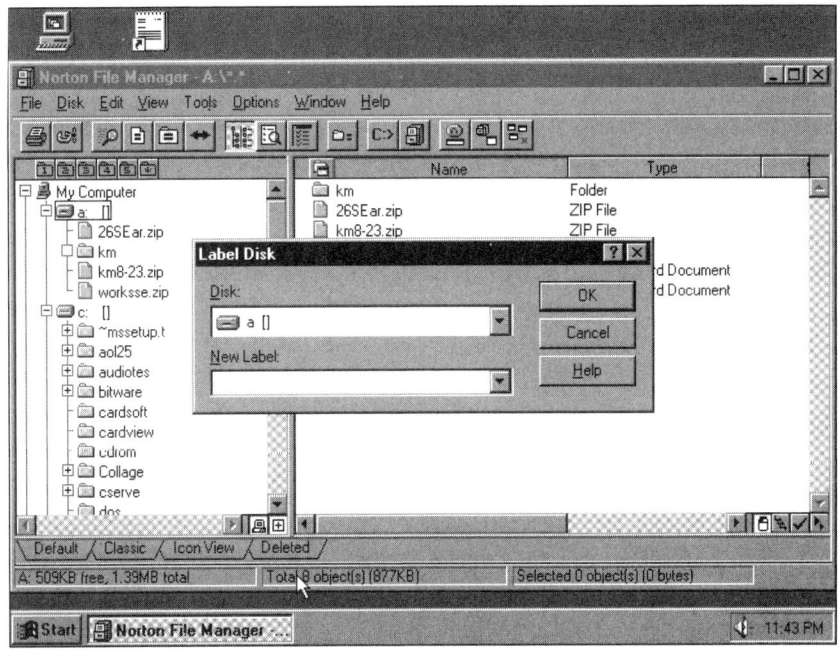

FIGURE 10.5 LABELING A DISK FOR EASY RECOGNITION.

Type a name of as many as 11 characters in the **New Label** textbox; then click **OK**. The label is applied to the disk.

Formatting Disks

As mentioned earlier, the process of formatting a disk is an important part of your overall computing picture. A disk cannot record your programs and data until you've formatted it.

To format a disk, insert the disk you want to format into the diskette drive; then open the Disk menu and choose **Format Disk**. The Format dialog box appears, as shown in Figure 10.6.

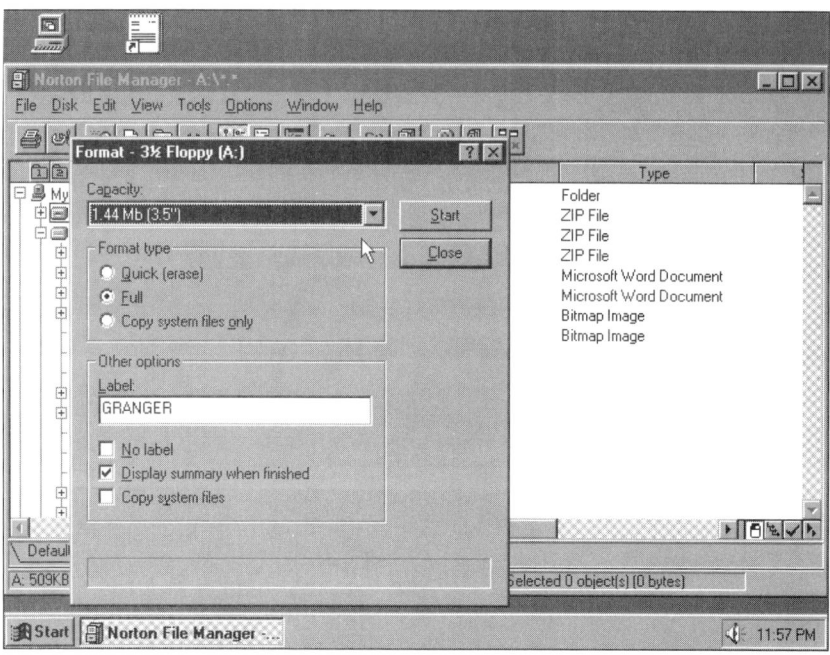

FIGURE 10.6 USING THE FORMAT DIALOG BOX TO SPECIFY FORMATTING OPTIONS.

The **Capacity** setting determines the amount of information that can be stored on the disk. For 3.5-inch disks, you can choose 1.44MB or 720KB capacities. For 5.25-inch disks, you can choose 1.2MB or 360KB.

NOTE How do you know which capacity to choose? In most cases, you can use the capacity Norton File Manager automatically displays. If you try to format a disk to 1.44MB when it can store only 720KB, Norton File Manager will alert you to the problem with no harm done.

The type of format you choose depends on what you want to do and how much time you have. (Note: Even the longest format takes only a minute—unless you're formatting a hard disk.) Choose from one of these format types:

+ **Quick (erase)** simply removes all data stored on the disk. Use this format type when you've been using the disk (it has been formatted previously) and simply want to remove the information currently on the disk.
+ **Full** format means that Norton File Manager divides the disk into tracks and sectors and prepares the disk to store data for the first time. You can choose **Full** format even when you've previously formatted a disk. Remember, however, that any information on the disk will be erased.
+ Copy system files only copies the startup system files to the disk so that after formatting, you can start the computer using the disk you've just formatted.

If you don't have a startup disk—also called a *boot* disk—that you can use to start your computer if your hard disk malfunctions, make one. Format a disk and use the **Copy system files only** option to copy the startup files to the newly formatted disk.

You can elect to change the label in the **Label** textbox. Just position the pointer in the **Label** box, double-click the text to highlight it, and then type the new label name.

Other options include selecting **No label** when you don't want the label copied. **Display summary when finished** which shows you how many tracks and sectors were copied successfully. **Copy system files** adds system files to either a **Quick** or a **Full** format.

When you're ready to begin formatting the disk, click **Start**. A Formatting status bar appears across the bottom of the Format dialog box.

NOTE: To stop the format at any time, click **Cancel**.

Scanning Disks

One of Norton File Manager's many talents is the ability to snoop out any viruses that may be lurking in your system. Additionally, Norton File Manager can find potential hardware problems. This means that if your disk drive is in danger of failing (a nice thing to know before it actually happens) or if there's something wrong with a program you've recently added, Norton has a good shot at finding it for you.

Use the **Scan Disk** command in the Disk menu to start the process of checking a disk. When you choose the command, the ScanDisk dialog box appears, as shown in Figure 10.7.

CHAPTER 10 WORKING WITH DISKS   211

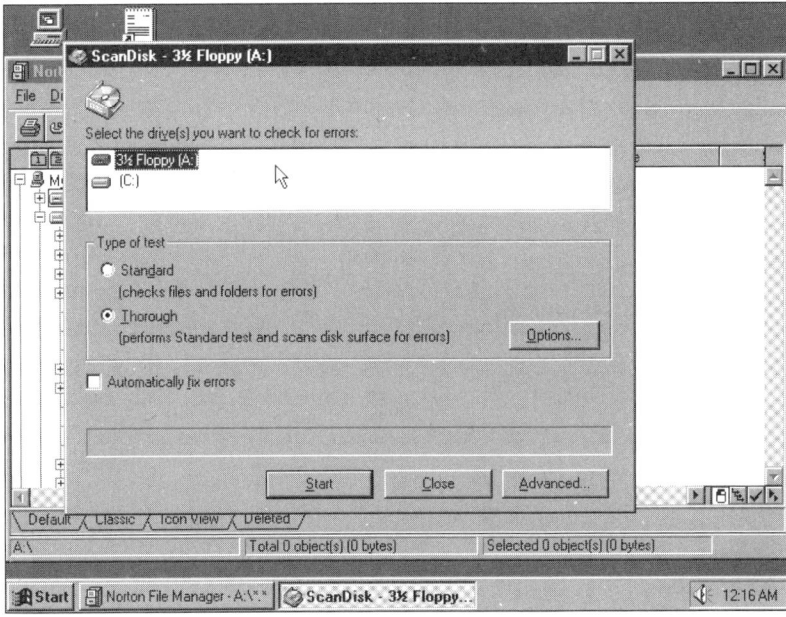

FIGURE 10.7 CHECKING THE HEALTH OF YOUR DISKS WITH SCANDISK.

ScanDisk gives you the option of checking the disk drive or your hard disk. Click the drive you want to scan.

 **NOTE** If you are scanning your disk drive, the check will probably take only a matter of minutes. If you are checking your hard disk, especially if you have a larger-capacity hard disk (say, about 210MB), be prepared to wait at least 30 minutes while Norton File Manager checks everything out.

After you choose the drive you want to check, select the type of test you want to perform. A **Standard** test essentially goes through the programs and data on your disk and looks for scattered data clusters and fragmented files. A **Thorough** check looks for problems with programs and data files and also scans the disk hardware to see whether there is anything physically wrong with the drive.

If you perform a **Thorough** scan, you can click the **Options** button to make additional choices about the scan (see Figure 10.8). You can select where you want ScanDisk to scan (all areas, the system file area only, or the data area only). You can also choose whether you want Norton File Manager to test writing something to the disk and whether the program automatically repairs problems found in system and hidden files.

In most cases, you'll use ScanDisk quickly when you're having a little trouble with a disk or wondering whether your disk drive is performing the way it should. For simple operations, unless something seems seriously wrong, the default options should do the trick for you.

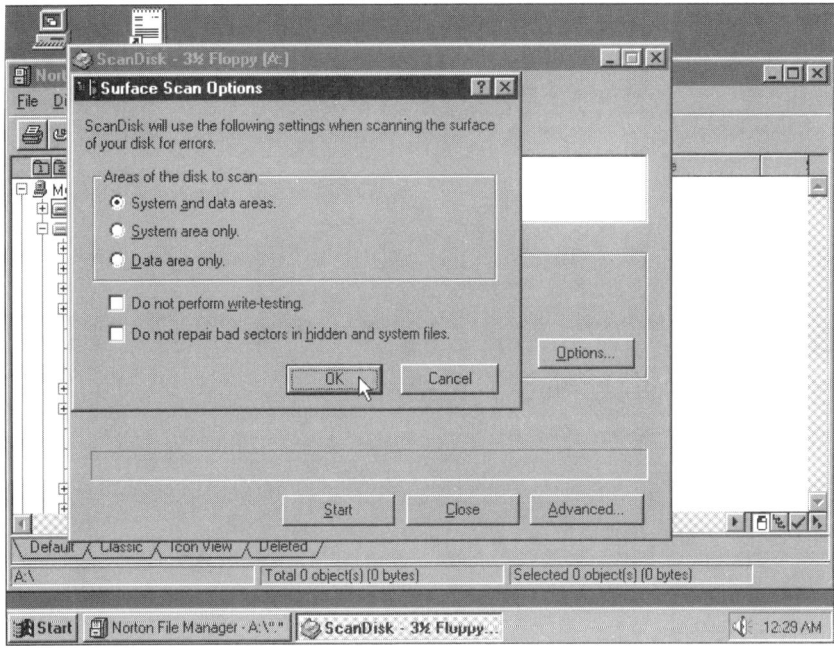

FIGURE 10.8 CHOOSING THE TYPE OF SCAN YOU WANT PERFORMED.

When you click **Advanced**, the ScanDisk dialog box offers you yet another popup box of options (see Figure 10.9). The ScanDisk Advanced Options dialog box appears. In this dialog box, you can choose whether you want the track and sector summary displayed, whether you want to replace the existing log file for the disk, what you want to do about cross-linked files and lost file fragments, and whether you want Norton File Manager to check for invalid file names, dates, and times. The final option, **Check host drive first**, tells Norton File Manager to check your uncompressed drive in the event you are using data compression on your system.

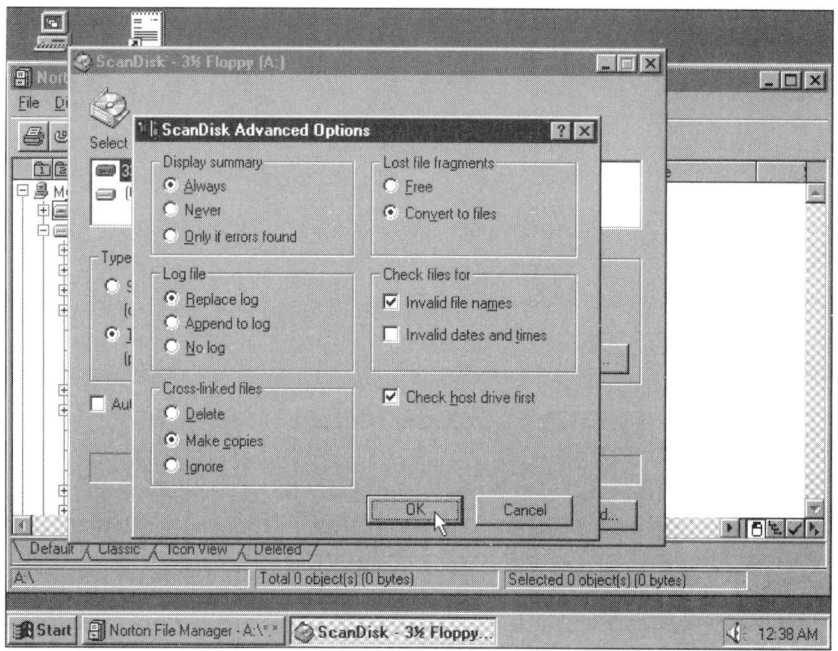

FIGURE 10.9 TAKING A LOOK AT THE SCANDISK ADVANCED OPTIONS.

To begin the ScanDisk operation, click **Start**. A status bar appears across the bottom of the screen to tell you how many clusters have been checked. When the scan is complete, the ScanDisk Results dialog box appears. It reports whether any errors were found and how the disk space is allocated (see Figure 10.10).

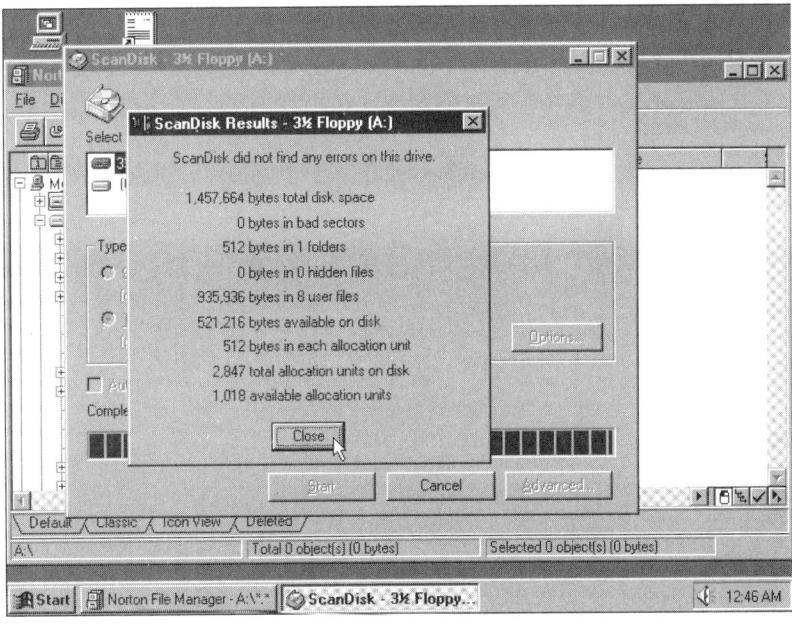

FIGURE 10.10 THE SCANDISK RESULTS SCREEN SHOWS ANY ERRORS FOUND IN THE SCAN.

To exit the ScanDisk Results dialog box and return to the ScanDisk dialog box, click **Close**. Click **Close** again to return to the Norton File Manager.

Working with Network Drives

If your computer is part of a larger network, at some point you may need to add a drive to those currently available on your system. To add a network drive to your Norton File Manager display, first check with your system administrator to make sure that the changes you're about to make are in line with your network guidelines. Then, to add the network drive, open the Disk menu and choose **Map Network Drive**. Choose the drive you want to add and click **OK**. Norton File Manager adds the drive to the directory tree on the left side of the File Manager.

NOTE If you ever need to remove the network drive, select the drive; then open the Disk menu and choose **Disconnect Network Drive**. Select the drive you want to disconnect and click **OK**.

THE NEXT STOP

In this chapter, you've covered the basics for working with, copying, formatting, labeling, and scanning disks. Chapter 11 takes you into more specialized File Manager procedures so that you can do things such as searching, sorting, indexing, and archiving files.

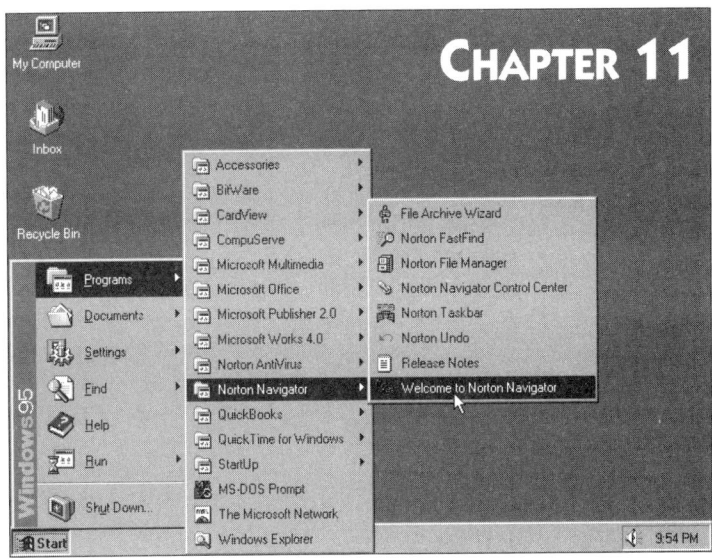

CHAPTER 11

SPECIAL FILE PROCEDURES: SEARCHING, SORTING, AND INDEXING

The more files you work with, the more you need efficient ways to organize, locate, and manage them. Norton Navigator includes special features that will help you to locate the files you use often, to search for specific files, and to sort files according to particular criteria.

Suppose, for example, that you want to find an Excel spreadsheet you know you created last month, but you can't remember the name of the file or even a letter or two of the folder you might have stored it in. You can use FastFind, a Norton Navigator feature designed to help you search for and find files easily, to locate the missing file. Additionally, you can save the search instructions so that you can find the file effortlessly next time.

This chapter explains how to search for files and groups of files using FastFind. You'll also discover how to sort and how to index files with Norton Navigator to help you find the files you need in the simplest manner possible.

Using FastFind to Locate Files

Norton's FastFind feature lets you create an index of files you use often and then use the index to search for specific files. FastFind can look for files in the folders you choose, or you can have FastFind search all the folders and subfolders on your hard disk.

You can start FastFind two ways:

- If you are starting at the Windows 95 desktop, open the Start menu, choose **Programs**, select **Norton Navigator**, and then choose **Norton FastFind**.
- If you are working in the File Manager, open the Tools menu and choose **FastFind**.

After you select **FastFind**, the FastFind dialog box appears, as shown in Figure 11.1.

The FastFind dialog box offers you three different tabs for fine-tuning the search:

- Name & Location
- Dates
- Advanced

The **Name & Location** tab, shown in default in Figure 11.1, is where you enter the type of files you're looking for. You tell FastFind what kind of files you want to locate, whether you want to search in folders and subfolders or look through files only, and whether you want to include special search characteristics, such as specific characters to search for or certain key words to locate.

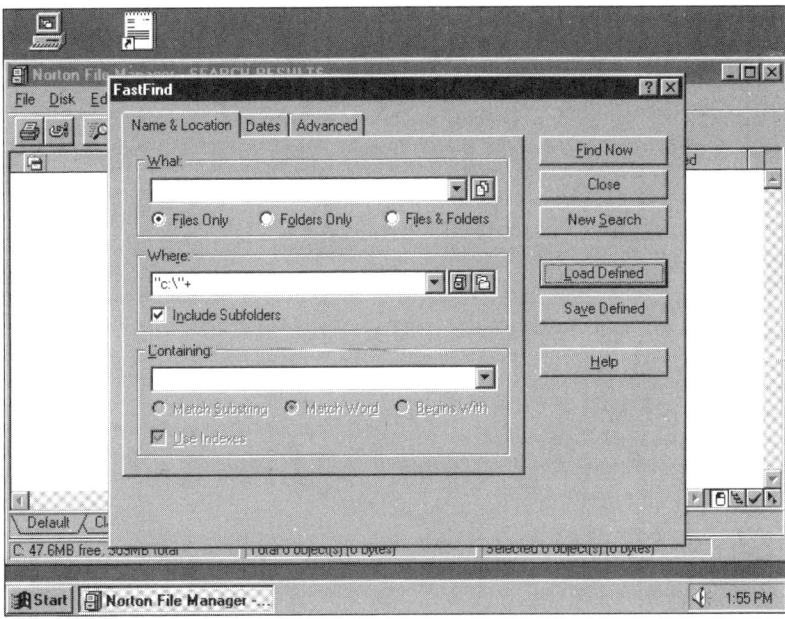

FIGURE 11.1 THE NORTON FASTFIND DIALOG BOX.

You can specify your searches in the **What** text box to tell FastFind what types of files you want to look for. For example, the following phrases would be acceptable with FastFind:

+ *.wks
+ *.*
+ rep*.*

To enter the search information, just click in the **What** box and type. To specify **Where**, enter the path you want FastFind to search (enclose the path in quotation marks).

SHORTCUT

You can enter more than one path for FastFind to search. Enclose the paths in quotation marks so that Norton Navigator knows where one path ends and another starts. For example, type **"c:\windows" "c:\works"** to have FastFind search both the Windows and the Works folders.

If you want FastFind to look for files with specific phrases, characters, or beginning words, type the necessary characters or words in the **Containing** textbox. You can also choose one of the additional options—**Match Substring**, **Match Word**, or **Begins With**—to further control the search conditions.

When you're ready to begin the search, click the **Find Now** button. FastFind scans the drive, folders, and files you specified in the **Where** box and displays the found files in the File Manager's Search Results window (see Figure 11.2).

CHAPTER 11   SPECIAL FILE PROCEDURES: SEARCHING, SORTING, AND INDEXING   221

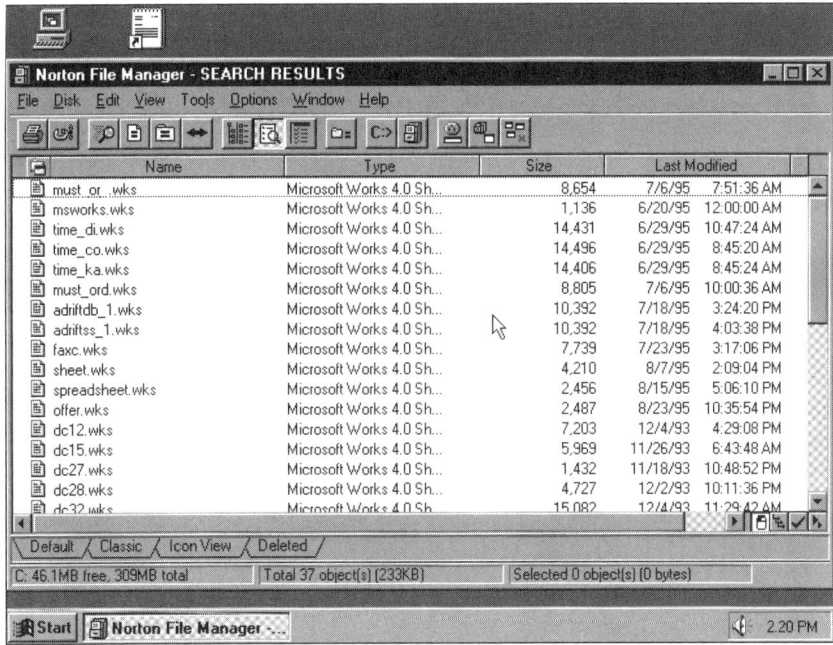

FIGURE 11.2 THE RESULTS OF THE FASTFIND ARE DISPLAYED IN THE FILE MANAGER'S SEARCH RESULTS WINDOW.

Once you display the found files in the Search Results window, you can work with them as usual—copying, deleting, zipping, or moving them to other folders or disks.

Using Indexes to Speed Up FastFind

The Norton Control Center provides you with an option you can use to speed up the FastFind searches you perform (see Figure 11.3). You can use **Norton Indexing** to create an index file that increases the search capabilities of FastFind.

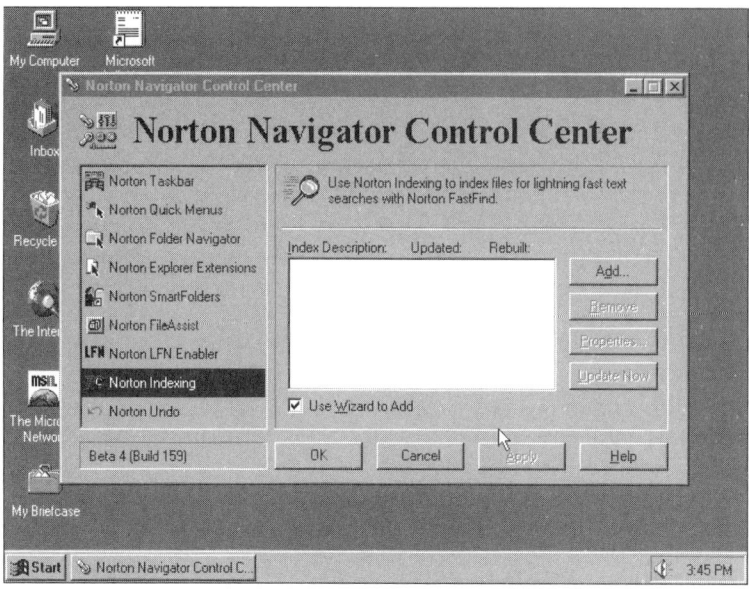

FIGURE 11.3 STARTING AN INDEX IN THE CONTROL CENTER.

To create an index, click the **Add** button. The **Use Wizard to Add** checkbox is selected by default at the bottom of the screen; a wizard appears and asks you questions about the index you want to create. First, enter a name that describes the index. For best results, use a phrase that you will easily recognize later (for example, **Publication files**). Click **Next**.

In the next window of the Add New Index wizard, enter the type of file and the location; then click **Finish** (see Figure 11.4). Norton Indexing displays a popup message box that tells you the operation may take a few minutes. To continue, click **Yes**. To cancel, click **No**.

CHAPTER 11 SPECIAL FILE PROCEDURES: SEARCHING, SORTING, AND INDEXING

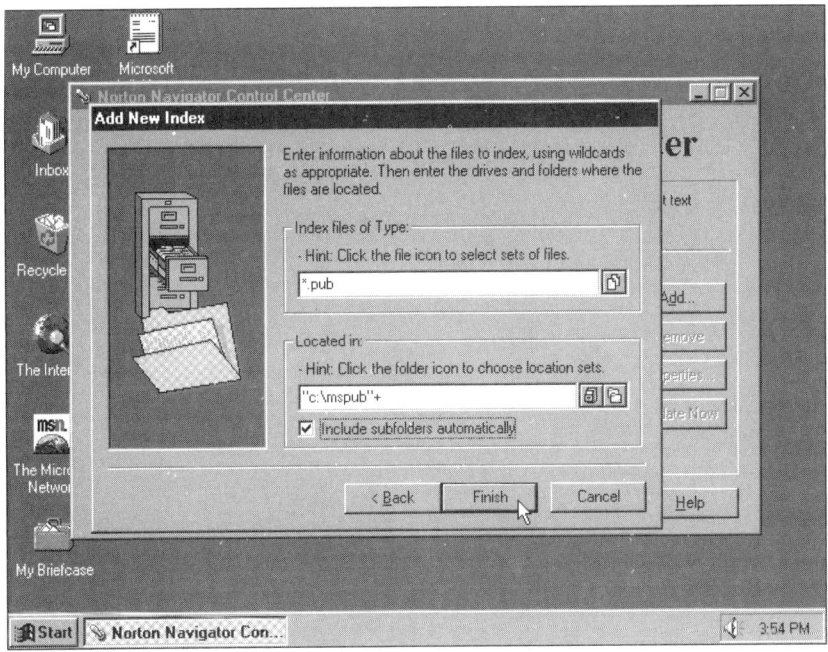

FIGURE 11.4 FINISHING THE INDEX ENTRIES.

After you click **Yes**, Norton begins to index the files. A status screen shows you the files that are checked as they are indexed. When the process is complete, Norton Indexing displays a message box telling you the index has been created and is up-to-date. Click **OK** to return to the Control Center window. The new index is listed in the **Index Description** area of the window (see Figure 11.5).

224 Inside Norton Navigator

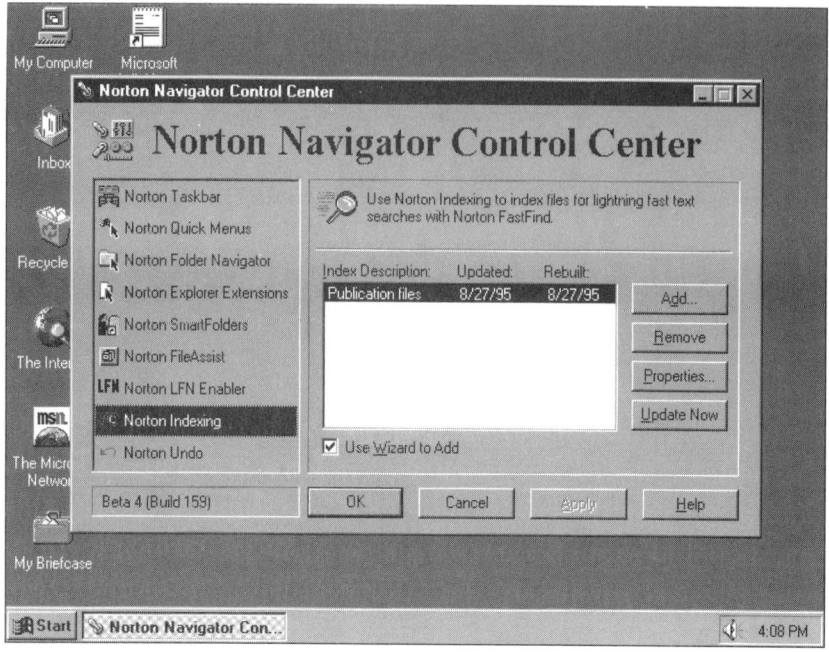

FIGURE 11.5 THE NEWLY CREATED INDEX.

 To have Norton Navigator update the index automatically, click the **Properties** button and make your selections in the **What & How** tab page.

SHORTCUT

Saving Searches

Once you design a search that finds the files you want to find, you can keep it and use it later. This comes in handy when you find yourself repeatedly searching for the same files. Perhaps you are always trying to find the most recent sales projections spreadsheet you created; or you often look for text files on a particular disk. You can save the search instructions so that you can perform the search in the future with just a few clicks of the mouse.

NOTE Before you save a search, be sure you've entered all necessary criteria. For example, if you want to include date or file size criteria, choose and enter the necessary information on the **Dates** and **Advanced** tab pages before you save the search definition. You learn to use these options later in this chapter.

To save a search you've just created, open the Tools menu when the results are displayed in the Search Results window; then choose **FastFind**. The FastFind dialog box appears, showing the last search information you entered. Click the **Save Defined** button.

The Save Search Criteria dialog box appears so that you can enter a description of the search. Type a phrase that best describes what the search information is looking for (see Figure 11.6). Then click **Save** to return to the FastFind dialog box. The search has been saved.

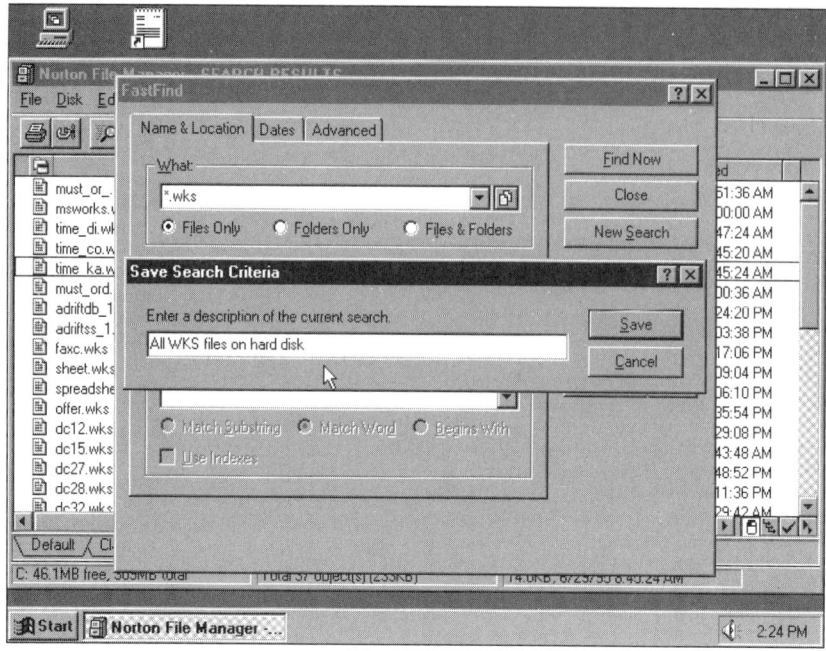

FIGURE 11.6 ENTERING A DESCRIPTIVE NAME FOR THE SEARCH INSTRUCTIONS.

Using an Existing Search

Norton FastFind includes several preset searches you can use to find files on your system. You can also add your own searches to the preset ones, following the instructions in the preceding section.

To use one of FastFind's preset searches, click the **Load Defined** button in the FastFind dialog box. The Defined Searches dialog box appears, along with a list of predefined searches. (We just added the last one—All WKS files on hard disk—in the last section.)

Simply click the search you want to use and click **OK**. FastFind returns you to the FastFind dialog box and enters the search information for you. Click **Find Now** to begin the search.

FastFind Search Options

In addition to the searches you can perform based on the name and location of files, you can also search for files by the dates they were created, modified, or last opened.

Click the **Dates** tab to display the different options for choosing dates. At first, all **File Dates** options are set to **Ignore**. You can select one of the different settings (**Ignore**, **On**, **Before**, **After**, **Between**, **Last**, **Prior to Last**) by clicking the down-arrow and choosing the option you want (see Figure 11.7).

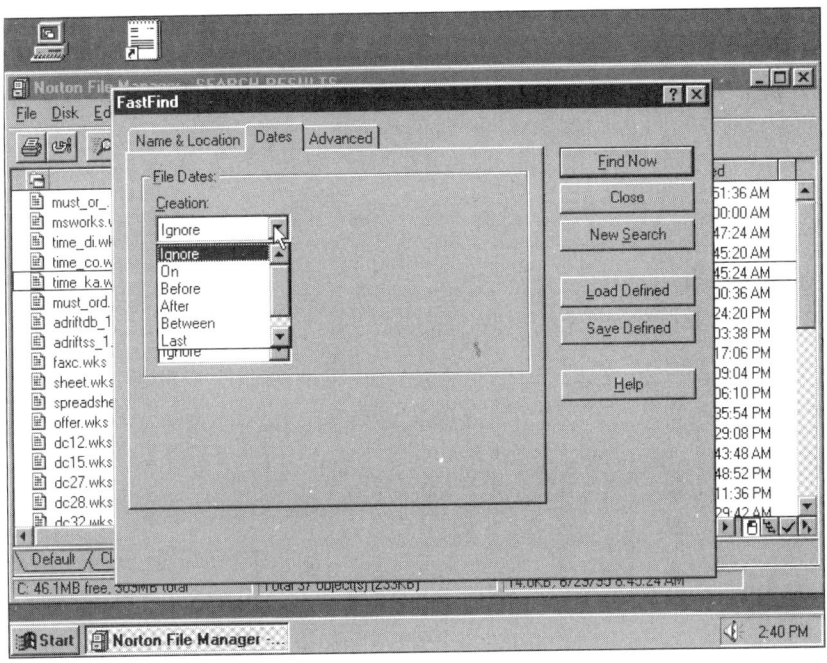

FIGURE 11.7 CHOOSING A DIFFERENT SETTING FOR THE **CREATION** DATE CRITERION.

When you've selected the date criteria, you can move to the **Advanced** tab page (see Figure 11.8). The **Advanced** tab page lets you search for files that are greater than or less than a specific size; have been assigned specific attributes; have duplicates; or have been deleted. Additionally, you can choose to append the found file(s) to the list displayed in the Search Results window.

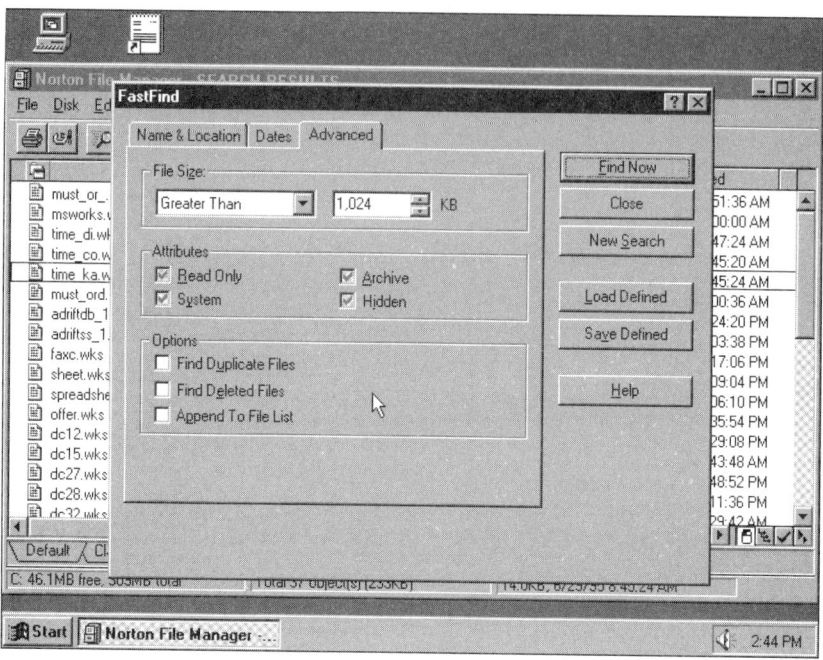

FIGURE 11.8 THE ADVANCED FASTFIND SEARCH PAGE.

When you've finished specifying **Advanced** search options, click **Find Now** to start the search or **Save Defined** to save the search instructions.

SORTING FILES FOR EASY ACCESS

Once you've found the files you're looking for, you may want to sort them in a particular order to locate important ones fast.

Chapter 11 Special File Procedures: Searching, Sorting, and Indexing

After you use FastFind to search and display the files you want, the files are displayed in the File Manager's Search Results window. Before you sort the files, open the Edit menu and choose **Select**; then choose **All Files**. The files are highlighted, ready for your sort instructions.

NOTE You can also sort files that aren't displayed in the Search Results window. In the File Manager window, make sure that the files in the list area are selected. Then open the View menu, choose **Sort**, and make your sort choices.

To sort the displayed files, open the View menu and choose **Sort**. The Custom Sort dialog box appears, as shown in Figure 11.9.

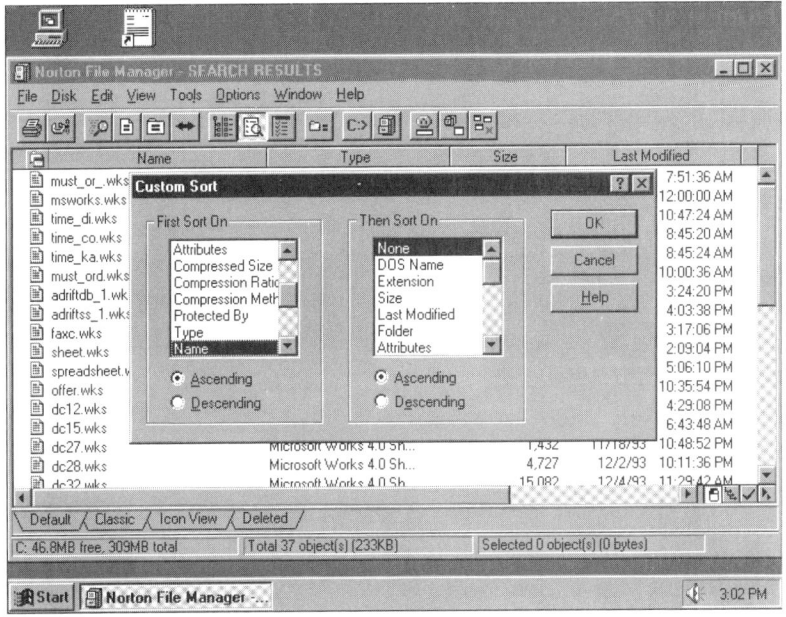

Figure 11.9 You can specify a special sort arrangement for your files in the Custom Sort dialog box.

Because of the way FastFind locates and displays the files in the Search Results window, they appear in no particular order. Actually, FastFind added the files to the window in the order they were located.

When you first display the Custom Sort dialog box, **Name** is chosen as the **First Sort On** setting. This means that Norton File Manager will sort the files alphabetically by filename. In the **Then Sort On** list, the **None** setting is selected. This means that no secondary sort is selected.

> **NOTE** A *primary* sort is the first sort setting used to sort the files. For example, if you choose **Type** as the primary sort, the files are sorted first by file type.

> **NOTE** A *secondary* sort is an additional sort criterion Norton File Manager uses after the files have been sorted according to the primary sort. For example, if you choose **Last Modified** as the secondary sort and **Type** as the primary sort, Norton will first display the files organized according to the type of file (Word, Works spreadsheet, and so on) and then by the date they were last modified. With **Last Modified**, you need to select whether you want ascending or descending order. If you choose **Ascending**, the dates are arranged from earliest modified to latest modified dates. In **Descending** order, the files are organized from most recently modified to earliest modified.

After you select the sort criteria you want, click **OK**. Norton File Manager performs the sort and displays the results in the Search Results window. Figure 11.8 shows the files in the Search Results window sorted first by file size (in ascending order, from smallest to largest file) and then by last modified date. You can see which files are the largest and oldest so that you can remove, zip, or archive them if necessary.

Using Sort Filters

When you are working in the File Manager window, you have the option of creating a sort filter to further control the files displayed in the list area. (In the Search Results window, you don't need to use filters because the displayed files have already been filtered according to your search instructions.)

To create a sort filter, select the folder containing the files you want to sort. Then open the View menu and choose **Filter**. The Custom Filter dialog box appears, as shown in Figure 11.10.

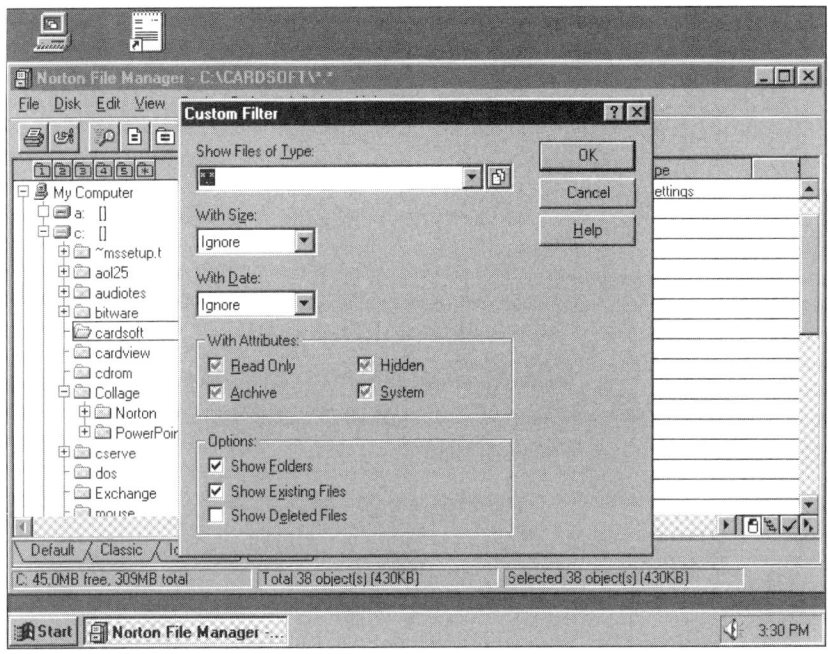

FIGURE 11.10 YOU CAN ENTER SORT INSTRUCTIONS IN THE CUSTOM FILTER DIALOG BOX.

In the **Show Files of Type** area, enter the type of files you're looking for. You can specify more than one type, if you choose, such as ***.txt**

*.doc, which tells Norton File Manager to look for all files that end with either **TXT** or **DOC**. You can exclude a particular type by entering a minus sign (a hyphen) before the file type you do not want to see: ***.*** - ***.wks**. This tells the File Manager to display all files *except* the ones that end with **WKS**.

In the **With Size** box, you can choose the size of the file you want to see. By default the setting is **Ignore**, but you can choose **Greater Than** or **Less Than**. If you choose one of the size criteria, another information box pops up to the right of the **With Size** box so that you can specify the size of the files you want displayed.

The **With Date** box lets you choose the date of the files displayed. If you choose one of the options other than **Ignore**, a second box appears so that you can select the date of the files you want to use.

In the **With Attributes** area, you can elect to search for files with specific attributes. All attributes—**Read Only**, **Archive**, **Hidden**, and **System**—are selected by default. If you wanted to display only the **Read Only** files, for example, you would click in each of the other three checkboxes to remove the check marks, causing Norton File Manager to use only the **Read Only** files in the sort.

The **Options** area lets you decide whether you want to show the folders in addition to files; show existing files only; or show also deleted files.

When you've specified all sort instructions, click **OK**. Norton File Manager sorts the files and folders according to your specifications and displays them in the list area.

THE NEXT STOP

Chapter 12 steps you through the final stop in *Inside Norton Navigator*, with a look at how you can make the Internet and your favorite FTP sites more accessible by using the tools available to you in the Norton File Manager.

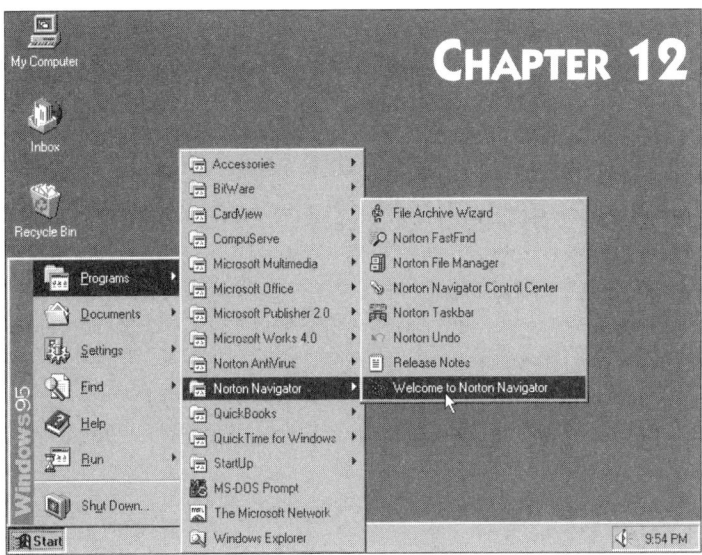

CHAPTER 12

MAPPING FTP INTERNET SITES

The world is getting smaller, right now. The reach of your computer—and the ability you have to access files all over the world—is expanding every day. With the millions of individuals, businesses, and universities already using the Internet and the millions more who will link up in the next few years, the world is becoming a tightly knit network of phone lines and fiber optic cable.

If you have never "surfed" the Internet, the challenge may seem awesome. Norton Navigator makes the Internet more accessible, giving you a front-end screen interface you're accustomed to by now—the File Manager.

Norton Navigator doesn't provide a fully functional, graphical interface for working with various aspects of the Internet, but it does give you a "way in" to your favorite places—FTP sites—for trading files and messages.

>  **NOTE** For more information on learning Internet basics and getting connected to the Internet, see *Internet in Plain English*, by Bryan Pfaffenberger, and *Internet Direct*, by Robert Miller and Elissa Keeler, both published by MIS:Press.

WHAT IS AN FTP SITE?

FTP is an acronym for *file transfer protocol*, which refers to the way in which your system and a remote system (in this case, the Internet server) communicate. An FTP site, then, is a site from which you download files for your system.

FTP Differences

You may have specific FTP sites that you access through an account and a password. For example, your business may have access to a site in your area of research or expertise that is not available to public users.

Some FTP sites are public sites, meaning that any user can log in to the FTP site and view and retrieve files in directories that are open to the public. This is known as *anonymous* FTP.

STARTING OUT WITH FTP

You use Norton Navigator to work with FTP sites by starting in the File Manager. If it isn't displayed, display the File Manager by clicking the File Manager **QuickLaunch** icon in the Taskbar. Or open the Programs menu, choose **Norton Navigator**, and select **Norton File Manager**.

If you scroll to the bottom of the tree area in the File Manager window, you'll notice that the tree displays an icon for FTP sites (see Figure 12.1). To display the FTP sites currently available on your system, click the **FTP Sites** icon in the tree area.

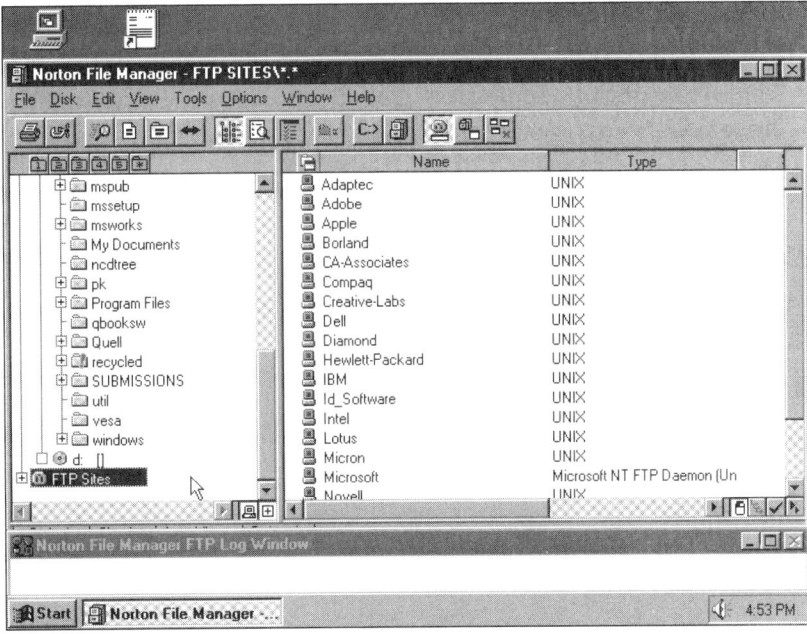

FIGURE 12.1 DISPLAYING THE FTP ACCESS SITES AVAILABLE ON YOUR COMPUTER.

WHAT DO I NEED BEFORE I CONNECT?

Assuming that your computer is equipped with a modem, you also need your own Internet connection before you can set up or use an FTP site with Norton File Manager.

How do you connect to the Internet? You may have an Internet access provider in your area that will enable you to establish an Internet account. (Check with local universities or computer retailers to find out about providers in your area.)

You can also connect to the Internet by using the access of popular information services such as CompuServe, Microsoft Network (new with Windows 95), or America Online. All three of these major services offer Internet access.

CONNECTING TO THE FTP SITE

When you are ready to connect to an FTP site from Norton File Manager, move the mouse pointer to the site name in the tree list and click the mouse button. Norton File Manager makes the connection.

Norton File Manager displays a message on the screen while the connection is being made. Then the File Manager and the FTP site are displayed side by side on the screen. Figure 12.2 shows the Microsoft FTP site. The active folder is one named **developr**, and subfolders are displayed.

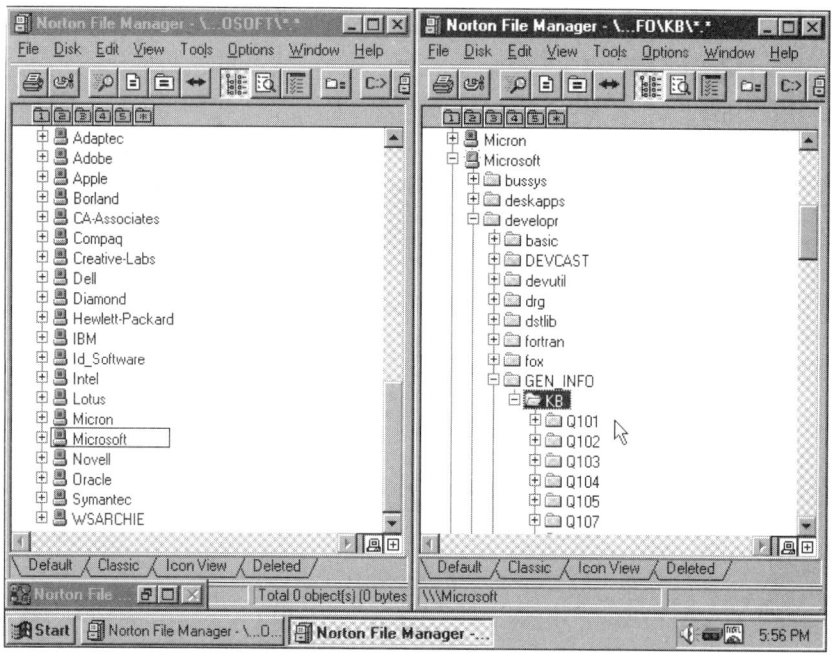

FIGURE 12.2 CONNECTING TO AN FTP SITE.

Displaying the FTP Log Window

To see what's going on with the connection, open the View menu and choose **FTP Log Window**. A small popup window appears at the bottom of the screen (see Figure 12.3).

CHAPTER 12 MAPPING FTP INTERNET SITES 237

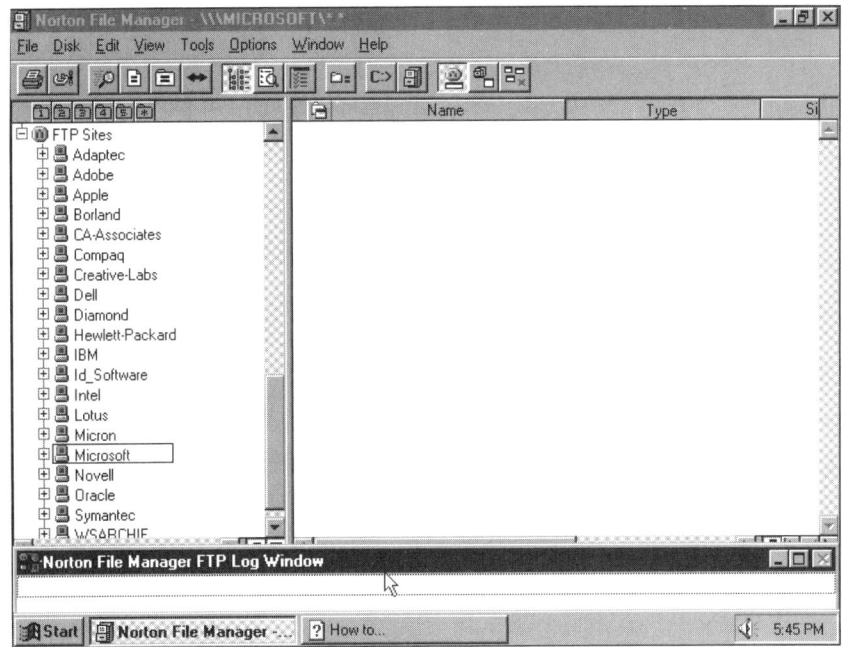

FIGURE 12.3 DISPLAYING THE FTP LOG WINDOW.

When you begin to retrieve files from the FTP site, you can keep an eye on the progress of the download by referring to the FTP Log Window. If you want to reduce the window, maximize it, or close it altogether, click the appropriate button on the right side of the FTP Log Window.

SHORTCUT

> You can also alternately display and hide the Log Window by clicking the **FTP Log Window** tool in the toolbar.

TRANSFERRING FILES TO NORTON FILE MANAGER

After the File Manager makes the connection, the FTP site appears as another folder and file list in the File Manager window. You can now work with the files at the FTP site as you would any other files in any other folders in the File Manager.

To copy one or more files from the FTP site to your computer, select the file or files you want to copy; then drag them to the desired folder.

Disconnecting from an FTP Site

When you are ready to disconnect from the FTP site, position the mouse pointer on the site name and click the right mouse button. When the popup menu appears, click **Disconnect Site** (see Figure 12.4).

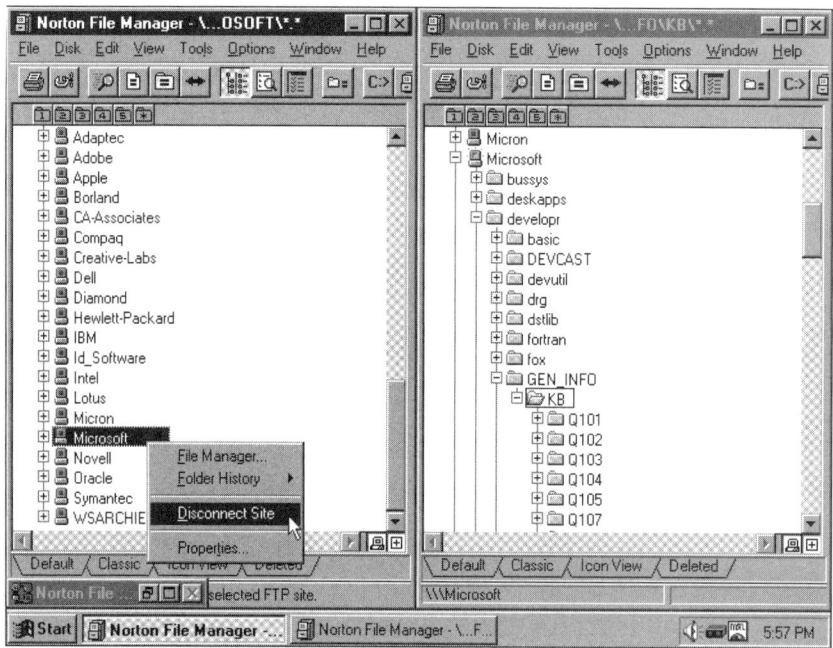

FIGURE 12.4 DISCONNECTING FROM THE FTP SITE.

ADDING A NEW FTP SITE

Chances are that sooner or later, you'll want to add your own FTP site to the File Manager. Whether you have a new site you want to check out on your own or your employer has asked you to research a new area of interest, you can easily provide the necessary setup information to add the site to File Manager.

Start by opening the Options menu and choosing **FTP Sites**. The Properties for FTP Connections dialog box appears, as shown in Figure 12.5.

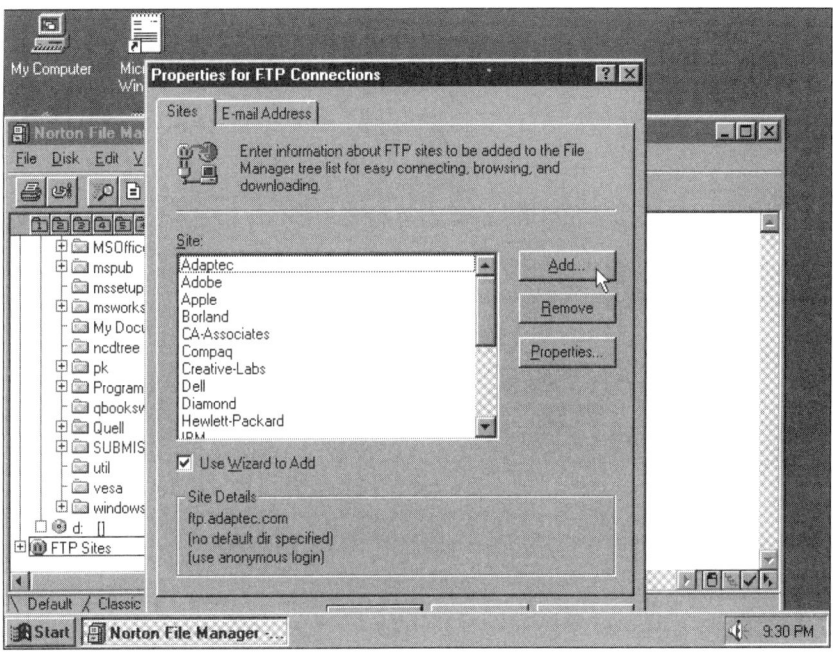

FIGURE 12.5 THE PROPERTIES FOR FTP CONNECTIONS DIALOG BOX LETS YOU ENTER A NEW FTP SITE.

The **Use Wizard to Add** checkbox should be selected by default. Click **Add**. The FTP Site Location dialog box appears. Type the **Site Description** (this will appear in the File Manager tree list) and the **Site Address** (this is what File Manager will use to access the site). Click **Finish** to add the site.

Next, click the **E-mail Address** tab. Here you enter your E-mail address for accessing Internet sites (see Figure 12.6). Even if you log in anonymously to an FTP site, you need your E-mail address in order to connect.

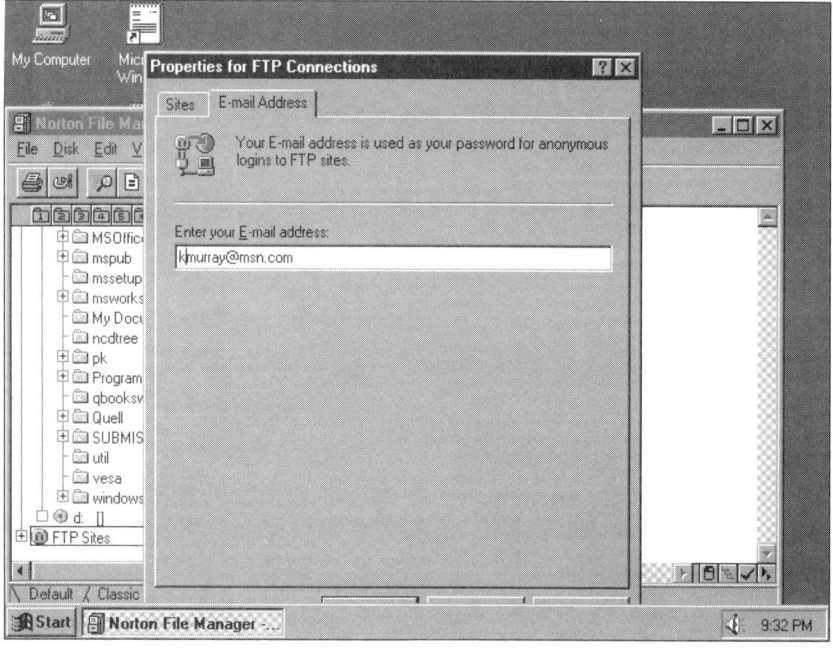

FIGURE 12.6 ENTERING AN E-MAIL ADDRESS.

When you set up any site, you can specify a folder. Norton moves to this folder automatically to store any files you retrieve from the FTP site.

NOTE You can choose a folder for your FTP files by positioning the mouse pointer on the folder, clicking the right mouse button, and choosing **Set as Login Folder**. This automatically assigns the selected folder to the FTP site you are currently using.

Setting FTP Properties

Once you create the FTP site, you can change its properties by clicking the **Properties** button in the **Sites** page of the Properties for FTP Connections dialog box. First, make sure the appropriate site is selected.

When you click **Properties**, the Properties dialog box for the site you selected appears, as shown in Figure 12.7. This dialog box includes three tab pages: **Location**, **Login**, and **Advanced**.

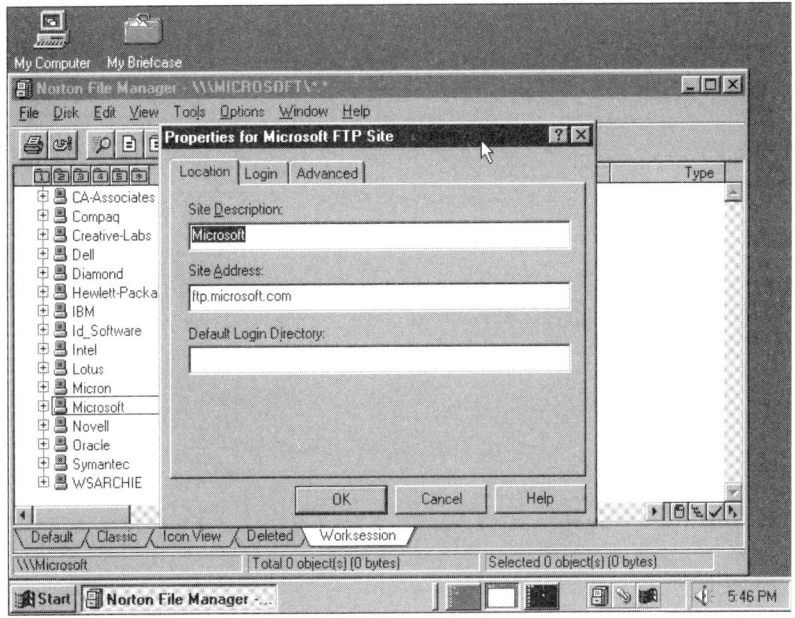

FIGURE 12.7 THE PROPERTIES DIALOG BOX FOR THE FTP SITE YOU SELECTED.

The **Location** tab page, shown by default, lets you change the **Site Description**, the **Site Address**, or the **Default Login Directory**. If you added this site, you entered this information in the Options menu's FTP Sites dialog box.

If this FTP site is one at which you have an account and a password, click the **Login** tab. Here you can enter your **Login Name**, **Password**, and **Account** number.

NOTE If the options in the **Login** tab are disabled, meaning that you cannot select them, the FTP site you have selected does not offer these types of setup. In this case, make sure that **Use anonymous login** is selected and be sure that you have entered an E-mail address in the Properties for FTP Connections dialog box.

The **Advanced** tab page lets you choose the operating system that is used at the FTP site. (**UNIX** is chosen by default.) You can also control the way the connection is made. If your computer encounters a busy signal, you may want to set a **Retry** value. By default, **Retry** is set to **0**. You can increase the number, if you choose, by clicking the up-arrow beside the entry.

The **Wait** option controls the amount of time your computer will wait for activity before disconnecting from the FTP site. The default is set to **65 seconds**, but you can increase or decrease the setting.

The **Connect at port number** setting is set to **21** by default. This is the port to which your computer connects when you access the FTP site. For best results, leave this number set to the default value unless specific instructions from your FTP site tell you to do otherwise.

Removing an FTP Site

You may have a number of FTP sites set up on your system, or you may have only a few. Whether you work with a limited or a large number of

FTP sites, there will be times when you want to remove the sites you no longer need.

To remove an FTP site, open the Options menu and choose **FTP Sites**. When the **Sites** tab page of the Properties for FTP Connections dialog box appears, click the site name in the **Sites** list. Then click the **Remove** button. The File Manager warns you that you're about to remove an FTP site. Click **Yes** to remove the site or **No** to cancel the operation.

The Next Stop

The ability to access and work with FTP sites is a unique and exciting feature of Norton File Manager that makes the Internet as simple to use as any folder on your hard disk.

This chapter rounds out our discussion of Norton Navigator, completing your tour through features that help you work with files, folders, and disks easier, faster, and smarter than ever before.

Keep exploring on your own, now that you know the basics...and happy navigating!

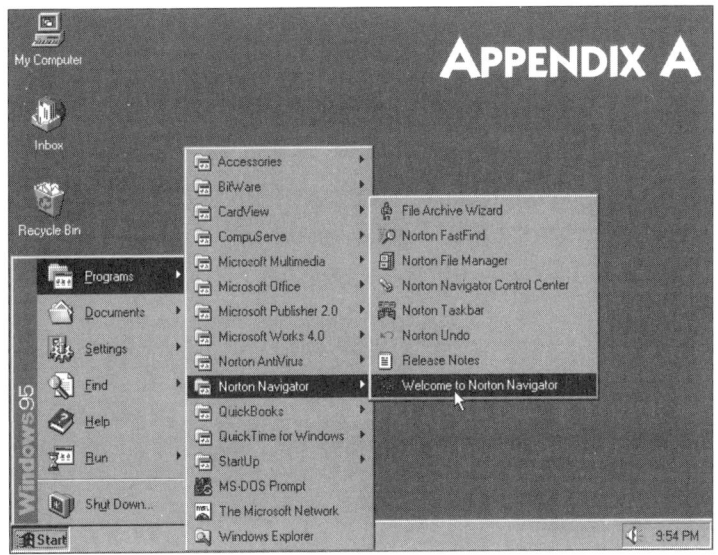

APPENDIX A

INSTALLING NORTON NAVIGATOR

If you have not yet installed Norton Navigator for Windows 95 on your computer, this is the place to start.

First, make sure that you have backed up your computer system recently and have copies of all important files. Additionally, free up as much hard disk space as you can—Norton Navigator requires slightly less than 3 MB. This isn't much, but the more room you have, the better.

STARTING INSTALLATION

First, insert the CD-ROM in your CD-ROM drive and double-click the **My Computer** icon on your Windows 95 desktop. The My Computer window opens and you see the Symantec icon, ready for installing (see Figure A.1).

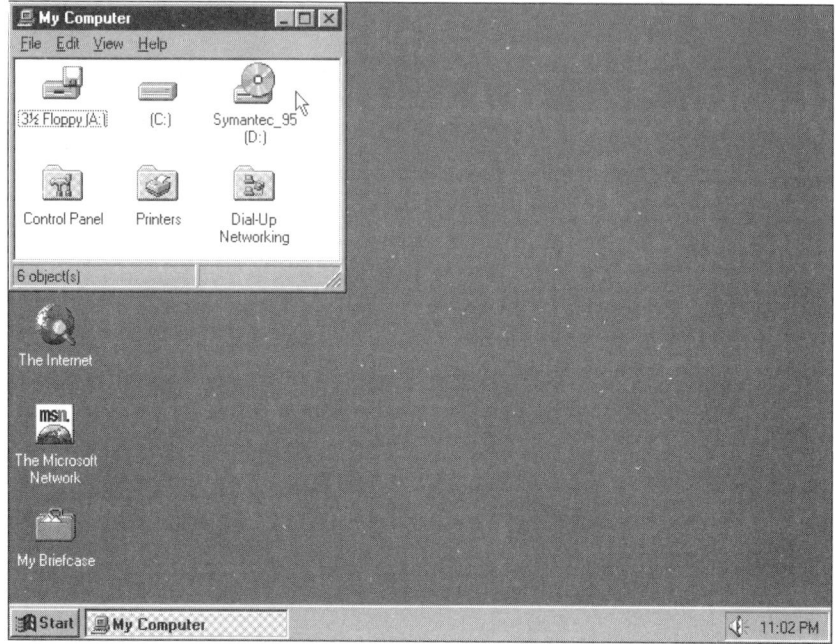

FIGURE A.1 GETTING READY TO INSTALL.

NOTE If you've opened the My Computer window and your CD-ROM drive is still showing the name of the last CD-ROM you used (the drive hasn't seen the Symantec_95 CD-ROM yet), open the View menu and choose **Refresh**. The window will be updated and the Symantec_95 icon will appear.

Next, double-click the **Symantec_95** icon. A window opens, showing a large number of files. Look for the **Setup** icon and double-click it (see Figure A.2).

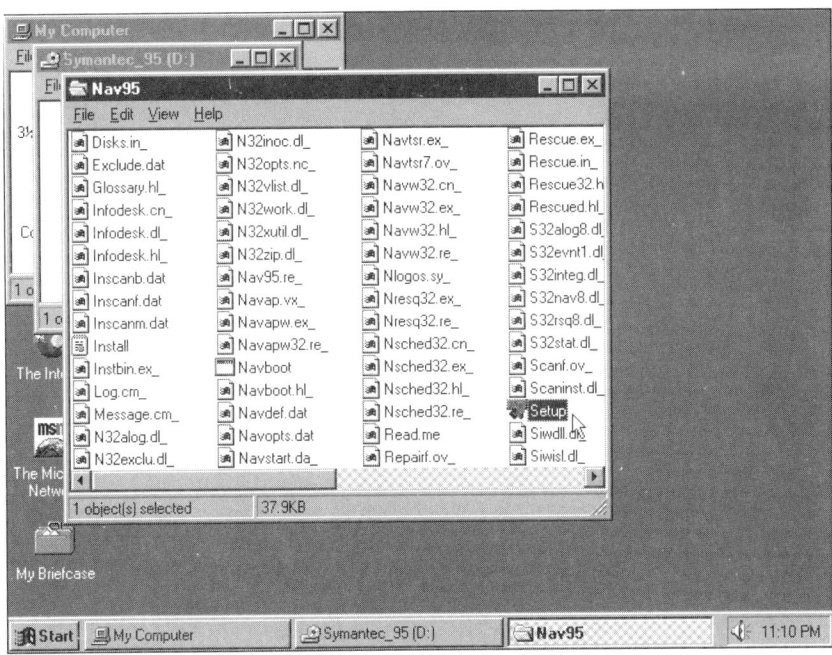

FIGURE A.2 CHOOSING **SETUP** TO START INSTALLATION.

Norton Navigator then starts its automated installation utility. Follow the prompts on the screen to provide information and choices as necessary. When installation is complete, Norton Navigator restarts your computer and Windows 95 automatically so that all changes will take effect.

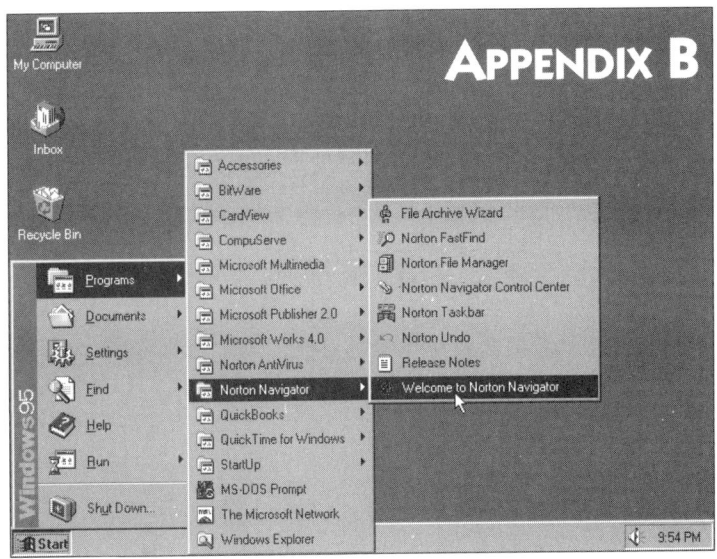

APPENDIX B

COMPARING WINDOWS 95 AND NORTON NAVIGATOR

With Norton Navigator, the enhancements of Windows 95 are more powerful than ever and easier to use. Here's the lowdown on the basic Windows 95 screen and how Norton Navigator can add to the features already there.

250 Inside Norton Navigator

✦ Start at the Start menu. If you choose, you can load the Norton Navigator Taskbar automatically at startup and display any desktop you choose.

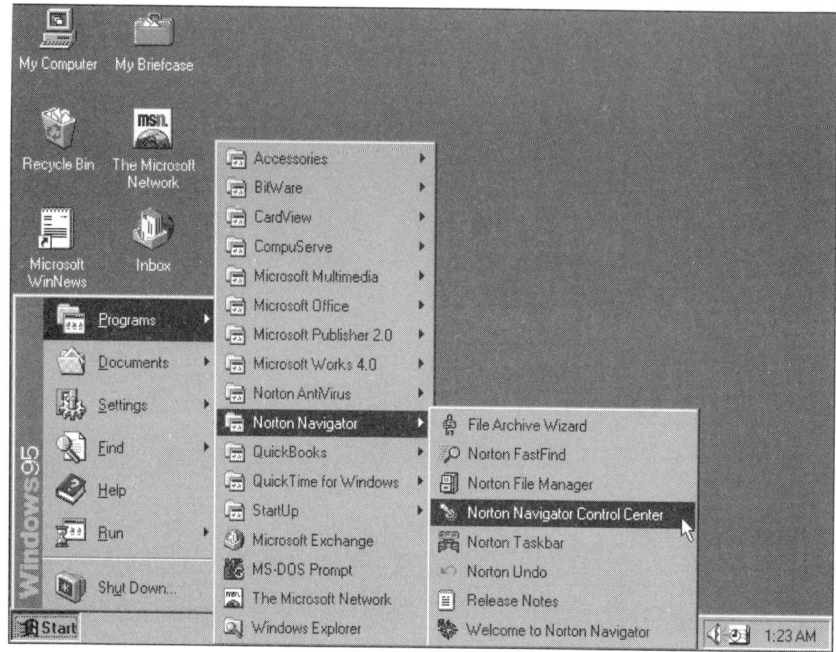

GETTING NORTON NAVIGATOR STARTED FROM THE WINDOWS 95 TASKBAR

APPENDIX B COMPARING WINDOWS 95 AND NORTON NAVIGATOR   251

✦ Cascading menus let you choose the programs you want. Norton Navigator gives you the option of reorganizing and showing history lists in some menus.

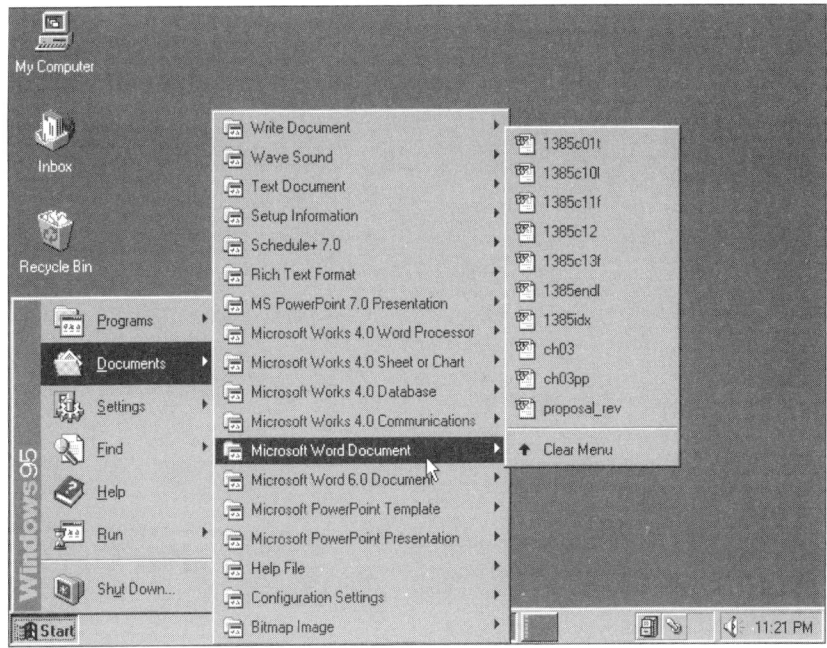

THE MODIFIED DOCUMENT MENU WITH A HISTORY LIST

252 Inside Norton Navigator

✦ Submenus offer additional choices. Norton Navigator lets you add shortcut menu choices to files and folders.

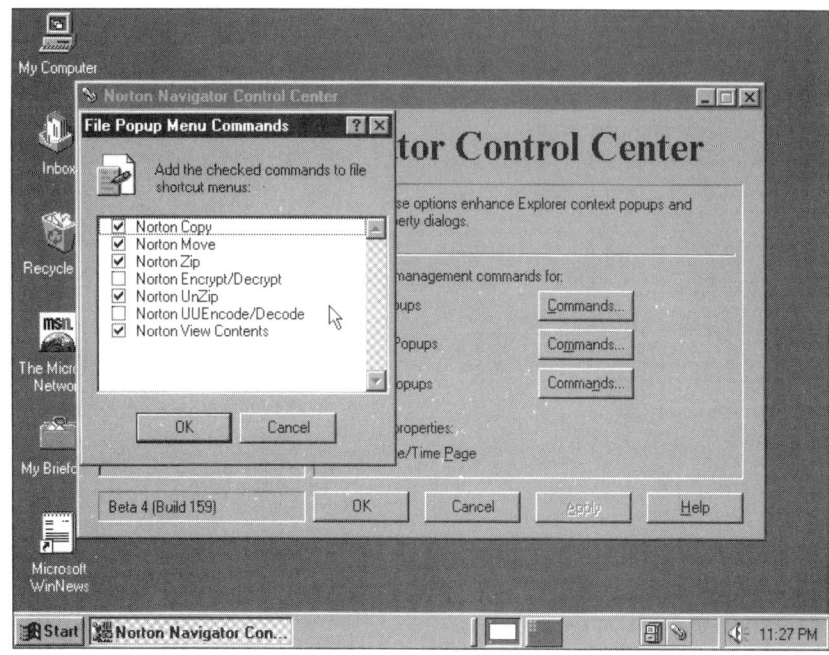

THE COMMANDS AVAILABLE TO ADD TO SHORTCUT MENUS FOR FILES AND FOLDERS

✦ Desktop shortcuts take you into programs and files quickly. With Norton Navigator, you can add programs and files you use often to the Taskbar QuickLaunch area.

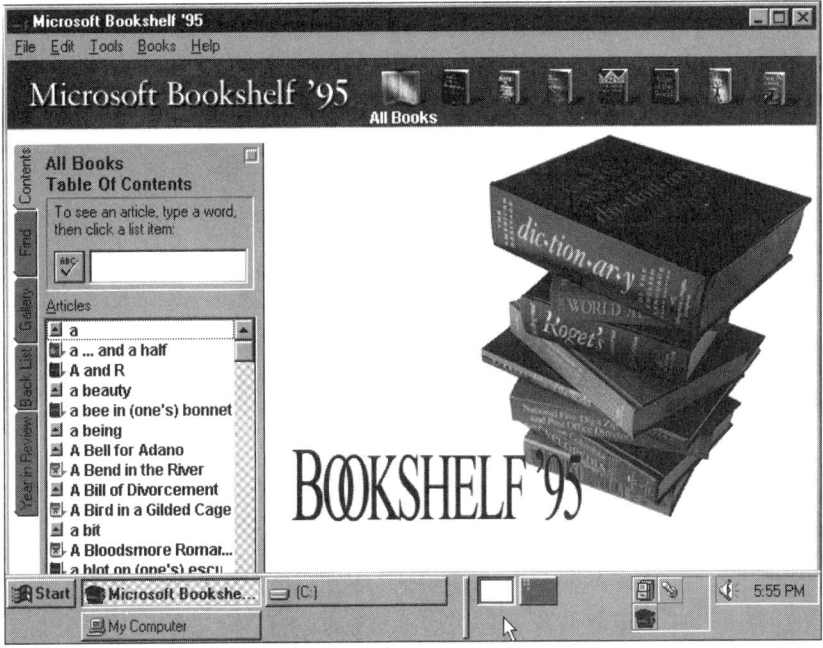

MICROSOFT BOOKSHELF 95 LAUNCHED FROM THE QUICKLAUNCH AREA.

254   Inside Norton Navigator

- You can still open windows by double-clicking their icons.
- The Windows Taskbar lets you move between programs easily. Norton greatly enhances the Taskbar for your applications.

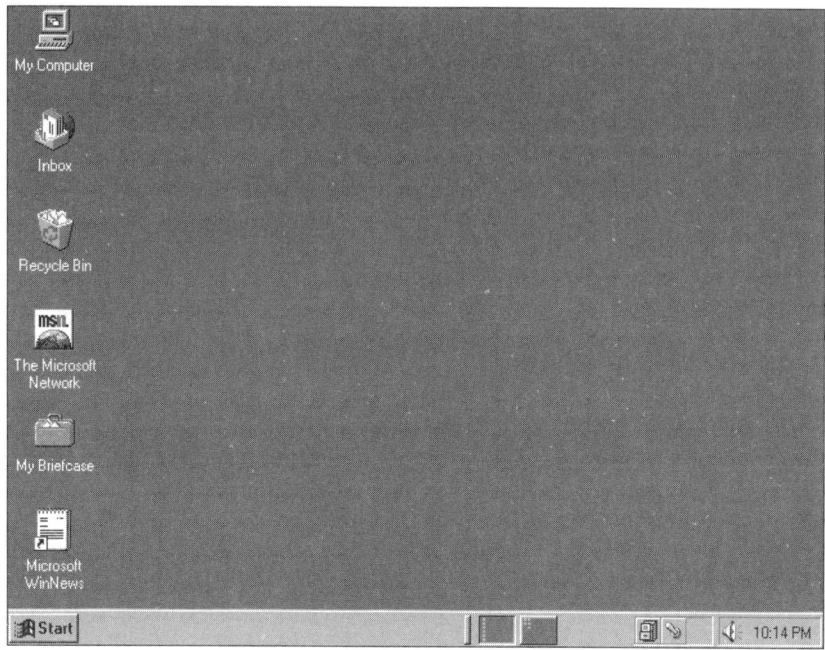

NORTON NAVIGATOR GREATLY ENHANCES THE TASKBAR

APPENDIX B COMPARING WINDOWS 95 AND NORTON NAVIGATOR   255

✦ Norton Navigator allows you to create and switch to multiple desktops with ease.

CHANGE TO A NEW DESKTOP WITH THE CLICK OF A BUTTON

✦ The Norton File Manager gives you greater power and flexibility than the Windows 95 Explorer

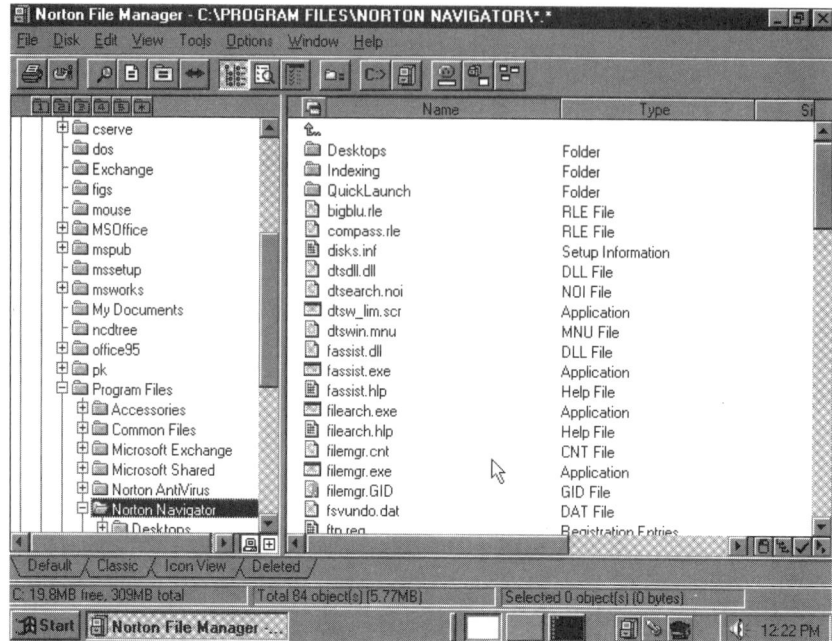

THE NORTON FILE MANAGER IN ACTION

✦ Integrated compression allows you to take greater control over your hard disk and many compressed files.

APPENDIX B   COMPARING WINDOWS 95 AND NORTON NAVIGATOR   257

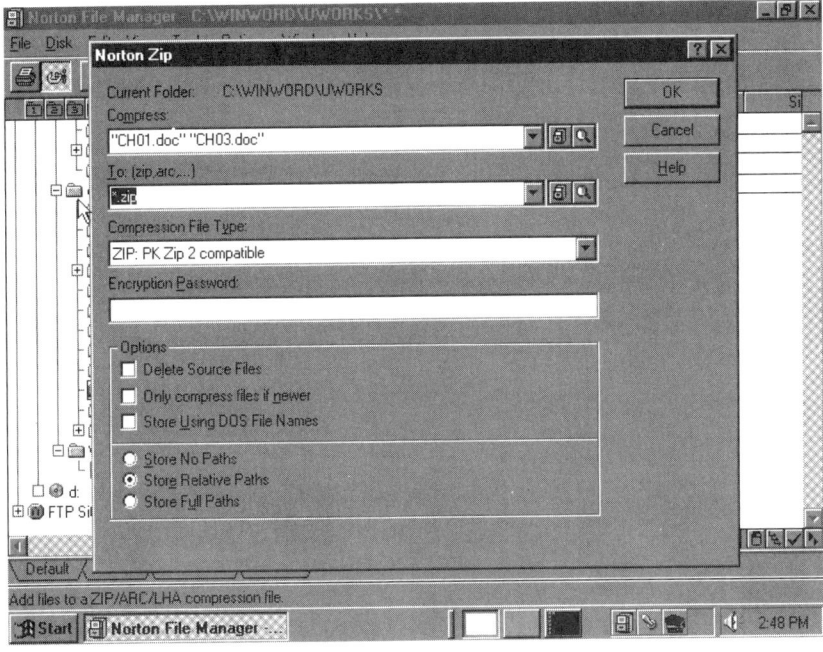

ZIPPING SELECTED FILES

Norton Desktop allows you to take greater control of your computer and to use it more effectively. Windows 95 has made using Windows much easier, but Navigator adds power to Windows 95 and allows you to take control of your system in exciting new ways.

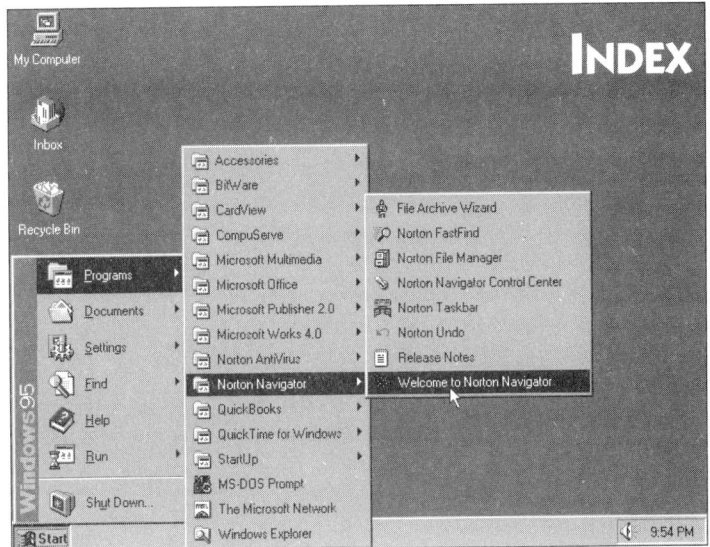

INDEX

A

adding
- a document history list, 54
- applets to Control Panel, 55-56, 118
- buttons to dialog boxes, 40
- commands to dialog boxes, 96-97
- desktops from other programs, 139
- Explorer Extensions, 57-58
- file-management commands to menus, 90-92
- folders to the tree display, 173-175
- FTP sites, 239-240
- items to desktops, 133-138
- Quick menus to Start menu, 115

Annotate option for adding notes, 29

applets, 118
- adding to submenu, 114

Applets button, 55-56

applications,
- launching from the Taskbar, 110-113

B

Back button, 27

backgrounds,
- desktops, 126
- wallpaper, 128-129

259

bad sectors,
    checking for, 64-66
Binary Compare, 193

C

changing
    desktop background, 126
    desktop patterns, 127-128
    desktop wallpaper, 129
    list display, 176-178
    Taskbar properties, 106-108
    toolbars, 168
clearing
    menus, 117
Command Menu button, 40
communications,
    mapping FTP sites, 233-236
comparing
    files, 191-195
compressing files, 70-72
Configure option, 23
connecting
    to the Internet, 235-238
Contents button, 27
Control Center
    adding Documents History List, 116-117
    customizing the screen, 103-118

displaying, 34, 83-84
elements of, 82
exiting, 100
exiting, 42
Explorer Extensions, 37, 57-58
FileAssist, 40, 96-97
Folder Navigator, 146-149
Folder Navigator, 37, 89-92
Indexing, 41, 100
LFN Enabler, 41-42, 98-99
options, 85-100
Quick Menus, 35-37, 52-56, 87-88, 114-115
SmartFolders, 38-39, 93-97, 150-157
Taskbar, 85
Taskbar, 86
Undo, 41, 100
working with desktops, 121-139
working with folders, 141-157
Control Center, 8, 11, 31, 52
Control Panel
    adding applets to 118
Control Panel command, 55-56
copying
    disks, 203-206
    files, 73-75, 188-189

creating
    an index file, 221-224
    desktops, 123-124
    SmartTabs, 182-183
customizing
    screen display, 103-118

D

deleting
    files, 75-76, 189
    SmartFolders, 156-157
deselecting
    files, 188
desktop
    Norton Navigator, 31-32
    overview of features for working with the, 15
desktops
    adding folders, 133-138
    adding items to, 133-138
    adding shortcuts, 133-138
    changing, 125
    choosing backgrounds for, 126
    choosing patterns for, 127-128
    choosing screen savers, 129-130
    choosing wallpaper for, 129
    creating, 123-124

    from other programs, 139
    multiple, 18, 122
    naming, 124-125
    properties, 126
    securing with passwords, 130-133
desktops, 121
dialog boxes
    adding buttons to, 40
    FileAssist, 96-97
directories
    see *folders*
disconnecting
    FTP sites, 238
    network drive, 216
Disk Doctor, 13
disk management, 33
disks
    basics, 200-202
    copying, 203-206
    formatting, 60-62, 207-210
    labeling, 206
    scanning, 62-66, 210-214
    selecting, 201-202
    viewing contents of, 73
    working with, 199-214
displaying
    Control Center, 34, 83-84

File Manager, 32-34, 162
Quick Menus, 35-36
Taskbar, 104
the FTP log window, 236
Document History button, 40
document history list, 54, 116-117
Drive Popups, 58
drives
mapping network, 215-216

E

editing
patterns, 127-128
exiting
Control Center, 100
Control Center, 42
File Manager, 77
Expandable Branches button, 172
Explorer Extensions, 56-58, 90-92
Drive Popups, 58
Folder Popups, 58
extensions
Explorer menu extensions, 37

F

FastFind, 8-9, 218-219
options, 220
search options, 227-228
speeding up, 221-226
File Archive Wizard, 8-9
file management basics, 161-183
File Manager
adding FTP sites, 239-241
basics, 161-183
changing folders, 60
compressing files, 72
copying files, 74-75
deleting files, 75-76
desktop, 32-34
displaying, 59-62, 162
exiting, 77
formatting disks, 60-62
FTP sites in, 10, 18
list display, 175-178
mapping FTP sites, 233-238
mapping network drives, 215-216
menus, 165-166
refreshing the window, 76
removing FTP sites, 242
ScanDisk, 62-66
selecting files, 66-70
SmartTabs, 178-183
sorting files, 229-232
tagging files, 70

INDEX

toolbar, 166-168

tree display, 169-175

undeleting files, 197

understanding the window, 163-164

working with disks, 199-214

working with files, 185-197

zipping and unzipping files, 194

zipping files, 72

File Manager, 8-10, 31

FileAssist, 40, 96-97

files

    adding file-management commands to menus, 90-92

    comparing, 191-195

    compressing, 70-72

    copying, 73-75, 188-189

    creating an index file, 221-224

    creating Document History List, 116-117

    deleting, 75-76, 189

    deselecting, 67, 188

    displaying properties of, 190-191

    FastFind, 218-228

    finding with existing searches, 226

    indexing, 41

    long file names, 17, 98-99

    moving, 189

    overview of features for working with, 14

    renaming, 190

    saving searches, 225-226

    selecting, 66-70

    selecting and tagging, 186-187

    sorting, 228-232

    tagging, 69-70

    transferring to FTP sites, 237-238

    undeleting, 196-197

    unzipping, 196

    using long file names with, 41

    viewing disk contents, 73

    working with, 161-197

    zipping, 10, 17, 70-72, 194-195

filters

    for sorting, 23-232

Folder History button, 40

Folder Navigator, 37, 89-92, 146-150

Folder Popups, 58

folders

    adding to desktops, 133-138

    adding to tree display, 173-175

    changing, 60

compared to directories, 145
creating SmartFolders, 38-39
defined, 142-144
displaying contents of, 33
Folder Navigator, 146-149
naming, 175
navigating, 37, 147-157
overview of features for working with, 15
SmartFolders, 150-157
tree display, 169-175
using Folder Navigator, 89-92
using SmartFolders, 93-97
folders, 141
formatting
    disks, 207-210
    disks, 60-62
FTP log window
    displaying, 236
FTP sites
    adding, 239-242
    connecting to, 236
    defined, 234-235
    disconnecting, 238
    mapping, 10, 18, 233-238
    properties, 241-242
    removing, 242
    transferring files, 237-238

H

help, 28, 42-47, 108-109
    Contents tab, 43
    Find tab, 45
    Index tab, 44
    Technical support, 46-47
    with Taskbar, 108-109
Help options, 28
hiding the Taskbar, 108

I

indexing, 41, 100, 221-224
installing Norton Navigator, 21, 245
Internet
    connecting, 235-238
    mapping FTP sites, 233-238
Introducing option, 23
Introduction to Norton Navigator, 2-18

L

labeling
    disks, 206
LFN Enabler, 41, 98-99
list display
    changing, 176-178

INDEX

File Manager, 175-178
loading
    Taskbar automatically, 35
locating files with FastFind, 218-228
long file names, 17, 41

M

mapping
    FTP sites, 233-238
    network drives, 215-2161
mapping FTP sites, 18
menus
    adding a Document History List, 116-117
    adding applets to, 114
    adding commands to, 37
    adding file-management commands, 90-92
    clearing, 117
    customizing, 165
    File Manager, 164-166
moving
    among folders, 89-92
    files, 189
    SmartFolders, 155-156
multiple desktops, 122
Multiple Select button, 68

N

naming
    desktops, 124-125
    folders, 175
navigating
    tree display, 172
networks
    mapping network drives, 215-216
Next Tip option, 23
Norton Desktop for Windows, 13
Norton Navigator
    adding Explorer Extensions, 57-58
    adding notes with Annotate, 29
    adding Quick Menus, 52-56
    compared to Windows 95, 1, 7, 249
    Control Center, 31-58, 82-157
    Desktop, 31-32
    desktop features, 15
    elements of, 30-47
    Explorer Extensions, 56-58, 90-92
    FastFind, 218-228
    FastFind, 8-9
    feature overview, 14-18

features added to Windows 95, 15-18

File Archive Wizard, 8-9

file features, 14

File Manager, 8-10, 31-34, 59-77, 161-216

folder features, 15

FTP sites, 233-242

getting help, 42-47

help options, 28

history of, 13

Indexing, 221-224

installation, 21

installing, 245

mapping FTP sites, 18

multiple desktops in, 18

Online Registration, 23-24

opening screen, 23

overview, 21-47

starting, 22, 50-51

system requirements, 16

taking the tutorial, 12

Taskbar, 8, 11, 26, 30-35, 42

tutorial, 24-27

Undo, 8, 12

using, 13

utilities in, 8-12

wizards, 39

Norton Taskbar, 8

notes

    adding with Annotate, 29

O

Online Registration, 23-24

opening screen, 23

Options button, 27

Organization of book, 2

Outline Mode button, 68

overview

    Norton Navigator, 21

P

passwords

    to secure desktops, 130-133

patterns

    desktops, 127-128

PC Tools for Windows, 13

PremiumCare support, 47

primary sort, 230

PriorityCare support, 47

properties

    changing Taskbar, 106-108

    desktop, 126

    displaying file, 190-191

    FTP sites, 241-242

Q

Quick Menus
    adding applets, 114-115
    changing the Start menu, 114-115
    displaying, 35-36
    using Control Panel, 54-56
    using Run, 53
Quick Menus, 52, 87-88
QuickLaunch, 110-113
QuickLaunch area, 42

R

Refresh command, 76
removing
    FTP sites, 242
renaming
    files, 190

S

saving searches, 225-226
ScanDisk, 210-214
ScanDisk utility, 62-66
scanning disks, 62-66, 210-214
screen
    customizing display, 103-118

screen savers
    choosing, 129-130
searches
    options, 225-228
    using existing, 226
secondary sort, 230
selecting
    a block of files, 69
    all files, 69
    disks, 66-70, 186-187, 201-202
    noncontiguous files, 69
shortcut keys (File Manager), 165
shortcuts
    adding to desktops, 133-138
Show All Drives button, 170
Show Entire Branch button, 68
SmartFolders, 38-39, 93-97, 150-157
    moving, 155-156
    removing, 156-157
    updating, 154
    using, 154-155
SmartTabs, 178-181
    creating, 182-183
sorting
    files, 228-232
    filters in, 231-232
    primary sort, 230

secondary sort, 230
StandardCare support, 46
Start menu
    changing with Quick Menus, 114-115
starting
    choices for, 51
    Control Center, 83-84
    File Manager, 162
    Norton Navigator, 22, 50-51
    Taskbar automatically, 52,
system requirements for running Norton Navigator, 16

T

Tag Mode, 187
Tag Mode button, 68
tagging files, 69-70, 186-187
Taskbar
    displaying, 104
    displaying at startup, 52
    elements of the, 105
    example of, 26
    getting help for, 109
    hiding, 108
    introduction to, 30-35
    loading automatically, 35

    properties, 106-108
    QuickLaunch area, 42
    QuickLaunching applications, 110-113
    starting the Control Center from the, 83
Taskbar, 8, 11, 85-86
Technical support
    PremiumCare, 47
    PriorityCare, 47
    StandardCare, 46
telecommunications
    mapping FTP sites, 233-236
toolbars
    changing, 168
    File Manager, 166-168
tree display
    File Manager, 169-175
tutorial
    taking the, 24-26
tutorial for Norton Navigator, 12

U

undeleting files, 196-197
Undo, 8, 12, 41, 100
unzipping files, 196
updating
    SmartFolders, 154

using

    SmartFolders, 154-155

V

viewing

    files, 73

W

wallpaper for desktop backgrounds, 128-129

Welcome to Norton Navigator tutorial, 8

Windows 95

    arrival of, 1-7

    compared to Norton Navigator, 249

    features Norton builds upon, 15-18

Wipe Delete option, 189

wizards

    adding an FTP site, 240-242

    creating SmartFolders, 39

    Index, 222

    Indexing, 100

    SmartFolders, 94

Z

zipping files, 10, 17, 70-72, 194-195